CONNECTIPLOMACY

CONNECTIPLOMACY

Using our Differences to Connect

Plus, step by step Insights from Iconic Leaders
"George Washington, Abraham Lincoln, Mahatma Gandhi,
Nelson Mandela, and Winston Churchill"

MARJORIE HOPE

XULON PRESS

Xulon Press
555 Winderley Pl, Suite 225
Maitland, FL 32751
407.339.4217
www.xulonpress.com

© 2023 by Marjorie Hope

All rights reserved solely by the author. The author guarantees all contents are original and do not infringe upon the legal rights of any other person or work. No part of this book may be reproduced in any form without the permission of the author.

Due to the changing nature of the Internet, if there are any web addresses, links, or URLs included in this manuscript, these may have been altered and may no longer be accessible. The views and opinions shared in this book belong solely to the author and do not necessarily reflect those of the publisher. The publisher therefore disclaims responsibility for the views or opinions expressed within the work.

Information provided for this book has been gathered from a variety of resources. The information provided in this book is offered for general informational purposes only; this book represents the opinions of the author and is intended as a book based on the author's opinions as such.

Library of Congress Control Number: 2023918760

Paperback ISBN-13: 978-1-66288-264-7
Ebook ISBN-13: 978-1-66288-265-4

DEDICATION

This book is a heartfelt dedication to all of you who have embarked on this journey of connecting with the world.

To my esteemed board of directors and advisors, who passionately embraced the idea of encouraging meaningful connections among people and understood that respect is the foundation that unites us. Unlike other organizations that solely engage with countries and governments, we believe in the power of individuals.

To my dearest mom, my unwavering confidante, whose love, support, and encouragement have been a constant source of strength throughout this endeavor.

To Chase and Carter, whose presence in my life has taught me the profound significance of connection and the beauty of shared experiences.

To my father, whose boundless wisdom and joy for life left an indelible mark on my heart. As I navigate the world without you, I carry your invaluable teachings with me. Your spirit remains a guiding force, inspiring me to confront challenges with courage and embrace the unknown. Your love continues to fuel my thirst for new experiences and my pursuit of genuine connections. The cherished memories of our conversations and the love we shared serve as a lasting tribute to your kind, compassionate, and loving nature. I am forever proud to be your child, and I strive to honor your memory every day with a smile.

ABOUT THIS BOOK:

Learn the steps for connecting the world.

You will be inspired that although our world has problems and we have cultural differences, you will find that we're not so different after all.

Our planet is fragile, in some areas clean drinking water is a luxury or natural disasters caused mass destruction.

The steps you can take can make a difference and geared to connect "step by step", with our world.

Starting with step 1. a "smile" is a universal communicator, expressing friendliness and gratitude because in every situation "people are people".

TABLE OF CONTENTS

Dedication v
About this Book vii
Acknowledgments xi
Preface xiii
Introduction xv

1. Building Bridges Across Borders 1
2. Cultural Diplomacy: A Journey through Time 19
3. The Power of Cultural Exchange 43
4. From Summits to Sporting events: the many faces of Diplomacy 65
5. How Diplomacy Can Change the World 79
6. World Events that Connect Us 103
7. Globalization: A Cause for Concern 121
8. Surviving in a Globalized World 157
9. Diplomacy and Politics: The intersection of Connecting 179
10. A World of Possibilities 209

In Closure 239
Insights 244
Epilogue 259
About the Author 263
Appendix: International Organizations 265
Endnotes 279

ACKNOWLEDGMENTS

I FEEL IMMENSELY FORTUNATE and grateful to have crossed paths with such extraordinary individuals who have played an integral role in the creation of this book.

First and foremost, to my cherished children, Chase, and Carter, to whom I dedicate this work. Your presence and unwavering support have been the driving force behind my journey as an author. You've shown me how to embrace life with wide-open eyes and a heart full of wonder, and I couldn't be prouder to be your mother.

To my beloved mother, Sondra Danoff, whose constant presence, support, and encouragement have been a guiding light throughout my life, I am deeply grateful. Her brilliance and resilience have inspired me in countless ways, and her steadfastness has been a rock to lean on during uncertain times.

In remembrance of my father, the late Dr. Alan Lee Danoff, whose impactful influence echoes through every day of my life. His unwavering determination and belief in me have shaped my worldview. His philosophical conversations remain etched in my mind, reminding me of our responsibility to the world and the significance of forging connections.

I am forever inspired by the lives of my grandparents—Frances, Ben, Phil, and Esther. Their courage and determination to embrace new adventures in a new world have left an indelible mark on my heart, and the love they showered upon me was truly special.

Gratitude also extends to my exceptional board of directors and advisors: Myra Adams, Armen Babajanian, Ken Carman, Ben Case, Jamie Dryer, Jim Eskin, John Largent, John Lenczowski, Tom McDevitt, Jeri Muoio, Aaron Rosen, Celeste Simon, Stanley Tate, and John Wobensmith. Your unwavering support and insights have been invaluable, propelling me forward on this journey.

To Jim Eskin in Texas, who lent a listening ear and believed in my dreams, thank you for seeing the potential in this endeavor and for being a constant source of encouragement.

A heartfelt gratitude to Myra Adams for her unwavering support and encouragement that constantly motivated me to strive for excellence. And to Ken Carman, whose invaluable assistance has been instrumental in shaping this work, I am deeply appreciative.

To my forever friends—Lisa, Paula, Sandy, Sarah, and Stacey—your unwavering support and lessons in love and acceptance have shaped me in profound ways.

In honor and remembrance of Yvonne Boice, whose influence opened my eyes to the world. Her words—"A candle loses nothing by lighting another candle."—and her belief in the power of giving continue to resonate within me.

A heartfelt appreciation to my project manager, Kim Small, whose organizational prowess kept me on track during this endeavor.

To Gina Flemming, my incredible editorial consultant, your expertise and guidance have been invaluable.

To all those who have inspired me and contributed to shaping the person I am today, I offer my deepest gratitude. Here's to the hopes and dreams that lie ahead, and may we embrace each day with boundless gratitude.

PREFACE

IN TODAY'S DYNAMIC and competitive world, where overwhelming complexities and rapid changes are constant, nurturing human connections and forging strong relationships emerge as pivotal strategies. These relationships enable us to channel our collective focus towards crucial global solutions, from world economic growth to pressing health challenges, all the while advocating for peaceful societies. Aziza Idris Ahmed's poignant question, "Tell me, what does a person want? Peace and safety, the rest comes after,"[1] resonates deeply with our universal longing for peace and security.

Cultural diplomacy stands as a potent tool for building relationships and promoting understanding among nations. Through the exchange of ideas, traditions, and practices, we can construct a cohesive global community founded on mutual respect and cooperation.

Connecting with others presents us with an invaluable opportunity to learn, respect, and embrace diversity. A smile on our faces and an open heart can dismantle barriers. Each person's unique story and perspective enriches the world, and by listening and learning from one another, we can develop a deeper appreciation for the complexity of human experience. Cultivating humility and remaining open to growth and change are essential as we seek common ground amidst our differences.

This book extends an invitation to explore the beauty of embracing diversity. By celebrating and honoring the uniqueness in everyone, we cultivate enduring bonds that shape a more interconnected and united world.

"A house divided against itself cannot stand", often attributed to Abraham Lincoln, holds profound relevance in our present world. Translated into our global context, "A world divided cannot stand." This echoes the essential truth that unity and collaboration are fundamental for the stability and progress of humanity and our world.

INTRODUCTION

Reviving Connections: The Lost Art of the Family Dinner

IN THE PAST, family dinners served as a vital avenue for open communication, where thoughts and concerns were freely expressed, fostering a sense of connection among family members. However, in today's "all about me" society, this skill seems to have vanished. Economic pressures led both parents to work, leaving little time for sitting down together and engaging in meaningful conversation. Instead, families turned to digital distractions like video games and social media, hindering genuine interaction.

The decline of family dinners had far-reaching consequences, affecting the ability of individuals to communicate effectively and empathize with others.

As we fast-forward to the present, electronic gadgets have taken center stage, replacing genuine human interaction with machines. An entire generation is raised by Google, fostering a lack of personal engagement and independence in seeking knowledge. Furthermore, outside influences can sway our actions, leading us astray from our own best interests.

Nonetheless, the value of sharing a meal cannot be underestimated. When dining with individuals from different backgrounds, we open ourselves to the world, learning, laughing, and breaking down barriers. The dining table has long been recognized as a forum for negotiation, settling differences, and building relationships, earning the moniker "dinner diplomacy" by Winston Churchill.

Through history, we find remarkable stories of leaders making profound decisions over a meal, harnessing the power of shared experiences to influence the world. Dining together brings diverse viewpoints and opinions, fostering a spirit of coexistence and evolution among nations.

Now, let us embark on a fascinating journey into the concept of cultural diplomacy, where iconic figures like George Washington, Abraham Lincoln,

Mahatma Gandhi, Nelson Mandela, and Winston Churchill engage in hypothetical dialogue. Their perspectives and experiences will shed light on how diplomacy can change the world.

So, pull up a chair, gather 'round the fire, and immerse yourself in Leaders Feasting on Ideas and Insights! Join us on this captivating journey as our table of five great leaders unites to offer a unique opportunity to connect, engage, and shape a harmonious global landscape.

Sharing a meal with others can lead to some of the most important conversations of our lives and connect us to the world in profound ways. Throughout history, the dining table has served as a unique forum for negotiations, conflict resolution, and the sealing of relationships, as noted by The Diplomat magazine in December 2022.

Renowned leaders, like Winston Churchill, recognized the power of bringing people together over a meal, coining the term "dinner diplomacy." In books such as Stuan Stevenson's "The Course of History–Ten Meals That Changed the World," intricate details of meals that shaped history offer insight into significant political contexts and plans.

Numerous extraordinary examples demonstrate how dining has connected us. For instance, during a dinner in June 1790, Alexander Hamilton, James Madison, and Thomas Jefferson decided how the Revolutionary War's debt should be allocated, putting personal differences aside and agreeing to locate the capital on the banks of the Potomac.

Food has been an essential medium for communicating important messages, even among American presidents. Alex Prud'homme's *Dinner with the President: Food, Politics, and a History of Breaking Bread at the White House* reveals how food choices conveyed political symbolism and intent.

Beyond the taste and flavor, dining together holds powerful emotional and hormonal influences, influencing our thinking and responses. Viscount Palmerston referred to dining as the "soul of diplomacy," and Hillary Clinton recognized the unique capacity of shared meals to transcend boundaries and build bridges.

The carefully chosen food items symbolized cultural references and relationships, representing a warmth breaking through barriers.

In 2018 at the Korean Peace Summit,[2] an enlightening example of this occurred. Everything on the table was there for a specific reason. The choice of minced croaker and sea cucumber as a dumpling filling referenced the hometown of South Korean President Kim Dae-Jung, while rösti, the traditional Swiss potato fritter, referenced where North Korean leader Kim Jong Un was from. A mango mousse, decorated symbolically with a map of a unified Korea, had a hard chocolate shell the leaders had to smash through while jointly holding a large hammer, representing the warmth of their relationship breaking through.

Eating is a necessity, but doing so in a way that supports everyone's objectives requires thoughtfulness. The relaxed nature of a meal provides an ideal environment for addressing diverse issues without inhibitions, fostering coexistence and evolution among nations.

Decisions and relationships of great significance have been forged over a meal, effectively communicating powerful messages to global leaders. The exchange of ideas, values, traditions, and other aspects are examples of cultural diplomacy. These exchanges help strengthen relationships with other people and countries and, in doing so, enhance social and cultural cooperation to find common ground with one another.

In exploring the concept of cultural diplomacy and its impact on the world, it is intriguing to consider how influential leaders from different eras might have approached these issues. By engaging in hypothetical dialogues, we bring together icons like George Washington, Abraham Lincoln, Mahatma Gandhi, Nelson Mandela, and Winston Churchill, representing diverse perspectives and experiences. Their insights provide valuable context in discussing how diplomacy can transform the world.

So, pull up a chair, gather 'round the fire, and immerse yourself in timeless talks: "Leaders Feasting on Ideas and Insights!" Each captivating chapter offers a unique opportunity to connect and engage with the world's great leaders.

Connecting people through cultural diplomacy, mutual understanding, trust, and contact with other cultures that promote better international relations.

ONE

BUILDING BRIDGES ACROSS BOARDERS

STEP BY STEP IN CONNECTING HISTORY TO PRESENT DAY DIPLOMACY

"THE ONLY WAY TO MAKE A REAL AND LASTING PEACE IS TO BUILD BRIDGES OF UNDERSTANDING BETWEEN NATIONS AND CULTURES."
- NELSON MANDELA

Chapter 1
BUILDING BRIDGES ACROSS BORDERS

> "Observe good faith and justice toward all nations. Cultivate peace and harmony with all."[3]
> George Washington

> "Cultural diplomacy is not a luxury, it is a necessity for nations that seek to build bridges, rather than walls."[4]
> Madeleine Albright

IN A WORLD brimming with untapped potential, the quest to construct bridges across borders emerges as a captivating and indispensable mission, igniting sparks of peace, stability, and prosperity that radiate far and wide. The very process of intertwining nations and cultures sets the stage for a mesmerizing global ensemble, transcending geographical barriers and a tapestry of profound understanding and boundless collaboration.

Measuring the strides in crafting global bridges becomes an exhilarating and nuanced adventure. From the captivating realm of foreign policy to the center stage of economic relations, and the enchanting art of cultural exchange, the canvas of possibilities unfurls with excitement.

Within the realm of foreign policy, these bridges of success manifest through the art of diplomatic dialogues, sparking an electrifying surge of international cooperation and peaceful resolutions to conflicts. Vibrant alliances and dynamic partnerships between nations serve as shining beacons of unity, embracing a collective journey toward shared goals and mutual interests, strengthening the very art of global ties.

Economic relations take center stage in building bridges across borders, as captivating initiatives like trade agreements, investment partnerships, and economic aid kindle a blaze of interdependence and mutual growth. Nations engaging in fair and open trade practices pave the way for a thrilling surge of prosperity, unveiling an awe-inspiring canvas of economic development that transcends continents.

At the heart of this remarkable journey lies the transformative power of cultural exchange, igniting the flames of understanding and appreciation for diverse traditions, customs, and beliefs. Enthralling artistic collaborations, exhilarating cross-cultural events, and educational exchange programs unite people from diverse backgrounds, weaving the fabric of a harmonious global community.

Yet, the measurement of progress in building bridges demands the exploration of uncharted depths and the continuous effort to nurture mutual respect, trust, and cooperation. Regular assessments fuel the excitement of gauging the impact of these initiatives, paving the way for breathtaking vistas of peace, stability, and global prosperity.

Moreover, progress in building bridges must be viewed through a captivating prism, acknowledging that it is not solely the responsibility of one nation but demands an electrifying chorus of collective efforts from countries worldwide. Collaborative endeavors, including dynamic international treaties and exhilarating forums, empower nations to embark on an extraordinary quest, confronting global challenges together, forging an enthralling path toward an interconnected world.

As our world evolves, so do the exhilarating metrics for measuring progress in building bridges across borders. Embracing the winds of change, adapting to emerging technologies, and navigating the ever-shifting geopolitical dynamics invigorate the thrill of fostering meaningful and impactful connections between nations.

Ultimately, building bridges across borders stands not as a mere destination, but as a journey that demands an electrifying spirit of dedication, understanding, and an unwavering commitment to promoting peace, stability, and prosperity for the entire global community. As we continuously nurture these breathtaking connections and unite in the face of shared challenges, we unlock the power to build a world pulsating with unity, strength, and harmony.

Connecting Nations: The Significance of Building Bridges Across Borders for Diplomacy

- **Promoting understanding**: By fostering relationships and facilitating communication between nations, diplomacy can help to build mutual understanding and reduce the likelihood of conflict.

- **Resolving disputes**: Diplomacy provides an opportunity for nations to peacefully resolve disputes and find mutually beneficial solutions.

- **Strengthening alliances**: Building bridges across borders can help to strengthen alliances and promote cooperation among nations on important global issues.

- **Encouraging trade and investment**: Diplomacy can also help to build economic ties and promote trade and investment between nations.

- **Advancing shared goals**: Through diplomacy, nations can work together to advance shared goals and tackle common challenges, such as climate change, terrorism, and poverty.

It is important to note that progress in building bridges across borders can also be hindered by a variety of factors, such as geopolitical tensions, economic disparities, and cultural differences.

Cultural diplomacy is the use of cultural exchange as a tool to build relationships and strengthen cooperation between countries. It involves the promotion of a country's culture abroad, as well as the promotion of cultural exchange and cooperation between nations.

One form of cultural diplomacy is the exchange of artists, musicians, and other cultural figures between countries. This can take the form of touring performances, exhibitions, and other cultural events. Cultural diplomacy can also involve educational exchange programs, such as study-abroad programs or the exchange of scholars and students between countries.

Cultural diplomacy can be an effective tool for building relationships and promoting understanding between nations. It allows people from different cultures to learn about and appreciate one another's traditions and values and can help to build mutual respect and cooperation.

The Vital Significance of Connecting Across Borders

Building understanding and appreciation of different cultures: Connecting with people from other cultures can help us to learn about and appreciate their traditions, values, and ways of life.

- **Promoting cooperation and collaboration**: By building connections with people from other countries, we can work together to address common challenges and achieve shared goals.

- **Strengthening international relations**: Connecting with others in the world can help to build more peaceful and harmonious international relations by fostering greater understanding and cooperation between nations.

- **Enriching personal and professional experiences**: Connecting with others can broaden our horizons and enrich our personal and professional experiences. It can expose us to new ideas, perspectives, and ways of life that can broaden our understanding of the world.

Cultural diplomacy, while valuable in promoting understanding and cooperation, is not without its controversies. Critics view it as a form of propaganda, presenting an overly positive and possibly distorted image of a country's culture. However, proponents argue that cultural diplomacy promotes dialogue and reduces tensions, encouraging peaceful relations between nations.

In acknowledging the challenges, building bridges across borders may encounter roadblocks that hinder effective cooperation and understanding between nations. Instances of unsuccessful efforts include situations where geopolitical tensions, economic concerns, or security issues pose obstacles to connectivity. Cultural or historical reasons might also play a role in hindering cross-border connections.

Addressing these challenges is essential in paving the way for successful cultural diplomacy, facilitating genuine exchanges of ideas, values, and traditions, and the connection of harmonious relationships between nations. Emphasizing cooperation and mutual understanding is vital for creating a more connected and peaceful global community.

When Diplomacy Hits Roadblocks: Exploring Alternatives and Solutions

- **Diplomatic breakdowns**: Diplomatic relations between countries can break down for a variety of reasons, such as conflicting interests, political disagreements, or unfulfilled commitments. In such cases, efforts to build bridges can be hindered or fail altogether.

- **Cultural misunderstandings**: Cross-border misunderstandings, often rooted in cultural differences, can create obstacles to building bridges and promoting cooperation.

- **Economic disparities**: Economic disparities between countries can create tension and lead to difficulties in building bridges, especially in trade and investment relations.

- **Geopolitical tensions**: Political tensions and conflicts, such as disputes over territory or resources, can create barriers to building bridges across borders.

- **Historical tensions**: Historical tensions, such as those stemming from past conflicts or injustices, can also make it difficult to build bridges across borders.

The United States Department of State[5] generally supports building bridges across borders as a means of promoting international cooperation and enhancing economic and cultural ties between countries. The department views bridges as symbols of connection and partnership using the construction of bridges to facilitate trade, travel, and exchange between nations. However, the specific stance of the Department of State on any bridge project would depend on a variety of factors, including the geopolitical context, economic impact of the project, and potential security risks.

Additionally, the United States Department of State views diplomacy as a critical tool for building bridges across borders and promoting peace, security, and economic growth around the world." [6] The department's mission includes advancing America's interests, values, and security through diplomacy and engagement with foreign governments, international organizations, and people. The State Department works to build and maintain relationships with foreign partners, resolve conflicts through diplomatic means, and support of America's businesses and citizens abroad. In this context, diplomacy is seen as a means of encouraging mutual understanding, cooperation, and trust between nations.

Here are a few references that we are familiar with and will talk about later in the book:

- **NATO**[7]: whose purpose is to safeguard the freedom and security of all its members by political and military means

- **The United Nations**[8]: whose goal is to maintain international peace and security, develop friendly relations among nations, and achieve international cooperation.

- **The Economist**[9]: which offers fair-minded, fact-checked coverage of world politics, economics, business, science, culture, and more.

- **The Council for Foreign Relations**[10]: an American think tank specializing in foreign policy and international relations.

- **America Connected**[11]: a non-profit organization embraces an entirely non-partisan, non-political and proactive approach to connecting people of the world closer together and discovering that they share much more in common than what separates them.

Each of these above have a strong role to play.

At last count, the world population is about 8 billion people living in 200 different countries. At the same time, each day and in every part of the world, we all become closer and closer to one another. Technology—that our parents and grandparents could never imagine—empowers us to do wonderful things together, but technology is just the hardware and software through which we connect.

Diplomacy has been bolstered by:

- Faster travel: Planes and trains can cover long distances much faster than other modes of transportation, such as ships or cars. This means that people can travel to other countries quickly and efficiently, reducing travel time and making it easier to connect with people in other countries.

- Increased accessibility: These modes of transportation have made it possible for people to travel to places that were previously difficult to reach. Remote locations, such as small towns or rural areas, are no longer inaccessible, which has opened new opportunities for tourism and business.

- Greater convenience: People can travel directly from one city to another without having to transfer or make multiple stops. This has made travel more convenient and efficient, making it easier for people to connect with other countries.

- Greater affordability: With the increased competition in the airline and train industries, travel has become more affordable for people. This had made it easier for people to travel to other countries for tourism, business, or to connect with family and friends.

In today's interconnected world, the progress in transportation means, such as planes and trains, has brought about a revolutionary change in how people connect with other countries. The remarkable speed, accessibility, convenience, and affordability of travel have paved the way for extensive cultural exchange, trade, and globalization.

Amidst this global outreach, it is essential not to overlook the profound human connections we experience in our daily lives through family, community, and personal and professional networks. This interconnectedness, now accessible on a global scale, is truly a gift that our world celebrates. With the advent of computers, laptops, smartphones, and the Internet, social media has opened doors to incredible possibilities, enabling us to connect with one another anywhere in the world.

In this dynamic landscape, cultural diplomacy emerges as a vital force, facilitating the exchange of ideas, values, and traditions. As we strengthen relationships with other countries, we connect greater social and cultural cooperation, finding common ground with people from diverse backgrounds. Embracing our differences and treating one another with respect will lead to a more progressive and developed world.

The goal of cultural diplomacy is to serve as a dynamic force, promoting connections between people through mutual understanding, trust, and engagement with diverse cultures. Its aim is to promote harmonious international relations by bringing nations and individuals closer together.

Every day, this unifying process unfolds, as people come together, connecting, and joining forces through a simple yet powerful act—breaking bread. Starting with food, barriers are broken down, and cooperation is fostered. It provides an opportunity to share opinions, embrace differences, and bridge gaps between individuals.

A personal experience in India exemplifies the transformative nature of this approach. Engaging in yoga together, the initial shyness and awkwardness dissipated once the session concluded, and the group decided to have tea together. As they sat around the table, the atmosphere changed, with laughter and conversation flowing effortlessly. The language barrier seemed to vanish as they shared the simple act of drinking tea, forming bonds of friendship despite having little in common beyond their interest in yoga. This encounter illustrated the power of sharing common experiences and breaking bread, leading to the sharing of joy, love, and trust—a testament to the potency of cultural diplomacy as a problem-solving tool.

While cultural diplomacy seeks to build bridges across borders, it is important to recognize that some countries may choose not to participate due to various reasons. Geopolitical tensions, economic concerns, and security issues may deter certain nations from engaging in such endeavors. Additionally, cultural, or historical factors might influence a country's reluctance to connect with its neighbors. In such cases, building bridges across borders may not be a priority or may be viewed as a potential threat to their interests.

The Connection of Hope

In the mosaic of human existence, hope, and connection join, forming an intricate pattern of interdependence. As defined by the Merriam-Webster dictionary, connection signifies the state of being linked or associated with another, revealing the profound relationship between two or more things. A timeless example of connection lies in the harmonious bond between peanut butter and jelly in a sandwich.

Hope, on the other hand, emerges as an emotion characterized by the fervent anticipation and desire for specific outcomes or wishes to materialize. It is the beacon that guides us through the intricacies of life, shining brightly even in the darkest of times.

In our unyielding quest to build and nurture meaningful relationships, we unravel the threads of hope, cultivating a profound sense of connectedness with the world around us. Strong bonds with family, friends, and colleagues provide us with the love, support, and sense of purpose that elevates our self-esteem. This innate feeling of belonging extends far beyond our immediate circles, enveloping a broader community and reaching out to individuals from diverse backgrounds and cultures worldwide.

Within these connections lie the keys to our pursuit of happiness, safety, and security, enriching our lives with resilience and contentment. Though the journey to foster and fortify these relationships demands effort and dedication, the invaluable rewards it bestows upon our lives are immeasurable.

As we engage with people from different countries and cultures, our understanding of the world expands, and our capacity to empathize and appreciate diversity deepens. We recognize that values and beliefs may differ, yet our collective pursuit of hope bridges these gaps. A simple, yet profound starting point is to embrace wholehearted listening, immersing ourselves in the perspectives of others. In doing so, we honor their uniqueness while finding common ground that unites us on a deeper level.

Together, hope and connection propel us forward on a shared journey toward a more interconnected and harmonious world. Building bridges across borders is not just an aspiration; it is the embodiment of hope in action. By fostering cultural exchange, mutual understanding, and cooperation, we create a symphony of hope that resonates across nations and cultures, nurturing a world where empathy, understanding, and a shared vision for a better tomorrow flourish."

The Transformative Power of Cultural Diplomacy

- **Cultural exchange programs**: Cultural exchange programs provide opportunities for people from different countries and cultures to learn from each other through immersive experiences. This can include language study, arts and cultural performances, and homestays with local families.

- **Diplomatic visits and cultural events**: Diplomatic visits and cultural events provide opportunities for political leaders and diplomats to engage in dialogue and build relationships through shared cultural experiences. This can include attending cultural festivals, visiting museums and historical sites, and participating in traditional ceremonies.

- **Media and digital platforms**: Digital platforms and social media can be used to connect people across borders and promote cultural understanding. This can include sharing stories and images that highlight cultural traditions and practices, promoting cultural events and festivals, and engaging in cross-cultural dialogue through online forums and social media groups.

- **Education and language learning**: Education and language learning programs can promote cultural understanding and help people to connect across cultural and linguistic divides. This can include language classes, cultural immersion programs, and educational exchanges that bring students and scholars from different countries together.

Through the celebration of our differences and the diverse mosaic of unique cultural traditions and practices, we have the power to shape a truly inclusive and interconnected world. This transformative vision rests on a bedrock of empathy, understanding, and mutual respect, binding us together as global citizens in a fabric of unity.

But What About the Twists and Turns of Democracy?

Democracy[12] is a political system that is built on the principle of equal representation and participation of citizens in government decision-making.

However, the implementation of democracy in practice often involves navigating twists and turns influenced by a variety of factors, such as political ideology, interests, power dynamics, and historical context.

One major twist in democratic systems is the challenge of striking a balance between individual rights and freedoms and the needs of the larger community. For instance, while freedom of speech and expression are essential components of democracy, they can also be exploited to spread hate speech or incite violence, leading to calls for speech restrictions.

Another challenge in democracy is the influence of money and special interest groups on the political process. Wealthy individuals and corporations can use their financial resources to sway elections and shape government policies in their favor, eroding the principle of equal representation.

Additionally, the growing polarization and division in society can pose a threat to democracy. When people become deeply entrenched in their beliefs and unwilling to listen to opposing viewpoints, reaching consensus, and making progress on critical issues becomes challenging.

Despite these challenges, democracy remains a popular and widely adopted political system because it offers citizens the opportunity to participate in government decision-making and hold elected officials accountable.

Take the January 6 insurrection,[13] what if people had turned right instead of left?

The events of January 6, 2021, when a mob of supporters of former President Donald Trump stormed the US Capitol building to disrupt the certification of the Electoral College vote, were a severe attack on American democracy. The outcome of the events could have been very different if the mob had turned right instead of left, or if several other factors had been different.

Yes, sometimes only a few things need to happen differently for big things to change. The fragility of democracy lies in its reliance on the willingness of citizens to engage in the political process in a peaceful and responsible manner and to respect the rule of law and the outcome of elections. When people lose faith in the democratic process, or when they believe that their voices are not being heard, it can lead to unrest and violence.

The events of January 6th serve as a reminder of the importance of preserving and protecting democracy and the need for all citizens to work together to defend its core principles. This includes respecting the outcome of elections, supporting peaceful and lawful protest, and rejecting violence and extremism in all forms.

Building bridges across borders is an indispensable approach to cultivating understanding and cooperation between different countries and cultures. In democratic societies, open and respectful communication and dialogue form the foundation of building these bridges and fostering unity.

Within the context of democracy, creating bridges across borders can cultivate a more connected and cooperative global community. When individuals from diverse countries come together to share ideas, perspectives, and experiences, they can learn from one another and establish trust. This, in turn, can lead to increased collaboration on global challenges, such as climate change, economic development, and security.

However, building bridges across borders also presents challenges. Differences in language, culture, and values can create barriers to understanding and cooperation, while political tensions and conflicts may hinder collaboration among nations.

Despite these challenges, the benefits of building bridges across borders are profound, and it remains crucial for democracies to strive for greater international cooperation and understanding. This can involve promoting cross-cultural exchanges, fostering diplomatic relations, and supporting initiatives that unite people from different countries. By working toward a more connected and cooperative global community, democracies can help promote peace, stability, and prosperity for all.

The problems faced by democracies, such as in America, often resonate across other countries and provide valuable lessons on the significance of preserving and strengthening democratic institutions and values.

For instance, maintaining a balance between individual rights and the needs of the larger community is a shared challenge among many democracies worldwide. Issues like hate speech, misinformation, and extremism can undermine democratic stability and integrity, necessitating thoughtful consideration on how to address these challenges while upholding democratic values.

Additionally, ensuring equal representation and reducing the influence of money in politics is a common struggle faced by democracies. The influence of special interest groups and the call for transparency and accountability in government are issues that require collective exploration and resolution.

In the thrilling world of global collaboration, democracies build bridges together, drawing strength from the vast treasury of shared experiences and wisdom. Fueled by this collective knowledge, they boldly confront challenges with unparalleled efficacy, forging an unbreakable alliance that propels them toward triumphant victories. This collaboration sparks ingenious best practices, transforming them into an unstoppable force that deftly unravels shared problems with brilliance and innovation, while holding high the torch of democratic values, illuminating the path to a brighter future.

Teaching democracy becomes a mesmerizing dance, gracefully weaving through diverse forms: from diplomatic endeavors that span continents to cultural exchange programs that transcend boundaries. Like a harmonious symphony, nations and governments engage with people from far-reaching lands, igniting fires of democracy that blaze passionately across the globe. With each stride, bridges of understanding and cooperation emerge, solidifying the foundation for enduring global peace and unshakable stability.

Unified, participating nations and governments stand as staunch guardians of democracy's sacred flame, their collective passion and unwavering resolve fortifying the very essence of just governance. With every step forward, the world they shape becomes a dynamic canvas of equality and hope, where the echoes of democratic ideals reverberate, ensuring that a more equitable and righteous world flourishes for all humanity.

In our upcoming chapter, we invite you to step into a journey through time, delving into the world of diplomacy. Join us as we uncover the fascinating evolution of diplomatic practices and the pivotal role they have played in shaping history.

> "Diplomacy is the art of understanding and respecting others, even when their opinions and actions differ from your own. It is the ability to find common ground and build bridges of understanding, rather than walls of division. True diplomacy is rooted in compassion, empathy, and the belief that peaceful coexistence is possible through dialogue and mutual respect."[14]
> Mahatma Gandhi

Timeless Talks: Leaders Feasting on Ideas and Insights

With the candlelight casting a warm glow on the table, the diplomatic leaders discuss the world becoming increasingly interconnected, and the leaders contemplate the significance of cultural diplomacy in fostering understanding and cooperation among nations.

> **George Washington** "Gentlemen, I believe that cultural diplomacy is of the utmost importance when it comes to understanding and building relationships with other nations. By gaining knowledge and understanding of the customs, beliefs, and values of other cultures, we can foster more effective communication and cooperation."
>
> **Abraham Lincoln** "I do not disagree with you, General, but I must remind you that sometimes war is necessary for the greater good. As leaders, it is our duty to protect our nation and its people, even if it means resorting to arms."
>
> **Nelson Mandela** "I understand your viewpoint Mr. Lincoln, but I must respectfully disagree. War brings only destruction, loss of lives, and trauma to the people. We as leaders have a responsibility to exhaust all peaceful means of resolving conflicts before resorting to war. We must always strive for peace and reconciliation, even in the face of adversity."

Mahatma Gandhi "I concur with Mr. Mandela. Nonviolence and mutual respect are the key principles to resolve conflicts and build a more just and equitable world. By engaging in dialogue and seeking common ground, we can work toward resolving conflicts and building a more just and equitable world."

Winston Churchill "I can understand all of your views, gentlemen. Diplomacy has the power to bring people from different cultures and backgrounds together and to promote understanding and cooperation between nations. It is essential for building a more peaceful and harmonious environment, a global community. However, I also understand the importance of being prepared for the worst and being ready to defend our nation."

George Washington "Diplomacy is a crucial tool in shaping the course of international relations. By building relationships and understanding with other nations, we can work toward common goals and create a more peaceful and harmonious world."

Abraham Lincoln "I agree, George. Diplomacy allows us to address conflicts and differences in a peaceful and constructive manner, rather than resorting to violence and war. It is essential for building a better world for all."

Mahatma Gandhi "I believe that diplomacy can be a powerful force for good, especially when it is based on the principles of nonviolence and mutual respect. By engaging in dialogue and seeking common ground, we can work toward resolving conflicts and building a more just and equitable world."

Nelson Mandela "My friends," Nelson Mandela says. "I agree with Mr. Gandhi. Diplomacy has the power to bring people from different backgrounds and cultures together and to promote understanding and cooperation between nations. It is a vital tool for building a more peaceful and united global community."

Winston Churchill "I agree with all of you. is essential for building a more peaceful and harmonious global community."

George Washington "Indeed, cultural diplomacy is the key to understanding and building relationships with other nations. It allows us to better understand the customs, beliefs, and values of other cultures, which can lead to more effective communication and cooperation. Cultural diplomacy can also be used to promote mutual understanding and respect between different cultures and nations, which can help to resolve conflicts and promote peace."

Abraham Lincoln "I agree that cultural diplomacy is important, but I must respectfully disagree with the idea that it can always resolve conflicts and promote peace. Sometimes war is necessary for the greater good. As a leader, it is our duty to protect our nation and its people, even if it means going to war."

Nelson Mandela "I understand your perspective, Mr. Lincoln, but I must respectfully disagree. War brings destruction, loss of lives, and trauma to the people. I believe that as leaders, we have a responsibility to exhaust all peaceful means of resolving conflicts before resorting to war. We should always strive for peace and reconciliation, even in the face of adversity."

Mahatma Gandhi "I believe that diplomacy can be a powerful force for good, especially when it is based on the principles of nonviolence and mutual respect. By engaging in dialogue and seeking common ground, we can work toward resolving conflicts and building a more just and equitable world."

Winston Churchill "I agree with all of you. is essential for building a more peaceful and harmonious global community. However, I also understand the importance of being prepared for the worst and being ready to defend our nation."

TWO

CULTURAL DIPLOMACY: A JOURNEY THROUGH TIME

STEP BY STEP IN CONNECTING HISTORY TO PRESENT DAY DIPLOMACY

"OBSERVE GOOD FAITH AND JUSTICE TOWARDS ALL NATIONS. CULTIVATE PEACE AND HARMONY WITH ALL"
- GEORGE WASHINGTON

Chapter 2

CULTURAL DIPLOMACY: A JOURNEY THROUGH TIME

> "Cultural exchange is like giving water to the
> roots of friendship and peace."[15]
> Mahatma Gandhi

EMBARK ON A thrilling journey through time as we uncover the exhilarating roots of cultural diplomacy. From ancient civilizations to the modern era, this powerful tool has been weaving vibrant connections between diverse groups. Explore the rich history of cultural exchange, where envoys and diplomats served as bridges between nations, cultivating profound relationships and instilling cooperation.

Discover the timeless wisdom found in *Deuteronomy 10:19*, where the commandment to "love the stranger" reverberates through the ages. This divine lesson of hospitality and compassion resonates in the hearts of humanity, urging us to embrace others with open arms, just as if we were once strangers in a foreign land.

As we delve into the depths of history, we encounter the profound words of Democritus, the ancient Greek philosopher, "To a wise and good man, the whole earth is his fatherland," a timeless testament to the universality of human connections and the boundless potential of cultural diplomacy.

But this captivating journey is not confined to the annals of history. In the modern world, cultural diplomacy continues to flourish in vibrant forms. Witness the exchange of artists, musicians, and cultural icons, breathing life into the essence of nations. Unravel the intricate tapestry of educational exchange programs, empowering individuals with knowledge and understanding.

Step into a realm where cultural initiatives transcend borders, propelling economic and social development with unmatched vigor. Embrace the power of cultural diplomacy as it surges forward, forging an integrated melody of connections across the globe.

Let the legacy of cultural diplomacy ignite your spirit, invigorating your perspective on the world. Embrace the magic of profound connections and the promise of a united, interconnected global community. As we continue to explore the ever-evolving landscape of cultural diplomacy, it may inspire us to create a world where love, respect, and compassion bring us together as one human family. This is the journey of a lifetime, an unforgettable experience that will leave you breathless with anticipation for the grand finale!

Democritus (born c. 460 BCE—died c. 370), an ancient Greek philosopher and a central figure in the development of the atomic theory[16] of the universe, said this about diplomacy: "To a wise and good man the whole earth is his fatherland."[17]

In more recent history, cultural diplomacy has taken many forms, including the exchange of artists, musicians, and other cultural figures; the promotion of educational exchange programs; and the use of cultural initiatives as a means of promoting economic and social development.

Cultural diplomacy has also been shaped by historical events and trends. For example, the Cold War[18] saw the use of cultural diplomacy as a means of competing for influence between the United States and the Soviet Union. In more recent years, the increasing globalization of culture has led to the proliferation of cultural diplomacy as a means of building relationships and understanding between nations.

Cultural diplomacy has a long history, with many countries participating in efforts to promote cultural exchange and build bridges across borders through the centuries.[19] Some of the most notable examples include:

- **Ancient Greece**[20]: The Greeks were known for their love of art, literature, and theater, and they spread their culture throughout the Mediterranean world through trade, colonization, and diplomacy.

- **Rome**[21]: The Roman Empire was renowned for its architecture, engineering, and legal system, and its influence extended far beyond its borders through military conquests and cultural exchange.

- **The Byzantine era**[22]: Also known as the Byzantine Empire, this era refers to the period spanning from the fourth century AD until the fall of Constantinople in 1453. The Byzantine Empire was a continuation of the Eastern Roman Empire and was centered around the city of Constantinople (modern-day Istanbul) as its capital.

    Some of the most significant events of the Byzantine era include the reign of Emperor Justinian I, who oversaw a period of territorial expansion and cultural flourishing in the sixth century AD; the Iconoclasm controversy of the eighth and ninth centuries, which centered on the use of religious images; and the Fourth Crusade, which led to the sack of Constantinople by Western European forces in 1204.

    The Byzantine Empire was also known for its significant contributions to art, architecture, and literature, with notable examples including the Hagia Sophia, the iconic church and later mosque in Istanbul, and the works of historians such as Procopius and Anna Komnene.[23]

- **Islamic Golden Age**[24]: During the Islamic Golden Age, which lasted from the eighth to the thirteenth century, the Islamic world made significant contributions to science, philosophy, and the arts and promoted cultural exchange with other civilizations through trade and diplomacy.

- **Renaissance**[25]: The Renaissance, which took place from the fourteenth to the seventeenth century in Europe, was a period of cultural, artistic, and scientific advancement, and many countries in Europe participated in cultural exchange through diplomacy and trade.

As transportation and communication technology advanced, it facilitated greater travel and connections among people from diverse parts of the world. This increased mingling of cultures and ideas brought both opportunities for cooperation and understanding, as well as new challenges with conflicts arising between unfamiliar groups.

During the nineteenth and twentieth centuries, European colonial powers expanded into Africa and Asia, leading to clashes with indigenous populations. These confrontations often stemmed from cultural, economic, and political disparities and involved groups who had not encountered each other before the colonial era.

In the modern era, globalization has intensified the interconnectedness of people and nations, yielding both positive outcomes, such as economic growth and cultural exchange, and negative consequences like new sources of conflicts and tensions among individuals with diverse backgrounds and traditions.

Cultural diplomacy remains instrumental in promoting cross-border understanding and collaboration, with countries like France, Germany, and the United States establishing cultural institutes and supporting exchange programs. In the face of our world becoming more interlinked, the roots of conflicts and disputes have grown more intricate and varied, involving individuals who lack personal knowledge of each other. Consequently, cultural diplomacy continues to evolve and adapt to address the changing needs of our linked humanity.

Outstanding Examples of Individuals Who Have Championed Cultural Diplomacy on a Global Scale

- **Pablo Casals**[26]: a Spanish cellist who used his music to bring people together and promote peace during the twentieth century.

- **Toni Morrison**[27]: an American author and Nobel Prize laureate who used her writing to promote understanding and bridge cultural divides.

- **Yo-Yo Ma**[28]: a French American cellist who has performed and collaborated with musicians from around the world to promote cross-cultural understanding through music.

- **Muhammad Ali**[29]: an American boxer who used his celebrity and charisma to promote peace and cultural understanding during the Civil Rights Movement and beyond.

- **Mstislav Rostropovich**[30]: a Russian cellist and conductor who used music as a means of promoting cultural diplomacy and human rights.

- **Youssou N'Dour**[31]: a Senegalese singer and songwriter who has used his music to promote African culture and unity.

- **Andres Segovia**[32]: a Spanish classical guitarist who helped to establish the guitar as a respected musical instrument and promote Spanish culture through his performances.

- **Martha Graham**[33]: an American dancer and choreographer who helped to promote American modern dance abroad and bring attention to American culture through her international tours.

- **Ravi Shankar**[34]: an Indian sitar virtuoso who helped to introduce Indian classical music and culture to the Western world and promote cross-cultural understanding through his performances and collaborations.

- **Mahatma Gandhi**[35]: (1869-1948), an educational teacher who taught education as a powerful tool to brings awareness to people.

- **Nelson Mandela**[36]: (1918-2013), a revolutionary anti-apartheid, philanthropist, politician and one of the great leaders of the world

- **Winston Churchill**[37]: (1874-1965), a British statesman, soldier, and writer who served as prime minister of the United Kingdom twice, from 1940 to 1945, during the Second World War, and again from 1951 to 1955. Apart from two years between 1922 and 1924, he was a Member of Parliament (MP) from 1900 to 1964 and represented a total of five constituencies.

- **Martin Luther King Jr**[38]: (1929-1968), globally renowned for his speech, "I Have a Dream" in Washington, MLK is one of the most celebrated souls across the globe and is named among the great leaders of the world. His leadership was fundamental to that movement's success in ending the legal segregation of African Americans in the South and other parts of the United States. He was awarded the Nobel Peace Prize in 1964.

- **Abraham Lincoln**[39]: (1809-1865), known as the sixteenth president of the United States, he was a revolutionary leader who ignited the "free nation" spirit in the USA.

- **Mother Teresa**[40]: (1910-1997), left a lasting dent in humankind. Because of her unforgettable devotion to empowering vulnerable groups, she has grabbed a notable mention in the list of great leaders of the world. She led a global community in her support, which avidly worked for opening orphanages, clinics, around the world.

- **Napoleon Bonaparte**[41]: (1769–1821), a reputed French military leader profoundly remembered as the Emperor of France as well as his significant role in the Napoleonic wars.

- **George Washington**[42]: (1732-1799), one of the Founding Fathers of America, the first and only nonpartisan political leader, and first president of America

- **Daliai Lama**[43]: (1935-present) among the great leaders of the world; working for non-violence, peace, and democracy for more than fifty years.

- **Julius Caesar**[44]: (100BC-44BC), a revolutionary personality and legacy is from the fact that his name is synonymous with leadership, and the month of July is named after him.

- **Franklin D Roosevelt**[45]: (1882-1945), known as FDR, was an American political leader who assisted his country during the Great Depression and WWII. FDR's leadership teachings are still applicable for business executives today, even more than eighty years later.

- **Ashoka the Great** [46]: (304 BC–232 BC) was the last emperor of the Maurya Empire and recognized as a Buddhist advocate who preached Buddhist principles and lessons from Buddha's life to the people.

- **Alexander the Great** [47]: (356BC – 323BC), known as "the man who conquered the world," is widely regarded as the greatest military leader of all time, controlling the greatest empire in history, stretching from Greece to Egypt to India. He accomplished the great feat of uniting numerous Greek city-states.

- **Margaret Thatcher**[48]: (1925–2013), known as the "Iron Lady," was elected prime minister, the first woman to hold the position. During her three terms, she cut social welfare programs, reduced trade union power, and privatized certain industries.

- **Maharaja Ranjit Singh**[49]: (1780–1839), known as the "Lion of Punjab," was the first Maharaja of the Sikh Empire who protected religious freedom inside his borders. People from all walks of life, religions, and castes were engaged in his empire. Infrastructure was renovated, trade was opened and developed, and the arts flourished under his rule.

- **Bill Gates** [50]: (1955–Present) vision and leadership has inspired an entire generation of innovators altering the way the world does business and communicates with information technology (IT), being used by millions of people all over the world.

Across diverse corners of the world and across various epochs, these remarkable individuals are bound together by their magnificent minds and extraordinary wisdom. Driven by their inspirational journeys, they have left an indelible mark on history, achieving extraordinary goals that continue to be revered to this day.

An introduction of another heroic figure and the exploration of this remarkable story.

Gary Powers[51] was an American pilot who was shot down while flying a U-2 spy plane over the Soviet Union in 1960. The incident caused a diplomatic crisis between the United States and the Soviet Union. Eventually, the crisis was defused through diplomatic negotiations and the exchange of prisoners, including Powers. He was released in February 1962 in exchange for a Soviet spy, Rudolf Abel. Powers' release was part of a larger prisoner exchange, known as the "Spy Swap." Along with Powers, the US released Soviet spy Rudolf Abel, who was captured in the United States, in exchange for several other individuals, including American student Frederic Pryor and West German national Gunther Guillaume.[52]

Reaching for the Stars Together: Notable Examples of International Space Cooperation

The space program has emerged as a powerful tool for cultural diplomacy, fostering stronger relations among nations. By promoting international cooperation in space exploration, it has united individuals from diverse countries in pursuit of a shared objective, nurturing cross-cultural understanding and collaboration.

- **International Space Station (ISS)**[53]: The ISS is a joint project between five space agencies: NASA (United States), Roscosmos (Russia), JAXA (Japan), ESA (Europe), and CSA (Canada). It has been continuously inhabited since November 2000 and serves as a platform for research in various fields, including biology, physics, and astronomy.

- **Hubble Space Telescope**[54]: The Hubble Space Telescope is a collaboration between NASA and ESA, launched in 1990. It has been responsible for many groundbreaking discoveries in astronomy and cosmology and has been serviced and upgraded by space shuttle crews from both agencies.

- **Mars missions**[55]: Many recent missions to Mars have been collaborations between multiple space agencies. For example, the Mars Exploration Rovers (Spirit and Opportunity) were a joint project between NASA and JAXA, while the Mars Express orbiter was a collaboration between ESA and Roscosmos.

- **Voyager missions**[56]: The Voyager 1 and 2 missions, launched in 1977, were a joint project between NASA and JPL (Jet Propulsion Laboratory). The spacecraft have explored the outer Solar System and beyond and are still transmitting data back to Earth today.

- **Lunar missions**[57]: Several recent missions to the Moon have involved international cooperation, including the Chang'e missions by China, the Lunar Reconnaissance Orbiter by NASA, and the Chandrayaan missions by India.

- **The Apollo-Soyuz Test Project**[58]: The first internationally manned space mission, which saw American Astronauts and Soviet cosmonauts link up in space in 1975, promoting improved relations between the two countries during the height of the Cold War joint missions between the United States and Russia to repair and upgrade the Hubble Space Telescope, demonstrating the power of international cooperation in space exploration.

Collaborative missions between Europe, Russia, and the United States to Mars and other destinations in our solar system demonstrate the potential for international cooperation in exploring our universe.

The ISS is a collaborative project between the space agencies of the United States, Russia, Europe, Japan, and Canada. The station is home to a rotating crew of astronauts and cosmonauts who conduct research in a wide range of scientific fields, including biology, physics, astronomy, and meteorology.

The ISS has been visited by more than 240 people from nineteen countries and is an example of international cooperation in space exploration. It serves as a platform for scientific research, technology development, and testing of new systems for future human exploration of space. The ISS is expected to be operational until at least 2024 and possibly beyond that.

These are just a few examples of how the space program has been used as a tool for cultural diplomacy and improving relations between nations.

China's Endeavors in Cultural Diplomacy

> "To have friends come from faraway places, is this not a joy?"
> Confucius[59]

China has been involved in cultural diplomacy throughout history. The country has a rich cultural heritage, and its government has often used cultural exchanges and initiatives to promote a positive image of China and improve relations with other nations.

- **The Silk Road Initiative**: A modern-day revival of the ancient Silk Road trade route, which aims to promote cultural exchange and economic cooperation between China and other countries in Asia and Europe

- **Confucius Institutes**: Cultural centers established by the Chinese government in countries around the world, which aim to promote Chinese language and culture and improve understanding between China and other nations.

- **Cultural exchange programs**: Includes visits by Chinese artists, musicians, and dancers to other countries and hosting international cultural events in China, which aim to promote cultural exchange and understanding between China and other nations.

- **The 2008 Summer Olympics in Beijing**: Served as a platform for China to showcase its culture and modern advancements to the world.

Uncovering the Threads of Russia's Diplomatic Web

Russia, like many other countries, has also used cultural diplomacy as a tool to promote a positive image of the country and improve relations with other nations. Throughout history, Russia has used cultural exchange programs, international cultural events, and other initiatives to showcase its rich cultural heritage and promote understanding between Russia and other countries.

Peter the Great,[60] also known as Peter I, was a Russian tsar who ruled from 1682 until his death in 1725. He is known for his ambitious reforms that modernized Russia and transformed it into a major European power. He was a skilled diplomat and visionary leader who recognized the need for Russia to modernize and reform to keep up with the other European powers.

One of Peter's most significant accomplishments was his effort to westernize Russia.[61] He traveled to Western Europe to learn about their customs, culture, and military tactics and then brought back these ideas to Russia. He implemented sweeping reforms that modernized the Russian military, government, and society, including the creation of a navy, the introduction of Western-style clothing, and the establishment of a new capital city, St. Petersburg.

Despite some controversies, Peter the Great's legacy is largely positive and as a skilled and successful diplomat.[62] During his reign, Peter sought to build strong diplomatic relationships with European powers to modernize Russia and expand its influence on the world stage. He conducted successful diplomatic missions to countries such as France, England, and the Netherlands and formed alliances with other European powers against the Ottoman Empire. This enabled Peter to see new architecture, new dress and customs, and arts, all of which he brought back to Russia, opening the curtains to the world. Peter also demonstrated his diplomatic abilities through his handling of internal politics. He skillfully navigated complex power struggles within the Russian nobility, consolidating power in the hands of the tsar, and implementing reforms to modernize the country.

- **The Bolshoi Ballet**[63]: one of the world's oldest and most famous ballet companies, which has toured extensively around the world and helped to promote Russian culture and dance to international audiences.

- **The Hermitage Museum**[64]: in St. Petersburg, one of the largest and most important art museums in the world, which has hosted international exhibitions and collaborated with museums around the world to promote the appreciation and understanding of Russian art and culture.

- **Russian cultural centers and institutes**: such as the Pushkin Institute,[65] established in countries around the world, which aim to promote Russian language and culture and improve understanding between Russia and other nations.

- **The 2014 Sochi Winter Olympics**[66]: which served as a platform for Russia to showcase its culture and modern advancements to the world.

Forming Alliances and Shaping the World: Diplomacy During World War II

During World War II,[67] cultural diplomacy was largely put on hold as countries focused their resources and attention on the war effort. In many cases, cultural exchange programs were suspended, and international cultural events were canceled.

However, even during the war, some countries continued to use cultural diplomacy as a tool for propaganda and to promote their own national interests. For example, both the Allies and the Axis powers used film and other forms of media to promote their own perspectives and ideologies and to sway public opinion in their favor.

In the post-war period, cultural diplomacy, once again, became an important tool for promoting cross-cultural understanding and improving relations between nations. The Marshall Plan,[68] for example, which provided aid to Western European countries in the aftermath of the war, included cultural exchange programs and initiatives aimed at promoting cultural understanding between the United States and Europe.

Overall, the impact of World War II on cultural diplomacy was significant, but it did not completely halt cultural exchange and diplomacy between nations. Cultural diplomacy continued to play an important role, both during the war and in the aftermath, in promoting cross-cultural understanding and improving relations between nations.

Today, cultural diplomacy continues to play an important role in promoting cross-cultural understanding and improving relations between nations. The world has become increasingly interconnected, and cultural diplomacy has become a key tool for nations to promote their cultures and values and build relationships with other countries.

Diplomacy can be classified into different types based on the context, objectives, and methods used. **Here are some common types of diplomacy**[69]:

- **Public diplomacy**: involves communicating with and influencing foreign public opinion through various means, such as cultural exchanges, media outreach, and educational programs.

- **Cultural diplomacy**: a form of public diplomacy that seeks to promote a nation's cultural heritage, arts, and values as a way of enhancing, understanding, and building relationships with other countries.

- **Economic diplomacy**: involves promoting a nation's economic interests and strengthening economic ties with other countries through trade agreements, investment partnerships, and other economic initiatives

- **Multilateral diplomacy**: involves negotiating and coordinating with other countries through international organizations such as the United Nations, World Trade Organization, and the World Health Organization

- **Track II diplomacy**: involves unofficial or informal diplomacy between non-governmental actors, such as academics, business leaders, and civil society organizations to foster dialogue and build trust

- **Bilateral diplomacy**: involves direct communication and negotiations between two countries to resolve specific issues or advance mutual interests

- **Digital diplomacy**: involves the use of digital technologies, such as social media and online platforms, to promote a nation's foreign policy objectives and engage with foreign audiences

- **Gunboat diplomacy**: a type of coercive diplomacy that involves using military force or the threat of force to achieve foreign policy objectives

- **Sports diplomacy**: a form of public diplomacy that uses sports as a means of promoting international understanding and building relationships between countries

- **Summit diplomacy**: involves high-level meetings between heads of state or government to discuss key issues and resolve conflicts

Reconnecting the Steps Amidst a Journey of Disconnect

The notion of democratic progress and liberal economics being irreversible has been challenged throughout history. The once-flourishing democracies of ancient Greece, along with the powerful Republics of Rome and Venice, ultimately succumbed to external pressures or internal shortcomings. Similarly, the evolving liberal economic order in Europe faced a collapse during the tumultuous 1920s and 1930s. Contrary to the belief that a better idea will naturally prevail, sustaining such principles necessitates the concerted efforts of great powers, extensive labor, and tremendous energy to uphold them in the face of opposing forces.[70]

During a period of British control over the seas and a delicate balance of great powers in Europe, a relative sense of security and stability prevailed. This conducive environment led to the growth of prosperity, the expansion of personal freedoms, and a world that became more closely interconnected through revolutions in commerce and communication.

However, the outbreak of World War I marked a turning point, as the era of settled peace and advancing liberalism, with European civilization nearing its zenith, came crashing down. Hyper-nationalism, despotism, and economic calamity took the stage, overshadowing the once-promising spread of democracy and liberalism. The momentum of progress halted, and a somber reversal occurred, leaving only a few outnumbered and besieged democracies to grapple with the challenges of an uncertain future.[71]

Who knows what might have happened if Nazi Germany and imperial Japan had prevailed.

Political Scientist G. John Ikenberry argues that American power may diminish, but "the underlying foundations of the liberal international order will survive and thrive."[72]

The Fragile Threads of Disconnection: Along the Journey of Mean, Degrading, and Dehumanizing Instances

As humans, we are remarkably adept at forming connections, but we are equally quick to disconnect along this journey. Unfortunately, there have been instances where this disconnection took a darker turn, manifesting in mean-spirited actions, degrading behaviors, and dehumanizing treatment. These experiences serve as poignant reminders of the fragility of our connections and the importance of fostering empathy and understanding in our interactions with one another. Let's delve into some of these disconnects and explore the impact they have on individuals and communities.

- **The Black Death**: Many people believed the Black Death in 1348[73] to be a punishment from God for the sins of the people. Some people blamed the Jews, even claiming that wells used by Christians had been poisoned with the plague. As a result, persecution was quick, with Jews having their property stolen, their homes burned, and their inhabitants killed.

- **The Inter Caetra**: In 1494, a year after Christopher Columbus's arrival in the new world, Pope Alexander VI issued the papal bull "Inter Caetra"[74] This significant document proclaimed that any land not inhabited by Christians was open to be "discovered by Christian rulers" and that the "Catholic faith and Christian religion be exalted and be everywhere increased and spread, that the health of souls be cared for, and that the barbarous nations be overthrown and brought to faith itself."

- **Doctrine of Discovery**: This document, later known as the Doctrine of Discovery[75] played a foundational role in the European colonization of the Americas. It provided a legal basis for the presumptuous claims of Western expansion, famously known as Manifest Destiny, and unfortunately, it also led to the genocidal killing and oppression of Indigenous people. The Doctrine of Discovery had profound and far-reaching implications, shaping the course of history in the Americas and the treatment of Indigenous communities for centuries to come.

- **Slavery**: Even before the first Africans arrived in the Jamestown colony in 1619, slavery had already been a prevalent institution worldwide. In ancient economies, such as those of Greece and Rome, slaves played crucial roles and were integral components of their societies.[76] In America, tobacco and sugar plantations in the Southern colonies required intensive labor. To cut labor costs, plantation owners turned toward slavery.

- **Indian Removal Act of 1830**: In 1830, the Indian Removal Act[77] was passed that allowed the government to move Indian tribes to the land west of the Mississippi.

- **California Gold Rush**: Gold was found in California, in the 1850s,[78] settlers rushed west as quickly as possible and destroyed the land that the Indians depended on for hunting and fishing.

- **Indian Reservation Policy**: At the beginning of the twentieth century, the American government started putting Indian tribes on reservations in the western part of the United States.

- **The Jewish People act in 1862**: General Ulysses S. Grant[79] ordered the Jewish people (aiming to suppress cotton speculation during the Civil War), as a class to leave the area under his jurisdiction, including parts of Kentucky, Mississippi, Tennessee, within twenty-four hours (Lincoln later revoked the order).

- **Central Pacific Railroad**: In 1863, the Central Pacific Railroad[80] built the western portion of the first transcontinental railroad by employing more than 10,000 Chinese laborers. Demanding shorter workdays, better treatment, and equal pay to whites, several thousand Chinese in the Sierra Nevada laid down their tools and walked off the job, returning to their camps along the line. The strike ended after the Central Pacific cut off all their food and supplies, which forced the Chinese back to work.

- **Black Codes**: In 1865, "Black Codes"[81] were laws passed throughout the South, starting around 1865, that dictated most aspects of Black peoples' lives, including where they could work and live.

- **The Chinese Exclusion Act of 1882**: This was signed by President Chester A. Arthur,[82] and lasted for ten years and was then extended for another ten years by the 1892 Geary Act, requiring people of Chinese origin to carry identification certificates or face deportation.

- **The Bubonic plague**[83]: This hit San Francisco in the early 1900s. Chinese Americans, because they looked different, were blamed for it.

- **The Mississippi Senate Vote**: In 1922, Mississippi's Senate voted to send all the state's Black people to Africa.[84] After passing the Senate, the bill went to the State House of Representatives, and on March 1, 1922, it was voted out. Why was it voted out? Well, believe it or not, it was voted out because of Representative John Holmes Sherard, who explained his opposition this way, "this meant the loss of labor where the Negro was needed."[85]

- **Japanese Americans**: In 1942, United States Government falsely blamed Japanese Americans[86] for assisting Imperial Japanese forces in their attack. Americans forced confinement of more than 120,000 Americans of Japanese ancestry. These Japanese Americans were held in camps[87] that often were isolated, uncomfortable, and overcrowded.

- **The Holocaust of 1933–1945**[88]: This was the systematic state-sponsored killing of six million Jewish men, women, children, and millions of others by Nazi Germany and its collaborators during World War II. The Germans called this "the final solution to the Jewish question."[89]

- **Racial profiling**: In the mid-80s, this was a practice that violated the US Constitution's core promises of equal protection under the law and freedom from unreasonable searches and seizures. It involved suspecting, targeting, or discriminating against individuals based on their ethnicity, religion, or nationality, which undermined the principles of fairness and justice enshrined in the Constitution.

- **September 11, 2001**[90]: A series of coordinated terrorist attacks were carried out by the extremist group al-Qaeda on the United States. These attacks, commonly referred to as "9/11," targeted major landmarks and institutions in the country, leading to significant loss of life and devastation. This led to a prevailing belief that Saddam Hussein had obtained chemical and nuclear weapons. However, a harmful and unfounded misconception emerged, wrongly implicating ALL Muslims as responsible for the devastating events of that day. Acknowledging and rectifying these misconceptions is crucial in fostering understanding and preventing the perpetuation of harmful stereotypes.

- **COVID-19 pandemic (2019)**[91]: During the COVID-19 pandemic 2019, some individuals and groups engaged in mean-spirited behaviors toward people of Chinese descent, wrongly blaming them for the virus's spread. This type of behavior is known as xenophobia and discrimination.

- **Timothy Wilson Attack Plan**[92]: In 2020 Timothy Wilson was killed in an FBI shootout in Benton, Missouri, on March 25, 2020, after planning to bomb a hospital, a school, a synagogue, and a mosque, declared that the virus had been "engineered by Jews as a power grab."[93] Other anti-Semites shared his view that Jews created it.

Maneuvering a Disconnected World

Charting our disconnected world presents a formidable challenge in an age of immense global interconnectivity. While technological advancements have enabled instantaneous communication and access to information, the paradoxical result is a world that often feels fragmented and divided. The disconnection can manifest in various forms, from political polarization and cultural divides to economic disparities and social isolation.

In the digital era, social media platforms and online echo chambers can reinforce pre-existing beliefs, creating virtual bubbles where people are exposed only to information that aligns with their viewpoints. This phenomenon can lead to a lack of understanding and empathy for those with different perspectives, further deepening the disconnect.

Moreover, geopolitical tensions and nationalist movements can foster an "us versus them" mentality, hindering international cooperation and exacerbating global challenges. Economic inequalities between developed and developing nations can widen the gap between privileged and marginalized communities, leading to a sense of disempowerment and exclusion.

In this context, navigating our disconnected world requires deliberate efforts to bridge the gaps and instill meaningful connections. Emphasizing dialogue, empathy, and mutual respect can help break down barriers and promote a shared sense of humanity. Encouraging open-mindedness and critical thinking can combat the pitfalls of misinformation and bias that contribute to disconnection.

Cultivating global citizenship and recognizing our collective responsibility in addressing pressing issues, such as climate change, poverty, and public health, can inspire collaborative solutions that transcend borders. Initiatives that promote cultural exchange, education, and diplomacy can foster understanding and appreciation for diverse perspectives.

Ultimately, the journey to navigate our disconnected world demands a commitment to building bridges across divides, embracing diversity, and seeking common ground.

Unplugged: Potential for Disconnection

History shows the world order is transient. Countries rise and fall, and the downfall of the Roman Empire brought an end not just to Roman rule but to Roman government and law.

Numerous foreign-policy experts perceive the current international order as the natural outcome of human progress, arising from the convergence of scientific and technological advancements, a rapidly expanding global economy, the reinforcement of international institutions, a new norm of international conduct, and the gradual but inexorable ascendancy of liberal democracy over alternative forms of governance.

The present order will only last if those who favor and benefit from it retain the will and capacity to defend it.

People tend to hold the belief that the chosen order endures because it represents what is fair and just, not just for us but for all. Presuming that the success of democracy signifies the triumph of a superior idea, and the prevalence of market capitalism denotes the supremacy of a better system, with the assumption that both are permanent and cannot be reversed.[94]

Francis Fukuyama's thesis about "the end of history"[95] has, for the most part, proven correct. Liberal democracy continued to spread after the Cold War as humankind evolved politically and socially. It has remained the most universally persuasive form of government around the world. Fukuyama's thesis was proven recently in nations where nobody expected there to be liberalization. For example, post-apartheid South Africa, Turkey, and eastern and central European nations that only decades ago felt the bondage of authoritarianism have become democratic countries. The idea of inevitable evolution means that there is no requirement to impose a decent order. It will merely happen.

Navigating a Diverse Diplomatic Landscape: Modern Forms of Diplomacy

Cultural exchange programs, such as student exchanges and cultural visits bring people from different countries together to learn about each other's cultures.

- **International cultural events**: Festivals, concerts, and exhibitions showcase the cultural heritage and contemporary achievements of different nations.

- **Cultural centers and institutes**: Examples include the British Council and the Goethe-Institute, which promote the language and culture of their respective countries and provide a platform for cultural exchange.

The world today is characterized by a diverse and dynamic landscape of cultural diplomacy, with countries using a range of initiatives and programs to promote cross-cultural understanding and improve relations with other nations. Giles Scott-Smith and David Snyder authors of *Cultural Diplomacy and International Relations in the Second World War and Its Aftermath* discuss that "Cultural diplomacy continues to be a key tool for nations to promote their cultures and values, build relationships with other countries, and contribute to a more peaceful and connected world."[96]

Join us in a captivating odyssey in the next chapter as we explore the remarkable world of cultural diplomacy, where art, music, and literature act as powerful bridges connecting people from diverse backgrounds. Discover how this enchanting form of diplomacy enables understanding, mutual respect, and appreciation for the richness of global cultures.

"Cultural Diplomacy is not a thing apart. It is an integral part of foreign policy, of which it should be the soul."[97]
Winston Churchill

Timeless Talks: Leaders Feasting on Ideas and Insights

With the candlelight flickering in the background, the statesmen delve into the topic of cultural diplomacy and its role in connecting cultures and communities throughout history.

George Washington "I must confess, my understanding of diplomacy in my time does not fully align with this concept of cultural diplomacy. In my era, diplomatic relations were primarily focused on forming alliances and treaties with other nations, not on exchanging culture."

Abraham Lincoln "I understand your skepticism, General Washington. However, I believe that cultural diplomacy has always been a part of diplomacy, but over time, as the world has grown more interconnected, the focus on cultural exchange has become more prominent."

Mahatma Gandhi "I believe that cultural diplomacy is essential for fostering understanding and cooperation between nations. By learning about and appreciating the cultures of other nations, we can build bridges and resolve conflicts in a nonviolent manner."

Nelson Mandela "I concur with Mr. Lincoln. Cultural diplomacy is a powerful tool for promoting peace and understanding between nations and cultures. It can help to break down stereotypes and create a more united and harmonious global community."

Winston Churchill "I, too, believe that cultural diplomacy is important for fostering understanding and cooperation between nations. In my time, we saw the power of cultural exchange to build bridges during difficult international relations."

George Washington "I can see the value in cultural exchange, but I must admit, it is hard for me to reconcile it with the traditional practices of diplomacy that I knew. It is fascinating how times have changed and how diplomacy has changed along with it."

Mahatma Gandhi "Gentlemen, I must express my concern that not everyone seems to understand the true nature of diplomacy. For it to be effective, it must be based on principles of nonviolence and mutual respect. Without these principles, diplomacy can devolve into power struggles and manipulation."

Abraham Lincoln "I share your concern, Mr. Gandhi. In my time, I saw how a nation divided can lead to the breakdown of diplomacy. It seems that when a nation is divided, diplomacy becomes a secondary concern, if not completely forgotten."

George Washington "I understand your concerns, gentlemen. However, I must remind you that diplomacy is not an easy task; it takes patience and understanding. In my time, I have seen how diplomacy can be effective in resolving conflicts and preserving peace. We must remember that diplomacy is not a one-time event. It is a process that must be constantly nurtured and maintained."

Nelson Mandela "I agree with General Washington, in my time, I have seen how diplomacy can be used to bring about change and promote peace in a non-violent manner. It is essential that we continue to work toward a more just and equitable world through diplomacy."

Winston Churchill "I concur with my esteemed colleagues. In my time, I have seen the power of diplomacy to build bridges and resolve conflicts. We must continue to work toward a more peaceful and harmonious global community through diplomacy."

Chapter 3

THE POWER OF CULTURAL EXCHANGE

"I Don't Like that Man. I Must Get to Know Him Better."[98]
Abraham Lincoln

Amidst a vibrant globe overflowing with diversity and unexplored opportunities, there lies a treasure trove of transformative experiences awaiting those who dare to venture into the realm of cultural exchange. The power it holds is nothing short of extraordinary – it can bridge chasms of misunderstanding, build unbreakable connections between nations, and ignite a global fire of creativity and innovation.

Just imagine a vibrant world of cultures, intricately latticed together through the exchange of ideas, art, language, and traditions. As individuals traverse this kaleidoscope of human experiences, they find themselves immersed in a journey of mutual understanding and appreciation. The barriers of ignorance crumble, replaced by a newfound empathy and respect for humanity.

But this exchange is not just a passive observation; it's a dance of harmony and unity. By joining hands with people from far-flung corners of the world, individuals become part of a global movement, a force that transcends borders and ideologies. The power of cultural exchange transforms mere acquaintances into friends and allies, forging alliances that bolster international cooperation and inspire dreams of a peaceful, shared future.

Venturing further into this magical world of cultural diplomacy, one uncovers its potential to shape the destiny of nations. Public diplomacy becomes an art, where the exchange of ideas becomes a symphony of diplomacy, art, and language. Countries project their best selves, not through propaganda, but through genuine connections, leaving a lasting impression of warmth and authenticity.

And as individuals delve deeper into the heart of cultural exchange, its economic prowess emerges. It sparks a global economic engine, driving tourism, trade, and investment to soaring heights. Nations become interconnected hubs of innovation and creativity, fueled by the fusion of diverse perspectives and unbridled talent.

But it's not all about tangible gains; the power of cultural exchange transcends the material world. It establishes a sense of pride in cultural heritage, preserving ancient traditions for generations to come. It nurtures a spirit of global citizenship, where every individual becomes an advocate for positive change, championing unity and cooperation to address the world's most pressing challenges.

In this realm of possibilities, the power of cultural exchange beckons, inviting people to unlock its wonders. It calls for explorers and dreamers, adventurers who seek to understand the world and themselves in ways they never thought possible.

It goes beyond mere entertainment or artistic expression; cultural diplomacy empowers individuals from different cultures to find common ground, advancing connections and mutual understanding.

At the heart of cultural diplomacy lies its significance in facilitating the exchange of ideas, values, traditions, and other cultural aspects. These enriching exchanges not only strengthen relationships between nations but also promote social and cultural cooperation. By helping people from foreign nations understand a country's ideals and institutions, cultural diplomacy garners broad support for economic and political objectives, making it a compelling tool for building influence.

In our daily lives, we witness the tangible effects of cultural diplomacy. Modern transportation and technology enable us to enjoy fresh fruits and vegetables year-round, sourced from various countries following in-season harvest times. Through the convenience of global trade, we can shop for and purchase items from different cultures, broadening our exposure and understanding of diverse societies. Engaging with movies and music from different parts of the world reminds us of the vastness and richness of our global community.

Cultural diplomacy plays a pivotal role in achieving several vital objectives. It serves as a bridge for cultural exchange and understanding, bringing people from diverse backgrounds together and cultivating an appreciation for each other's traditions and values. By enhancing understanding of other cultures, cultural diplomacy builds mutual respect and cooperation between nations, contributing to peace and harmony. Moreover, it acts as a powerful tool to reduce tensions and conflicts by promoting greater understanding and appreciation of other cultures.

Lyndon Johnson's inaugural address on January 20, 1965, was to help the country with a somberness from the shock of the tragic shooting of President Kennedy and the Vietnam situation. In his speech, he said, "For this is what America is all about. It is the uncrossed desert and the unclimbed ridge. It is the star that is not reached and the harvest sleeping in the unplowed ground. Is our world gone? We say 'Farewell.' Is a new world coming? We welcome it—and we will bend it to the hopes of man."[99]

In a world shaped by globalization and international relations, the importance of diplomacy in stimulating connections and understanding between nations cannot be underestimated.

Enter the Diplomacy Connectors, a trio of diplomats committed to promoting mutual understanding and unity through the power of cultural exchange, economic diplomacy, and public diplomacy.

- **Cultural Diplomacy**: One of the Diplomacy Connectors, Cultural Diplomacy, recognizes the potential of sharing ideas, art, language, and culture among nations. By facilitating these rich exchanges, Cultural Diplomacy aims to build bridges of understanding and empathy, fostering enduring connections between people from diverse backgrounds and traditions.

- **Economic Diplomacy**: Another vital member of the trio is Economic Diplomacy, who understands the significance of leveraging economic tools to achieve national interests. Through strategic trade relationships and collaboration, Economic Diplomacy seeks to promote economic growth and prosperity, breaking down barriers and facilitating cooperation between nations.

- **Public Diplomacy**: The third Diplomacy Connector excels in direct communication with foreign publics. Public Diplomacy's approach revolves around engaging in meaningful dialogues and seeking common ground. By expanding open communication and understanding, Public Diplomacy lays the foundation for peace and cooperation among nations.

Together, the Diplomacy Connectors embark on a global journey, organizing vibrant events that blend art, language, and music from various cultures. They facilitate trade agreements and cooperation that enhance prosperity and foster development for nations worldwide.

Their impactful message resonates deeply within international organizations like the United Nations, symbolizing the epitome of cooperation. The Diplomacy Connectors stand before a diverse audience, representing nations from all corners of the globe. Their words spark a powerful transformation, dismantling walls that once divided nations and replacing them with bridges of mutual understanding.

As people from different cultures reach out to one another, eager to learn and connect, the Diplomacy Connectors achieve their mission. The power of cultural exchange, economic diplomacy, and public diplomacy unites nations, ushering in an era of cooperation and peace.

The legacy of the Diplomacy Connectors serves as a reminder of the enduring impact of connection and the boundless possibilities that arise when people come together in mutual understanding and respect. Their efforts have transformed the world into interconnected hearts and minds, forever changed by the power of diplomacy and cultural exchange.

In a world that seeks unity and understanding, the Diplomacy Connectors stand as beacons of hope and inspiration, reminding us of the immense potential that lies within the exchange of ideas, culture, and cooperation. Their vision for a harmonious global community continues to inspire generations, highlighting the transformative power of diplomacy in instilling a more peaceful and interconnected world.

Strengthening Diplomatic Connections: Programs and Initiatives

Diplomacy plays a crucial role in connecting different countries and cultures, facilitating understanding, and promoting peaceful interactions. Several organizations and initiatives contribute to this noble endeavor:

- **Embassies and consulates**: Diplomatic missions staffed by knowledgeable individuals facilitate connections between countries. These entities provide valuable information on diplomatic events, programs, and initiatives that promote cultural exchange and understanding.

- **Cultural institutes and centers**: Many countries establish cultural centers or institutes abroad to showcase their heritage, language, and arts. These institutions organize events and programs that facilitate dialogue and cultural exchange.

- **International organizations**: Notable examples include the United Nations, World Bank, and International Monetary Fund, bringing together people from diverse backgrounds to work toward common goals. These organizations often host events and programs promoting cultural understanding.

- **Professional associations**: Organizations like the International Association of Cultural and Creative Industries unite individuals and entities from various countries and cultures working in the same field. These associations foster networking and collaboration among their members.

- **Educational programs**: Through the establishment of universities and the exchange of educators, educational initiatives promote cross-cultural learning. American study programs, conferences, and prestigious scholarships, such as Fulbright Scholarships, enable individuals to broaden their horizons and connect with others globally.

Effective Communication Channels

- **Broadcasting**: Traditional broadcasting has proven successful in disseminating ideas to foreign audiences. Initiatives like "America Connected TV–Get Connected" offer an unfiltered medium for distributing information and ideas to regions where media access might be limited.

- **Literature**: Newsletters, brochures, and posters are powerful tools for conveying information and education. They serve as effective means to share ideas, culture, and understanding.

The Power of Offering

Gift-giving serves as a profound gesture of thoughtfulness, respect, and care for others. The effects of meaningful gifts are enduring, fostering bonds, and strengthening diplomatic ties.

These programs of diplomacy and communication channels actively contribute to bridging the gaps between nations and cultures. Through these initiatives, understanding is cultivated, mutual respect is nurtured, and cooperation is fostered, laying the foundation for lasting and harmonious international relations.

Promoting the Unity of Mind, Body, and Soul in Global Diplomacy

In our interconnected world, the harmony of mind, body, and soul is paramount to achieving true health and fostering lasting peace and cooperation. This interconnectedness extends to the realm of diplomacy, where embracing the concept of mind, body, and soul can lead to more effective and empathetic interactions on a global scale.

Mindfulness in Diplomacy: Practicing mindfulness is a powerful tool for diplomats to cultivate patience, understanding, and empathy. By training the mind to remain present and focused, we can better comprehend the perspectives and needs of others, laying the groundwork for building trust and cooperation.

- **Emotional intelligence**: Diplomacy relies heavily on emotional intelligence, the ability to understand and manage emotions. By honing this skill, we can navigate complex and sensitive situations with empathy and tact, fostering understanding and mutual respect.

- **Physical health for effective diplomacy**: Maintaining good physical health is crucial to cope with the demands of long hours and frequent travel. A healthy body also supports a healthy mind, empowering effective decision-making and problem-solving.

- **Spiritual well-being**: We are often exposed to stress and challenging situations, and spiritual well-being can provide a sense of purpose and grounding.

- **A holistic approach to life**: The concept of mind, body, and soul emphasizes the interconnectedness of human existence and encourages a holistic approach to life. By prioritizing physical health, emotional well-being, and spiritual fulfillment, as individuals we become more balanced and harmonious, enhancing interactions with people from diverse cultures and backgrounds.

- **The connection between cultural diplomacy and unity**: By promoting cultural diplomacy and the unity of mind, body, and soul, we break down barriers and build a global community that celebrates our shared humanity.

Plus, embracing the unity of mind, body, and soul in diplomacy is essential for building a world where empathy, understanding, and cooperation thrive. By cultivating a holistic approach to life and promoting cultural diplomacy, we create a global community bound together by mutual respect and shared values.

The Synergy of Health and Diplomacy in a Globalized World

In an interconnected and globalized world, the realms of health and diplomacy intertwine in various ways, forging bridges of cooperation and understanding among nations. Health diplomacy serves as a powerful means to strengthen relationships between countries, as they unite to combat shared health challenges, such as the global response to the COVID-19 pandemic. Through joint efforts and collaboration, countries find common ground in addressing pressing health issues, fostering mutual trust, and reinforcing bonds of friendship.

Beyond combating health crises, health diplomacy also extends its reach to promote social and economic development across borders. One country's aid in improving another's healthcare system or tackling public health concerns, such as infectious diseases and chronic conditions, not only enhances well-being but also nurtures long-lasting partnerships founded on shared goals of prosperity and progress.

The promotion of global health emerges as a pivotal aspect of foreign policy, recognizing the intrinsic link between health and a nation's economic and social advancement. By championing healthier populations worldwide, countries pave the way for enhanced cooperation and greater global stability. As health becomes a shared priority, it becomes a catalyst for building stronger alliances and collaboration.

Amidst the diversity of global diplomacy, yoga emerges as a unique tool with the potential to facilitate harmonious international relations. As the popularity of yoga grows globally, it serves to enhance physical and mental health, reducing healthcare costs and paving the path for healthier societies. This shared journey toward well-being connects mutual understanding, cooperation, and empathy among countries, breaking down barriers and strengthening a spirit of unity.

Beyond its physical benefits, yoga's roots in ancient Indian philosophy and culture offer a profound opportunity for cultural exchange and appreciation. By embracing the practice of yoga, countries can transcend borders, encouraging cultural bridges, and strengthening bonds between diverse nations.

Moreover, yoga's emphasis on mindfulness and meditation contributes to a more peaceful and harmonious international environment. As individuals cherish inner peace and reduce stress through yoga, these positive changes ripple outward, advancing a climate of tranquility and reducing tensions between nations. In a world where conflicts can arise from misunderstandings, yoga offers a pathway to tranquility, encouraging nations to approach diplomacy with a clear and peaceful mindset.

In this interconnected world, public diplomacy plays a critical role, encompassing cultural, educational, political, and informational instruments. Health and yoga, as integral elements of this global landscape, offer invaluable opportunities to shape the narrative of international relations, promoting wellness, understanding, and cooperation among nations.

The Power of Global Connections: Cultural Diplomacy in a Globalized World

In today's globalized world, the importance of connection and cultural diplomacy cannot be overstated. Public diplomacy encompasses a diverse array of diplomatic instruments, from cultural exchanges to educational initiatives, all with the aim of building relationships with people from other countries and influencing foreign opinion. The desire to connect with others is a universal trait shared by all cultures, serving as the adhesive that binds us together and helps us understand not only others but also ourselves.

Through meaningful connections, we transcend mere individuality and become a cohesive community. The act of connecting with others enriches our lives, leading to greater happiness, improved health, and longevity. As we cultivate stronger connections with people from different backgrounds, our sense of well-being expands, including a global community that thrives on diversity and mutual understanding.

Instead of fearing differences and anticipating divisive responses, embracing our diversity becomes the key to genuine connection. Every human being is unique, shaped by different life experiences, but it is precisely these differences that forge bonds and bridge cultural divides. By valuing and connecting through diversity, we pave the way for a more harmonious and inclusive world.

Cultural diplomacy serves as a powerful tool in shaping foreign perceptions and understanding. It leverages the arts, education, history, science, and various other aspects of culture to influence foreign fields of thought positively. By showcasing the richness and vibrancy of a nation's culture and ideas, cultural diplomacy seeks to create a positive view of the country, its people, and its policies among other nations. This approach advocates for greater cooperation with the nation, advances policy change, and cultivates political and cultural understanding to prevent conflicts with foreign adversaries. Ultimately, cultural diplomacy plays a vital role in building bridges of empathy and respect, contributing to improved global relations.

In this interconnected world, cultural exchange becomes a gateway to deeper connections and mutual appreciation. By promoting cross-cultural interactions through arts, customs, sports, and more, countries can break down barriers, dispel misconceptions, and introduce a climate of international collaboration.

Understanding and embracing the cultural customs and traditions of others align with the broader goal of nurturing global harmony and unity.

Connection and cultural diplomacy serve as essential pillars in our globalized world. By valuing diversity, forging meaningful connections, and promoting cultural exchange, we can cultivate a world where mutual understanding, respect, and cooperation thrive. The power of cultural diplomacy lies in its ability to shape perceptions, build bridges, and cultivate an atmosphere of friendship.

Religion as a Bridge: Interfaith Cultural Diplomacy in a Globalized World

Religion plays a significant role in shaping international relations and foreign policy. Inter-religious dialogue emerges as a powerful tool for fostering understanding and cooperation among people from diverse religious backgrounds. By highlighting the common threads and moral values found in traditions like Islam, Christianity, and Judaism, we can bridge divides and alleviate hostilities between communities.

The concept of "Abrahamic traditions" serves as a unifying force, demonstrating the shared heritage and moral order among these religions. By emphasizing these commonalities, interfaith cultural diplomacy can pave the way for constructive conversations and peaceful resolutions to religious issues.

Cultural diplomacy becomes a crucial enabler in this context, serving as the foundation upon which inter-religious dialogue can flourish. Building solid relationships through cultural exchanges, educational initiatives, and intellectual engagement allows people to come together in a spirit of mutual respect and understanding.

Knowledge of religion is an asset in this diplomatic effort. Diplomats and leaders equipped with a nuanced understanding of religious beliefs and practices can navigate sensitive religious issues with greater empathy and insight. By combining religious knowledge with diplomatic skills, they can instill an environment conducive to dialogue and reconciliation.

Moreover, interfaith cultural diplomacy not only addresses existing hostilities but also helps prevent conflicts rooted in religious misunderstandings. By promoting cross-cultural understanding and appreciation of different religious traditions, we lay the groundwork for a more tolerant and inclusive global community. In a world where religious diversity is increasingly intertwined with political and social dynamics, interfaith cultural diplomacy holds the potential to transcend borders, creating a vision of unity.

From Neighborhoods to Nations

Heroes manifest in diverse forms, with real-life exemplars of kindness, helpfulness, and bravery found within our communities. Fred Rogers, the cherished host of Mister Rogers' Neighborhood, keenly grasped the significance of "the people in the neighborhood."

The bedrock of diplomacy and cooperation, however, takes root at the local level, where positive relationships flourish, and communities rally around shared objectives. Active engagement with neighbors and involvement in local communities facilitates unity that can transcend immediate boundaries. This unity, a catalyst for understanding across divergent groups, ultimately nurtures a broader atmosphere of peace and goodwill. Genuine transformation commences from grassroots endeavors, and interconnected communities wield the strength to illuminate a path toward a more cooperative world.

- **Forging unbreakable bonds**: Earlier epochs in America thrived on profound connections. Tight-knit neighborhoods mirrored extended families, their enduring bonds providing solace and joy. But concealed within their security often lay apprehension and distrust of outsiders. Studies from the American Psychological Association[100] spotlight how fear often arises from unfamiliarity. This underscores the pivotal role of cultivating empathy and comprehension across cultures and communities. Cultivating robust ties among people from varied backgrounds has the power to disperse apprehension, giving rise to a society that is inclusive and compassionate.

- **Embracing global linkages**: While nurturing local bonds remains paramount, so does extending this to encompass our globally interlinked society. In the contemporary landscape, the import of diplomacy cannot be overemphasized. Diplomacy, the bedrock of advancing mutual trust, respect, and understanding among nations, lays the cornerstone for constructive worldwide interaction. Its role in addressing intricate global quandaries, including democracy, human rights, and the creation of peaceful societies, is Unyielding. Neglecting diplomacy risks eroding the credibility and potency of employing military might.

To secure enduring solutions and champion well-being across the planet, diplomacy's engagement and unwavering endorsement of peace are prerequisites. Ultimately, uniting with neighbors and embracing global ties are intertwined aspirations. By supporting respect and understanding on both local and international fronts, we craft a world that celebrates diversity, empathy replaces fear, and cooperation reigns supreme. Within this interconnected sphere, we can usher in a future that encompasses all of humanity.

Global Connections Through Human Diplomacy

- **The unexpected**: In the year 2022, the world experienced airline flight shortages, resulting in numerous canceled flights and stranded passengers. Among them was Carlos Cordero, who found himself stuck at the terminal, yearning to return home while also seeking to extend a helping hand to fellow travelers. In a bold move, Carlos shouted out to those around him, proposing a solution: "We're renting a van to Knoxville, Tennessee," the destination of their original scheduled flight. Little did he know that this spontaneous act of kindness would have a profound impact, reaching far beyond the terminal.

- **Global impact**: A video of Carlos's invitation spread like wildfire across social media, attracting attention from people worldwide. The two-minute clip, viewed five million times, captured the hearts of individuals from various corners of the globe. Thirteen passengers, complete strangers until that moment, found themselves united in an unexpected journey to Knoxville. Despite having nothing in common but a canceled flight, they embarked on a shared adventure, connecting with one another in ways they could not have anticipated.

- **The power of human diplomacy**: The van ride spanning 652 miles was not merely a means of transportation; it became a testament to the power of human diplomacy. Human Diplomacy is a concept that highlights the pivotal role of individuals and their interactions in shaping diplomacy, transcending the traditional focus solely on state-to-state relations. In this chance encounter, the passengers demonstrated how ordinary people, through their acts of kindness, empathy, and camaraderie, can foster genuine connections that bridge borders and cultures.

- **Creating lifelong bonds**: As the journey unfolded, introductions turned into conversations, and laughter filled the van, the group of once-strangers transformed into a tight-knit community. A passenger named Michelle spoke on behalf of her fellow travelers, expressing that they had become friends for life. This heartwarming incident exemplifies the potential of human diplomacy to create lasting bonds that transcend geographical boundaries.

- **A global message**: Carlos's impromptu act of organizing the van ride and the subsequent viral video delivered a powerful message to the world. It reminded us that in times of uncertainty and crisis, the spirit of human connection can overcome barriers and unite people from diverse backgrounds. The unexpected journey to Knoxville exemplified the potential of human diplomacy to foster understanding, compassion, and a sense of shared humanity, resonating with individuals worldwide.

In a globalized world, where technology connects us like never before, human diplomacy presents a unique opportunity for individuals to be agents of positive change. By nurturing relationships, engaging in acts of kindness, and embracing diversity, ordinary people can contribute to a more connected and harmonious world, one interaction at a time

Global Diplomacy in Times of Disasters

Disasters strike with devastating force, impacting communities worldwide and leaving behind long-term physical, economic, and psychological scars. In the aftermath of such calamities, cultural diplomacy emerges as a powerful tool to foster cross-cultural understanding and support, helping to rebuild resilience and strength in affected communities.

- **Cultural diplomacy for recovery**: Cultural diplomacy comes into play as nations share their experiences and cultural practices, offering support through cultural events and exchanges. This collaborative approach aids in promoting a deeper understanding of the values and beliefs of affected communities, forging positive relationships, and providing vital support during the challenging recovery phase.

- **Humanitarian gesture transcending boundaries**: In times of crisis, countries often put aside political differences and provide disaster relief assistance to those in need as a humanitarian gesture. Guided by principles of humanity and the desire to alleviate suffering, nations come together to offer aid and support. Such actions, rooted in compassion, can transcend political and cultural barriers, showcasing solidarity with those facing adversity, regardless of their nationality or beliefs.

- **Encouraging goodwill amidst adversity**: Remarkably, disasters can bring about unexpected alliances. After the 9/11 attacks, even countries historically adversarial toward the United States, like Iran and Iraq, offered condolences and support. Similarly, natural disasters prompt countries with political tensions to extend a helping hand to one another. In these moments, disaster relief and humanitarian aid act as agents of goodwill, fostering positive relationships beyond traditional alliances.

- **Global response to 9/11 and other disasters**: The September 11, 2001, terrorist attacks triggered a strong international response, with countries offering condolences, aid, and resources to support the recovery effort. Countries like Canada, Japan, and Australia lent assistance during the Tsunami in Southeast Asia (2004), and Canada, Mexico, and European countries aided the United States in the aftermath of Hurricane Katrina (2005).

- **A shared responsibility**: The international community views disaster response as a shared responsibility, where countries collaborate to provide support regardless of political differences. From Cyclone Nargis in Myanmar (2008) to the Haiti earthquake (2010) and the Japan earthquake and tsunami (2011), nations worldwide sent rescue teams, humanitarian aid, and financial support to help affected regions recover.

In the face of disasters, diplomacy becomes an essential tool, transcending borders and fostering cooperation on a global scale. The examples of international assistance during these crises demonstrate the power of diplomacy in uniting nations, promoting understanding, and providing a lifeline to communities in need. Through the spirit of cultural diplomacy and humanitarian gestures, the global community stands strong, ready to support one another in times of dire need.

The September 11, 2001[101] terrorist attacks in the United States resulted in a strong outpouring of international support and solidarity. In the aftermath of the attacks, many countries offered condolences, sent aid and resources, and assisted with the recovery effort. For example, several countries, including Canada and Germany, sent rescue and aid teams to assist in the aftermath of the attacks, and many countries also offered to assist with the investigation and prosecution of those responsible. The United Nations and many individual countries also made donations to support relief efforts. The international response to the 9/11 attacks demonstrates the power of diplomacy in coming together to support one another in times of crisis, transcending political and cultural differences to promote greater understanding and cooperation.

Here are some other examples of diplomacy during times of disaster:[102]

- **Tsunami in Southeast Asia**[103] **(2004)**: Many countries, including the United States, Japan, and Australia, sent aid and resources to help with the recovery effort.

- **Hurricane Katrina**[104] **(2005)**: Several countries, including Canada, Mexico, and several European countries, aided the United States during the aftermath of Hurricane Katrina.

- **Cyclone Nargis in Myanmar**[105] **(2008)**: Several countries, including the United States, Japan, and the European Union, provided aid and resources to support recovery efforts.

- **Haiti earthquake**[106] **(2010)**: Several countries, including the United States and France, sent rescue and aid teams to Haiti after the earthquake, as well as humanitarian and financial aid.

- **Japan earthquake and tsunami**[107] **(2011)**: Several countries, including the United States, Australia, and South Korea, sent rescue and aid teams to Japan, as well as humanitarian and financial aid.

- **Turkey/Syria earthquake**[108] **(2023)**: Countries across the world, America, China, Russia, the European Union, the UK, and offers of assistance from all over the world offered aid and resources.

These examples demonstrate how diplomacy can play an important role in promoting international cooperation and support in times of disaster, helping to alleviate the impact on affected communities.

The Diplomatic Climate After the Disaster

The impact of a disaster on the relationship between countries that do not get along can vary widely. In some cases, the act of providing or receiving disaster relief can help to improve relationships and build trust between nations. For example, during a crisis, collaborative efforts to effectively respond can bring people from different countries together, facilitating mutual understanding of each other's perspectives and needs.

However, the effect of a disaster on international relations can also be more complex and can depend on a variety of factors, including the political climate prior to the disaster, the nature and scale of the disaster, and the response of the affected country. In some cases, the provision of aid can become a point of contention and can be used as leverage in international negotiations.

Ultimately, the impact of a disaster on international relations is difficult to predict and can vary widely depending on the specific circumstances. However, disasters have the potential to bring people and countries together in a shared effort to address a common humanitarian crisis, and the provision of aid can be an important tool for building bridges and improving international relationships.

But How Does Diplomacy Fare When War Erupts?

During a war, the diplomatic efforts of nations involved in the conflict often shift from negotiating peacefully to securing support from allies and trying to find ways to end the conflict as quickly and favorably as possible. Diplomatic relations between nations that are at war can be severely damaged and may take years to repair, even after the conflict has ended.

In some cases, neutral nations may still engage in diplomatic efforts to try to bring about a ceasefire or a peace agreement. International organizations such as the United Nations may also play a role in trying to negotiate a peaceful resolution to the conflict.

It is important to note that diplomacy should continue to be pursued, even during times of war, as it can help to reduce the duration and severity of the conflict and prevent the situation from escalating further.

Is It Still Possible for Us to Pursue Friendship with That Nation?

Yes, it is possible to maintain friendly relationships with nations that have been involved in a war or conflict, although it can be challenging. After a conflict has ended, the process of reconciliation and rebuilding relationships can begin. This often requires a willingness on both sides to forgive and move forward, as well as a commitment to addressing the root causes of the conflict.

Mending diplomatic relationships can take time and effort, but it is important for the stability and peace of the international community. Diplomatic relations can be restored through various means, such as through negotiations, peace agreements, and cultural exchanges.

In some cases, nations that have been in conflict may eventually develop strong, cooperative relationships and even become allies. However, the legacy of the conflict can linger and affect future relationships, so it is important to approach the reconciliation process with a commitment to healing and resolution.

Unity: Togetherness in a Globalized World

All I ever needed to know I learned in kindergarten[109] is a popular essay written by Robert Fulghum, which was published in 1986 as part of a collection of essays under the same title. The essay has become well-known and widely circulated in various forms, including as a book, posters, and greeting cards.

The essay suggests that many of life's most important lessons are taught in early childhood, specifically in kindergarten. Fulghum identifies basic values such as sharing, being kind, cleaning up after oneself, and apologizing when one has wronged another as the foundation of a happy and fulfilling life.

The essay has become popular because of its timeless wisdom, which applies to people of all ages and backgrounds. Its central message is that the principles of kindness, cooperation, and mutual respect that we learn in kindergarten are fundamental to living a happy and fulfilling life and should be carried with us into adulthood and applied in our interactions with others.

And "when you go out in the world, it is best to hold hands and stick together,"[110] emphasizes the importance of unity and teamwork in facing the challenges of life. It suggests that we should support and work together with others rather than trying to navigate the world alone. Holding hands and sticking together symbolizes the idea of working in unison, sharing ideas and resources, and offering each other emotional support.

In essence, this poem encourages us to maintain a childlike sense of wonder, curiosity, and kindness throughout our lives and to approach the world with a spirit of cooperation and unity.

The power of cultural exchange lies in its ability to bring people from different countries and cultures together to learn about each other's ways of life and build relationships based on understanding and respect.

Cultural exchange programs and initiatives can:

- **Promote cross-cultural understanding**: By exposing people to different cultures, languages, and traditions, cultural exchange programs can help to break down barriers and promote a deeper understanding and appreciation of other cultures.

- **Foster mutual respect and tolerance**: Through cultural exchange, people can learn to appreciate the differences and similarities between cultures and develop a greater respect for diversity.

- **Strengthen relationships between nations**: By building relationships between individuals and communities, cultural exchange programs can help to strengthen relationships between nations and promote peace and cooperation.

- **Encourage creativity and innovation**: By exposing people to new and different ways of thinking, cultural exchange programs can inspire creativity and innovation and contribute to cultural and economic growth.

Let the power of cultural exchange reverberate within your soul. As we immerse ourselves in the revelations of cultural exchange programs and trailblazing initiatives, brace yourself as diversity unfurls before your eyes, crafting together a mesmerizing collage of shared experiences and boundless potential. Feel the pulse of unity strengthen as nations forge unbreakable bonds, and the bridges of understanding span far and wide. This is your moment to seize the opportunity, to take steps that will forever transform your perception of the world. Welcome the brilliance of our shared humanity, and let it illuminate the path to a future of interconnectedness and harmonious coexistence. The promise of a brighter, more united world beckons, driven by the positive power of cultural exchange.

In the forthcoming chapter, we will set out on an exhilarating journey through pivotal moments in history, where Diplomacy at Summits and Sporting events play pivotal roles in shaping the course of nations and fostering a shared vision for a brighter and interconnected world. From the United Nations General Assembly to the World Cup Finals, the excitement of Diplomacy's transformative power awaits us as we explore how these events continue to reshape our world today.

> "Observe good faith and justice towards all nations; cultivate peace and harmony with all."[111]
> George Washington

Timeless Talks: Leaders Feasting on Ideas and Insights

As they enjoy their meal, the leaders begin to discuss the power of cultural exchange and its potential to bring nations and cultures together.

George Washington "I must say, I am impressed with how far cultural diplomacy has come since my time. Back then, diplomacy primarily focused on forming alliances and treaties. But now, cultural exchange is an integral part of it. It is like comparing a simple letter sent by a messenger to the advanced communication systems of today."

Abraham Lincoln "I agree, George. The world has grown more interconnected, and as a result, cultural diplomacy has become more prominent. It is vital for building understanding and cooperation between nations, just like how a house divided cannot stand."

Mahatma Gandhi "I disagree. I believe that cultural exchange is important, but it should not be the primary focus of diplomacy. Nonviolence and mutual respect should be at the heart of diplomacy, just like how a chain is only as strong as its weakest link. It is these principles that truly change the world."

Nelson Mandela "I agree with Lincoln. Cultural diplomacy plays an essential role in promoting peace and understanding between nations and cultures, just like how education is the most powerful weapon which you can use to change the world. It helps break down stereotypes and create a more united and harmonious global community."

Winston Churchill "I also think that diplomacy should not be mainly focused on cultural exchange. It should be centered on finding common ground and resolving conflicts in peaceful ways. Cultural exchange may be just a secondary point, like how the ability to forgive and forget is one of the greatest qualities of a great leader."

George Washington "It is fascinating to see how the role of cultural diplomacy has evolved over time, like how a tree that is bent too far will break. Each of you brings a unique perspective, and there are different ways of looking at the importance of cultural exchange in diplomacy." "I remember during my time as commander-in-chief, I had to navigate diplomatic relations with Native American tribes. It was not easy, but through cultural exchange and understanding, we were able to form alliances and treaties that benefited both sides."

Abraham Lincoln "I understand the importance of cultural diplomacy from my own experiences. During my presidency, I had to navigate delicate diplomatic relations with foreign nations during the Civil War. I remember how important it was to understand the perspectives and cultures of our allies to effectively communicate and cooperate with them."

Mahatma Gandhi "I can attest to the power of cultural diplomacy from my own experiences in India. By understanding and appreciating the cultures of the British colonizers, I was able to effectively communicate and negotiate for Indian independence through nonviolence."

Nelson Mandela "I, too, have seen the power of cultural diplomacy in my own experiences. During my struggle against apartheid in South Africa, I emphasized the importance of understanding and appreciating different cultures to promote unity and reconciliation."

Winston Churchill "As a leader during World War II, I understand the importance of cultural diplomacy in navigating international relations. I remember the importance of understanding and appreciating the cultures of our allies to effectively communicate and cooperate with them to defeat the Axis powers."

George Washington "Cultural diplomacy has been a powerful tool throughout history, and it will continue to be so in the future. It is important that as leaders, we continue to prioritize cultural exchange and understanding in our diplomatic efforts."

FOUR
FROM SUMMITS TO SPORTING EVENTS: THE MANY FACES OF DIPLOMACY

STEP BY STEP IN CONNECTING HISTORY TO PRESENT DAY DIPLOMACY

"SPORTS AND GAMES ARE A VITAL PART OF HUMAN LIFE, AND DIPLOMACY IS NO EXCEPTION."
- WINSTON CHURCHILL

Chapter 4

FROM SUMMITS TO SPORTING EVENTS: THE MANY FACES OF DIPLOMACY

> "Sport has the power to change the world. It has the power to inspire, it has the power to unite people in a way that little else does it speak to youth in a language they understand. Sport can create hope where once there was only despair." [112]
> Nelson Mandela

Contests and Assemblies: The Worldwide Harmony of Diplomacy

PICTURE AN AWE-INSPIRING performance where diplomacy conducts a mesmerizing world event, intertwining threads to unite nations across the vast expanse of the world. But hold on tight, for this is no ordinary orchestration; it transcends the limits of tradition, embracing ever-changing forms that reflect the dynamic landscape of international relations.

Summits and cultural extravaganzas set the stage for this epic spectacle. Visionary leaders converge in high-stakes gatherings, wielding the baton of traditional diplomacy to resolve conflicts and forge historic agreements. Yet, it is the vibrant canvas of cultural exchanges and sporting events that paints the diplomatic landscape with splashes of informality and raw strength. Here, nations proudly showcase their unique talents, and mutual understanding blurs political boundaries.

Prepare for a multifaceted marvel that transcends expectations. Economic collaboration orchestrates the steps of trade and investments, weaving a robust network of bonds between nations. As if that weren't enough, peacekeeping missions take center stage, orchestrating a breathtaking arrangement that joins together international forces in conflict zones, crafting a chorus of stability and safeguarding civilians.

The spotlight then shifts to the Digital Frontier, where a new crescendo awaits. Witness the thrilling performance of digital diplomacy as technology and social media strings resonate with citizens across borders, creating harmonies of international dialogue and understanding in this ever-changing global rhythm.

Diplomacy casts its spell, uniting nations in a mesmerizing pursuit of peace, stability, and mutual prosperity. Diverse activities and spirited collaborations fuse into a crescendo of a sense of shared vision and camaraderie. As nations entwine in this magnificent dance of diplomacy, their bonds grow stronger, understanding flourishes, and a shared vision of an interconnected world emerges. Feel the pulse of our rapidly intertwining planet, as diplomacy emerges as the heartbeat that unites nations and propels them toward an electrifying future of shared progress and profound respect.

Economic diplomacy: Brace yourself for a high-octane dance of trade and investment, as countries harmonize their interests and forge unbreakable bonds. Witness the spectacular power of economic cooperation as it elevates nations, and prosperity.

But the adrenaline doesn't stop there! Enter the realm of humanitarian diplomacy, a dynamic force combating global challenges head-on. With unwavering resolve, this epic endeavor fights against poverty, disease, and natural disasters, spreading a canopy of relief and hope over those in need. Prepare to be moved as diplomatic heroes leap into action, transforming lives and touching hearts around the world.

Yet, the most electrifying crescendo awaits—the breathtaking drama of peacekeeping diplomacy. Hold your breath as international forces descend upon conflict zones, heroes of diplomacy working tirelessly to nurture stability and protect civilians caught in the crossfire. This pulse-pounding mission is a testament to the power of unity and the resilience of the human spirit.

Join us on this invigorating quest, where diplomacy knows no limits, and the spirit of cooperation conquers all obstacles!

Are you ready to witness the world being transformed by the indomitable spirit of diplomacy? Welcome to a voyage that will leave you breathless, forever changed, and passionate about the limitless possibilities of unity.

Showcasing the Diverse Expressions of Diplomacy[113]:

- **Summit Diplomacy**[114]: The G20 Summit, held annually to bring together leaders of the world's largest economies, is an example of summit diplomacy. At the summit, leaders discuss a range of economic and political issues and work toward reaching agreements on global challenges.

- **Sporting Diplomacy**[115]: The Olympic Games is a well-known example of sporting diplomacy. The games bring together athletes from around the world to compete, promoting international goodwill and understanding.

- **Economic Diplomacy**[116]: The North American Free Trade Agreement (NAFTA) between Canada, Mexico, and the United States is an example of economic diplomacy. The agreement removed trade barriers and helped to increase trade between the three countries.

- **Humanitarian Diplomacy**[117]: The World Health Organization's response to the Ebola outbreak in West Africa is an example of humanitarian diplomacy. The WHO worked with governments and other organizations to provide medical aid and support to those affected by the outbreak.

- **Peacekeeping Diplomacy**[118]: The United Nations Mission in South Sudan (UNMISS) is an example of peacekeeping diplomacy. UN peacekeepers are deployed to the country to maintain stability and protect civilians, supporting the peace process and promoting a lasting settlement.

- **Digital Diplomacy**[119]: The use of social media by the US State Department to promote American foreign policy goals is an example of digital diplomacy. The State Department uses Twitter and other platforms to communicate directly with citizens of other countries and promote American values and interests.

- **Cultural Diplomacy:** A significant impact on the world can be had by promoting cultural exchange and understanding between countries. By bringing people from different cultures together and promoting the appreciation of different traditions and values, cultural diplomacy can help to build mutual respect and cooperation between nations.

Unlocking the Power of Cultural Diplomacy

Cultural diplomacy possesses a hidden key that can unlock more peaceful and harmonious international relations. By fostering a deep appreciation and understanding of diverse cultures, it holds the potential to alleviate tensions and conflicts between nations, paving the way for a world of greater understanding and unity.

But that's not all; cultural diplomacy's influence transcends borders and delves into the realm of economic development. Through promoting cultural exchange and cooperation, countries can tap into the boundless potential of tourism, trade, and investment. These avenues of growth and prosperity contribute to shaping vibrant economies and fostering global development.

Yet, while cultural diplomacy dazzles with its promise of unity, sports also wield the power of public diplomacy, albeit in a different guise. Hosting spectacular mega-events like the Olympics and FIFA World Cup becomes a grand stage for nations to showcase themselves and gain international prestige. Still, the impact of these sporting extravaganzas on achieving diplomatic goals is a subject of ongoing debate.

Take, for instance, China's 2008 Olympics—a spectacle that sought to unveil its openness to the world. Yet, some argue that despite the spectacle, the lasting diplomatic gains may have been less pronounced. On the other hand, Germany's 2006 FIFA World Cup emerged as a shining example of successful sports diplomacy. Facing a stained national image due to its history, Germany focused on investing in public diplomacy. The foreign office went all-in, investing heavily in creating a positive global perception. They mastered the art of communication, employing multilingual ambassadors to spread their message of goodwill, leading to a transformation in how the world viewed Germany.

Both cultural and sports diplomacy hold remarkable potential. They are vessels of soft power, capable of reshaping international relations, building bridges of understanding, and leaving lasting impacts on the world stage. As these avenues for diplomacy continue to evolve, their potential to create a more connected, cooperative, and harmonious world remains ever more promising.

Constructing Bonds and Shaping History through Summits

A summit is an assembly of state's leaders or governments at the international level.[120] They usually have significant media coverage, strong security, and a fixed agenda. The term "summit" was coined by Winston Churchill in 1950. Summits became a central element of the new contemporary diplomatic practice in the second half of the twentieth century, with meetings such as Kennedy and Khrushchev in Vienna in 1961[121] and Reagan and Gorbachev in Reykjavik in 1986.

Various Major International Summits:

- **G7 Summit**: This is a meeting of the leaders of seven of the world's largest and most advanced economies—Canada, France, Germany, Italy, Japan, the United Kingdom, and the United States.

- **G20 Summit**: This is a meeting of the leaders of nineteen countries and the European Union, representing the world's largest economies. The countries include Argentina, Australia, Brazil, Canada, China, France, Germany, India, Indonesia, Italy, Japan, Mexico, Russia, Saudi Arabia, South Africa, South Korea, Turkey, the United Kingdom, and the United States.

- **NATO Summit**: This is a meeting of the heads of state and government of the North Atlantic Treaty Organization, which is a military alliance of thirty North American and European countries.

- **UN General Assembly**: This is a meeting of all 193 member states of the United Nations to discuss and coordinate various global issues.

- **APEC Summit**: This is a meeting of leaders from twenty-one Pacific Rim countries, including Australia, Canada, China, Japan, Russia, South Korea, and the United States, among others.

- **ASEAN Summit**: This is a meeting of the leaders of the ten member states of the Association of Southeast Asian Nations, which include Brunei, Cambodia, Indonesia, Laos, Malaysia, Myanmar, the Philippines, Singapore, Thailand, and Vietnam.

- **EU Summit**: This is a meeting of the heads of state or government of the European Union member states, as well as the president of the European Council and the president of the European Commission.

- **BRICS Summit**: This is a meeting of the leaders of the five major emerging economies—Brazil, Russia, India, China, and South Africa.

- **Commonwealth Heads of Government Meeting**: This is a meeting of the heads of government of the fifty-four member countries of the Commonwealth of Nations, which is a political association of former British colonies and current dependencies.

Note that there are many other international summits that take place on various topics and at different levels, but these are some of the most prominent ones.

Unleashing the Power of Summits: Bridging Nations, Forging Bonds

In the ever-evolving landscape of diplomacy, summits have risen to prominence as a vital tool for forging connections and shaping international relations. G8 and G20 summits have become the norm, drawing political leaders from around the globe to engage in bilateral and multilateral meetings that hold immense significance in policymaking.

A remarkable advantage of these summits lies in the active participation of leaders themselves. Armed with the power to make critical decisions in their nations, leaders possess the nimbleness to respond swiftly to challenges presented at summits, unencumbered by the need for consultation. This preparatory advantage ensures leaders come to the table informed and ready for action.

But the significance of summits extends beyond policymaking. These gatherings offer leaders the invaluable opportunity to build positive relationships with their counterparts. As they familiarize themselves with one another, barriers of mutual distrust crumble, paving the way for smoother negotiations and fostering broader relationships based on trust. In this arena, leaders have an added incentive to charm and enchant their foreign counterparts for mutual benefit.

History has borne witness to the varying degrees of success that summits, and sporting events can achieve as diplomatic tools. From the 1936 Berlin Olympics, which eased tensions amid looming world conflict, to the more recent US-North Korea summit in Hanoi, with limited denuclearization progress, their effectiveness hinges on a complex interplay of motivations, goodwill, and global events.

Nevertheless, their significance remains undeniable. These summits provide a rare and precious platform for world leaders to engage in face-to-face negotiations, fostering trust and mutual understanding—a critical prerequisite for addressing interstate issues. As political leaders recognize their symbolic value and potential for strengthening bonds between nations, summits have become a testament to a government's commitment to act on critical issues.

Beyond immediate results, these gatherings contribute to the long-term exchange of views and cement the foundations of trust and cooperation. As the outcomes of a summit slowly unfold, the seeds of diplomatic success take root and bear fruit, manifesting in improved international relations and a world united by mutual understanding and common purpose.

A Myriad of Triumphs: Past Summit Success Stories

- Nuclear arms reduction: In 1986, President Ronald Reagan and Soviet General Secretary Mikhail Gorbachev met in Reykjavik, Iceland, for a summit on arms control. While the summit ended without a formal agreement, the discussions paved the way for the Intermediate-Range Nuclear Forces Treaty,[122] which eliminated an entire class of nuclear weapons.

- **Trade agreements**: In 1994, the leaders of the United States, Mexico, and Canada signed the North American Free Trade Agreement (NAFTA), which reduced trade barriers between the three countries and stimulated economic growth.

- **Environmental protection**: In 2015, world leaders gathered in Paris for the United Nations Climate Change Conference. The conference resulted in the Paris Agreement,[123] a landmark accord that set a goal of limiting global warming to below 2 degrees Celsius above pre-industrial levels and provided a framework for countries to reduce their greenhouse gas emissions.

- **Human rights**: In 1993, the United Nations convened the World Conference on Human Rights in Vienna, which led to the adoption of the Vienna Declaration and Program of Action.[124] The document reaffirmed the universality of human rights and established a framework for countries to work together to protect and promote human rights around the world.

- **Diplomatic breakthroughs**: In 2018, the leaders of North Korea and South Korea held a historic summit in which they agreed to work toward denuclearization of the Korean peninsula and establish a peace treaty to formally end the Korean War.

- **The 2019 G20 Osaka Summit:** Where leaders from the world's largest economies discussed issues such as trade, climate change, and international security

- **The signing of the Abraham Accords:** In 2020 between Israel and the United Arab Emirates (UAE) and Israel and Bahrain, in the declaration of peace.

- **The 2021 NATO Summit**, where leaders of NATO member countries discussed issues such as collective defense, cybersecurity, and emerging security challenges[125]

Summitry serves as a very important method of conducting international relations and, as a part of the diplomatic process, a symbolic role that provides trust building between leaders and states.

The Potential of a Connected World

In our interconnected and globalized world, the power of connectivity has brought about positive changes and opportunities for growth and progress. The internet and data networks have linked us in unprecedented ways, allowing for the seamless exchange of information and ideas across the globe.

Broadband access has become a crucial factor in driving innovation, economic development, and educational advancements. The World Economic Forum's Global Information Technology Report 2014[126] and other studies show that digitization has a positive, measurable effect on economic growth and job creation by increasing GPD.

Author Tae Yoo is senior vice-president of Corporate Affairs at Cisco[127] and explains, "Broadband access helps break down the barriers to a quality education. This capability dramatically changes how we define schools and increases education opportunities. Better yet, it equips people to find sustainable jobs and lifelong careers, allowing them to maximize their contributions to their community and economy."[128]

Global health impacts individual wellbeing and national security around the world. NIH (the Fogarty International Center) works with other institutes to research global health research, infectious disease, and non-communicable disease.[129]

It opens doors to global access to education, healthcare, and economic empowerment, transforming lives and communities. Through the power of connections, we can revolutionize how we approach critical human needs, creating a more inclusive and sustainable future.

Global health is another area profoundly impacted by connectivity. Collaborative efforts between countries, such as those led by organizations like the Fogarty International Center, have resulted in significant strides in research on infectious and non-communicable diseases. By working together, we can address health challenges that affect individual well-being and national security on a global scale.

Public diplomacy plays a pivotal role in shaping international relationships based on trust and mutual understanding. Building connections with people, not just governments, is crucial in fostering peaceful interactions and preventing misunderstandings. Dr. John Lenczowski, chancellor of the Institute of World Politics[130] in Washington, DC. explained "why it is so important to have public diplomacy all the time, to develop relationships with trust with people and not just with governments." John spoke about "a time when in Indonesia, a paper was forged by someone who lied about America. We were able to prove the forgery was fake. Wars can literally be averted by sitting down and making the effort to talk to each other, to connect to respect."[131] Engaging in dialogue, like Dr. John Lenczowski emphasized, helps to dispel misinformation, and forge genuine connections between nations.

In the pulsating arena of global diplomacy, summits and sporting events emerge as dynamic tools, igniting a composition of opportunities for leaders to converge, engage in spirited negotiations, and spark a brilliant exchange of ideas. As they unfold across the world stage, these events unfurl their magic, kindling flames of unity, goodwill, and unparalleled cooperation among participating nations.

In this interconnected age, the thrilling power of communication and collaboration knows no bounds, defying barriers, and boundaries to unveil a panorama of growth, development, and lasting peace. Embracing the art of diplomacy, we initiate on a thrilling voyage of connectivity and mutual respect, forging a resolute path through the labyrinth of global challenges. With each stride forward, we illuminate a beacon that leads us to a tomorrow brimming with harmony and hope for all of humanity.

In the upcoming chapter, we will delve into the transformative power of diplomacy in shaping the world. We will explore how diplomacy, with its strategic brilliance, has the potential to revolutionize global dynamics and bring about profound changes on the world stage. Join us as we unravel the captivating tales of diplomacy's impact on nations, forging paths to a more interconnected and harmonious world.

> "With malice toward none, with charity for all, with firmness in the right as god gives us to see the right, let us strive on to finish the work we are into bind up the nation's wounds, to care for him who shall

have borne to care for him who shall have borne the battle and for his widow and his orphan to do all which may achieve and cherish a just and lasting peace among ourselves and with all nations."[132]
Abraham Lincoln

Timeless Talks: Leaders Feasting on Ideas and Insights

As they sip their tea, the leaders begin to explore the various forms of diplomacy, from high-level summits to sporting events.

George Washington "A long time ago, diplomacy mainly took the form of official summits and treaties, not really sporting events, but it is fascinating to see how it has evolved over the years."

Abraham Lincoln "Indeed, diplomacy has taken many forms over the years, and we can now see it in sporting events and cultural exchange as well as in more traditional forms such as summits and treaties."

Mahatma Gandhi "I believe that diplomacy should be based on nonviolence and mutual respect; it can take many forms, including summits and sporting events, but the core principles must remain the same. Could you tell me more about the different kinds of sports used in diplomacy?"

Nelson Mandela "Sports that are widely recognized around the world, such as soccer, basketball, and track and field, can be powerful tools for fostering understanding and cooperation. They bring people together and break down barriers. The common bond of sport can be used to start difficult conversations and engage people who might not have been able to connect otherwise."

Winston Churchill "I also agree. Sports like cricket and rugby can bring nations together, promote mutual understanding and respect, and serve as a positive force for change, not only on the field but also in the diplomatic sphere."

George Washington "It's interesting to see how the role of diplomacy has evolved over the years, now it not just summits and treaties, but also sporting events and cultural exchange." "Aye, diplomacy has evolved greatly since my time. It's like comparing a simple letter sent by a messenger to the advanced communication systems of today. And now it can take on different forms, such as sporting events and cultural exchange."

Abraham Lincoln "Indeed, diplomacy has taken many forms over the years, and we can now see it in sporting events and cultural exchange, just as a river that starts small can become a mighty force. It is important to remember that diplomacy is not just about formal summits and treaties but also about building connections and understanding between people."

George Washington "Indeed, sports can be a unifying force, bringing people from different backgrounds and cultures together. It can promote understanding, cooperation, and foster a sense of community."

Abraham Lincoln "I couldn't agree more, George. Sports can be a powerful tool for fostering mutual understanding and respect between different cultures and nations."

Mahatma Gandhi "I also agree. Sports can be a powerful force for good. It can promote nonviolence, healthy competition, and bring people together in a peaceful way."

Nelson Mandela "And gentlemen, I agree. Sports have the power to unite people and break down barriers. It can be a platform for promoting peace, understanding, and reconciliation between different cultures and nations."

George Washington "Indeed, it seems that we are all in agreement that sports can be a powerful unifying force. It allows people from different backgrounds and cultures to come together and find common ground."

FIVE

HOW DIPLOMACY CAN CHANGE THE WORLD

STEP BY STEP IN CONNECTING HISTORY TO PRESENT DAY DIPLOMACY

"WE MUST STRIVE TO BE AN EXAMPLE TO THE WORLD, SHOWING THAT PEACE, TOLERANCE, AND JUSTICE CAN PREVAIL."
- NELSON MANDELA

Chapter 5

HOW DIPLOMACY CAN CHANGE THE WORLD

"The considerations which respect the right to hold this conduct. It is not necessary on this occasion to detail. I will only observe that according to my understanding of the matter that right, so far from being denied by any of the belligerent powers, has been virtually admitted by all."[133]
George Washington

THIS QUOTE REFLECTS Washington's practical and straightforward approach to dealing with people concerning a right to certain powers. In his diplomatic efforts, Washington was known for his ability to maintain cordial and respectful relationships with foreign leaders, even in times of disagreement or tension. He believed in the importance of civility and courtesy in international relations and often emphasized the need for patience, persistence, and mutual respect in achieving diplomatic goals.

Washington's 1793 Neutrality Proclamation[134] declared the United States' intention to remain neutral in the ongoing conflict between France and Great Britain. In the proclamation, Washington emphasized the importance of diplomacy in resolving international conflicts and expressed his hope that the United States could avoid being drawn into the war. It highlights the idea that diplomacy requires a careful understanding of the positions and interests of all parties involved and that it is possible to find common ground even in conflict or disagreement.

And now, a Thrilling Diplomatic Odyssey: Uniting Nations through Cultural Diplomacy

Prepare to be mesmerized as we step into the enchanting world of cultural diplomacy, where the timeless art of connection transcends borders and epochs.

From the dawn of civilization to the modern era, this captivating practice has woven an intricate weave of harmony, understanding, and mutual respect.

Journey back to the vibrant civilizations of the Near East, where great kingdoms engaged in a dazzling dance of diplomacy. Marvel at the brilliance of the Amarna system, where clay tablets etched with wisdom and eloquence crisscrossed the region, paving the way for peace, trade, and cultural exchange. Witness the profound recognition among Great Kings that cooperation, not conflict, reigned supreme—a lesson echoing through the corridors of time.

Venture forth to ancient Greece, a crucible of democracy and enlightened discourse. Behold the illustrious Hellenes as they engaged in riveting public negotiations, driven by the battle of ideas and rational thought. The amphitheaters echoed with the resounding voices of diplomats, gift-givers, and athletes, forging alliances and treaties that resonate with the essence of modern diplomacy.

Amid the dazzling Renaissance, witness the birth of modern diplomacy in the resplendent Italian city-states. The Peace of Lodi brought an era of peace, a triumph of Renaissance diplomacy, where permanent missions and foreign affairs ministries came alive, shaping the trajectory of global relations.

Eons may pass, but one thing remains eternal—the power of cultural diplomacy. Through art, sports, literature, and music, nations have found common ground, paving the way for understanding and cooperation. The echoes of shared values and traditions have spanned centuries, leaving an indelible mark on the world stage.

Today, cultural diplomacy stands tall as a masterpiece of global interaction. In a hyper-connected world, technology has shattered barriers, allowing cultural ambassadors to traverse oceans and time zones, reaching hearts and minds across the globe. It is a force that unites, transcending language and borders, and ignites the fire of peace and stability in our interdependent world.

So, brace yourself for this exhilarating journey, where the past and the present converge in a symphony of unity and collaboration. Cultural diplomacy—the timeless art of building bridges—is a beacon of hope, lighting the way for a world where understanding, compassion, and mutual respect reign supreme. Step into this remarkable odyssey and witness how diplomacy, with its ever-evolving forms, can truly change the world.

The Diplomatic Marvels of Empires

Hold onto your seats as we venture into the dazzling world of ancient empires and their mastery of diplomacy! From the grand Byzantine Empire to the strategic finesse of Ancient China and the captivating realm of Bharatvarsha, each chapter in history unfolds with awe-inspiring diplomatic prowess.

Let's begin our expedition with the Byzantine Empire, a formidable force that spanned Southeastern Europe and Asia. Against all odds, their remarkable survival hinged on the art of diplomacy, a skill they wielded like a potent weapon. Alexander A. Vasiliev recognized their brilliance, as they navigated their long borders with limited military strength, upholding the golden rule—avoid war at all costs—to preserve their realm. Witness the rise of this bridge between ancient and modern diplomacy, a defining chapter in the annals of history.

But our journey doesn't stop there! Ancient China awaits, where the wisdom of Sun Tzu's *The Art of War* laid the foundation for diplomatic strategies that endure to this day. Enter the enchanting world of the tributary system, projecting Chinese power and influence across the region. Marvel at the strategic marriage alliances, diplomatic missions, and military collaborations that showcased the art of Chinese diplomacy, a mesmerizing blend of hard and soft power strategies.

Next, we venture into the captivating tale of Bharatvarsha, where the ancient Indian civilization thrived with diplomatic finesse. The timeless treatise, the Arthashastra, guided their realm, offering invaluable insights into dispute settlement and governance. Delve into the concept of the Chakravarti Samrat, a universal emperor commanding respect and influence, as we unveil the ancient wisdom that shaped Indian diplomacy.

And the excitement doesn't stop there! Tracing the threads of American diplomacy, we encounter four distinct worldviews that have shaped the nation's approach to foreign affairs. From Hamiltonian's economic prowess to Jeffersonian's cautious diplomacy, to Jacksonian's unyielding defense, and Wilsonian's pursuit of international cooperation, the journey through America's diplomatic evolution is nothing short of thrilling.

Unveiling early encounters between European explorers and Native Americans, we witness the complex web of connections and alliances that shaped the course of history. From trade partnerships to cultural exchanges, we uncover the delicate balance of diplomacy in a new world.

So, join us on this epic journey through time, where empires rise and fall, leaving behind a legacy of diplomatic marvels that continue to inspire and shape the world we live in today. From grand empires to intimate encounters, the power of diplomacy is boundless, an enduring force that weaves the tapestry of global history with splendor and intrigue. Brace yourself for an unforgettable adventure as we explore the diplomatic secrets that have forever shaped the course of human civilization!

The Timeless Art of Cultural Diplomacy: Building Connections Across Nations

Cultural diplomacy, an age-old practice spanning centuries, exerts a formidable influence in uniting people through diverse channels like art, literature, music, science, business, and economy. From historical trade routes to contemporary interactions, the exchange of languages, religions, ideas, arts, and societal structures has consistently improved relations among diverse communities. This art of diplomacy serves as a bridge, facilitating the flow of information and cultural treasures between nations, promoting understanding and cooperation.

At its essence, cultural diplomacy revolves around the interchanging of ideas, values, and traditions. Harnessing mediums such as music, sports, exchange programs, and educational initiatives, nations can reinforce connections, advance their interests, and forge productive alliances. This approach engenders a sense of unity, aligning the philosophies of individuals, communities, and nations, and ultimately enriching the global community's fabric.

In our current world of globalization and intricate interconnections, advanced communication technologies have profoundly transformed how we connect, rendering cultural diplomacy even more potent. As our planet grows increasingly interwoven, the practice of cultural diplomacy emerges as a powerful instrument in supporting peace, stability, and mutual comprehension on a global scale.

The Global Evolution of Diplomacy: An Enduring Journey Across Time

From the earliest epochs of human civilization, engaging in communication with other societies has stood as a paramount requisite for survival and prosperity. The exchange of messages between messengers and distant communities wielded the potential to mold the fates of entire societies, determining whether they would flourish or grapple with adversity.

In these ancient epochs, diplomacy, in its most primitive forms, arose organically as a response to the shared political imperatives that united all. As human societies expanded and intermingled, the art of diplomacy adapted to navigate the intricacies of interdependence and collaboration. From the ancient trade routes that interlinked diverse cultures to the establishment of diplomatic envoys and embassies, the practice of diplomacy cemented its position as an indispensable facet of international relations.

Throughout the history of time, diplomacy has held a pivotal role in mitigating conflicts, forging partnerships, and reciprocal understanding among nations. As the world's interconnectivity blossomed through trade, exploration, and technological leaps, diplomacy transcended geographical confines, evolving into a truly global enterprise.

In the swiftly evolving landscape of today's globalized world, diplomacy endures as a bedrock of international engagement, nurturing discourse across nations. From traditional state-to-state negotiations to the burgeoning influence of cultural, economic, and digital diplomacy, this unbroken path of diplomacy persists as an influential catalyst in shaping the direction of human history.

The Mysterious and Enchanting Realm of the Near East

The Ancient Near East, encompassing Mesopotamia, Egypt, and Persia, witnessed the rise of powerful "Great Kingdoms" ruled by formidable "Great Kings" from the early seventeenth to the early twelfth century BCE. This region, spanning modern-day Turkey, Iran, the Levant, and Egypt, became a stage where these kingdoms vied for control and supremacy. Interestingly, it was their adeptness in diplomacy and effective communication that played a pivotal role in their success.

Among the most expansive and ancient diplomatic systems was the *Amarna System*,[135] initiated by the Egyptian Pharaoh Akhenaten during the fourteenth century BCE. The system took its name from Akhenaten's capital city, Amarna, and involved a vast network of diplomatic correspondences with various rulers across the ancient Near East.

The Amarna Letters, written in cuneiform script on clay tablets, provide invaluable insights into the mechanics of this diplomatic system. Exchanged during the reign of Pharaoh Akhenaten, these over 300 letters shed light on diplomatic relations, political alliances, and regional affairs of the time. Composed in Akkadian, the language of diplomacy in the ancient Near East, the letters originated from rulers of prominent city-states and kingdoms, such as Babylon, Assyria, Hatti, and Mitanni.

Intriguingly, the Amarna Letters facilitated peaceful communication and negotiation among states that might otherwise be in conflict. They also facilitated the exchange of goods like precious metals, textiles, and livestock, fostering trade and cooperation between the various states. This diplomatic system was instrumental in maintaining Akhenaten's power and Egypt's influence in the region.

A fundamental aspect of this system was the recognition among the Great Kings that no single power could attain hegemony. Instead, they understood that the region was vast enough for Great Kings to satisfy realistic territorial ambitions. Peaceful interaction between these peers yielded numerous benefits, including international trade opportunities and access to sought-after materials from distant lands.

The Amarna system stands as an early example of the significance of diplomacy in preserving peaceful relations between states. Its enduring legacy can be observed in modern diplomacy and international relations, where the power of communication and cooperation continues to shape the course of human history.

The Illustrious Hellenes

In ancient Greece, diplomacy took on a distinctive form, centered around public negotiation, rational thought, and competition. Their democratic ideals were forged through the battle of ideas and the exercise of power, aiming to gain trust and support from the people. Interestingly, the concept of "common peace" from ancient Greek diplomacy became a cornerstone for the League of Nations and the United Nations Charter.

Diplomacy played a crucial role among city-states in ancient Greece, facilitating trade, alliances, and military support. Ambassadors and envoys were appointed to represent city-states' interests and negotiate with others. Gift-giving, public speeches, and athletic competitions were used to build trust and foster relationships.

Treaties played a vital role in formalizing diplomatic relationships, setting boundaries, and regulating trade. The Amphictyonic League, established in the seventh century BCE, served as an essential diplomatic organization, regulating religious practices, and resolving disputes among its members.

Athens emerged as a major diplomatic center due to its size, wealth, and political power. Skilled diplomats from Athens negotiated alliances and treaties, establishing the Delian League, a military alliance that boosted their regional influence.

Culture and religion also influenced diplomatic relations, with shared language, heritage, and beliefs promoting cooperation and alliances. However, despite diplomatic efforts, conflicts and wars among city-states were common, sometimes leading to the use of military force to resolve disputes.

In the art of ancient Greece, diplomacy played a crucial role, enabling city-states to maintain relationships, negotiate agreements, and strive for peace whenever possible.

Renaissance Diplomacy: The Birth of Modern Diplomacy

The Italian Renaissance marked a golden age for diplomacy, from 1454 to 1494, with the signing of the Peace of Lodi bringing an end to wars between Milan, Naples, and Florence. This period ushered in a remarkable era of peace after a century of conflicts, establishing the foundations of modern diplomacy as we know it today.

Italian city-states in the fifteenth century played a pioneering role in this Renaissance diplomacy, developing permanent diplomatic missions and a rudimentary foreign affairs ministry with diplomatic archives at its core.

The Roman Empire stands as a testament to the sophistication of ancient diplomatic practices. To expand its influence and control over vast and diverse territories, Rome employed a multifaceted approach, blending military might, political alliances, and cultural assimilation.

Central to Roman diplomacy were treaties and alliances forged with other nations, fostering mutual defense, trade, and cultural exchange. Hostage diplomacy, where conquered individuals were taken as guarantees of treaty compliance, was another shrewd tactic used by Rome.

The Romans skillfully combined military strength with a policy of establishing client states, granting them some autonomy in exchange for loyalty. Furthermore, they embraced diplomacy to assimilate conquered cultures, adopting local customs to foster integration.

A Masterpiece of Propaganda

Roman diplomacy also entailed a masterful use of propaganda to project an image of benevolence and justice. Through art, literature, and public monuments, Rome celebrated its achievements and virtues, crafting a compelling narrative of its empire.

In essence, Roman diplomacy was an intricate web of strategies that left an indelible mark on the political and cultural landscape of the ancient Mediterranean world. Its legacy reverberates through history, shaping the diplomatic practices of subsequent civilizations.

The Byzantine Empire: Diplomatic Mastery in the Mediterranean World

Stretching across Southeastern Europe and Asia, the Byzantine Empire emerged from the eastern remnants of the Roman Empire, thriving until 1453 when Constantinople fell to the Ottoman Turks. In the face of countless rulers and border crises, the empire's remarkable survival hinged on the art of diplomacy.

Alexander A. Vasiliev noted that diplomacy became a necessity for the Byzantines, as their long borders could not be adequately defended by their limited military strength. Their elite upheld a golden rule—avoid war at all costs—to preserve their realm.

Distinguished as a bridge between ancient and modern diplomacy, the Byzantine era was a defining chapter in diplomatic history. Spanning from 324 CE to 1453 CE, the empire demonstrated a sophisticated approach to diplomacy that played a pivotal role in its Mediterranean influence.

Key Aspects of Byzantine Diplomacy:

- **Marriage alliances**: Byzantine emperors skillfully solidified loyalty among neighboring rulers through strategic marriage alliances. Such unions forged bonds of kinship and mutual obligation, cementing political relationships.

- **Diplomatic missions**: The Byzantines dispatched ambassadors, envoys, and emissaries to foreign courts for crucial negotiations. Their diplomats, adept linguists, and negotiators navigated the complex politics of the Mediterranean world.

- **Tribute payments**: Employing a common practice of the ancient world, the Byzantines paid tribute to enemies or potential adversaries to secure temporary peace and foster friendly relations.

- **Military alliances**: The empire forged military alliances with like-minded powers, rallying their troops to fight alongside allies or provide aid in exchange for support.

- **Religious diplomacy**: Religion held significant sway in Byzantine diplomacy, with the emperor serving as both the secular and religious leader. The Byzantines used religion to form alliances with fellow Christian powers and assert dominance over non-Christian groups.

Famed for their flexibility, pragmatism, and adept negotiation skills, Byzantine diplomacy expertly adapted to changing circumstances. Through centuries of diplomatic prowess, the Byzantines upheld their power and influence in the Mediterranean world, leaving an enduring legacy in the annals of diplomacy.

Ancient China: Mastering the Art of Diplomacy

In his seminal work, *Diplomacy and Strategy of the Chinese Empire*, K. C. Wu explores the intricate world of Ancient China's diplomatic prowess. Richard L.

Walker's *The Multi-State System of Ancient* China also delves into the fascinating era, shedding light on the early realist in international relations theory, Sun Tzu.

Living during a time of shifting dynamics and rivalries among states, Sun Tzu's *The Art of War*[136] laid the foundation for diplomatic strategies. The need for diplomacy arose as warring states sought allies, bartered land, and signed peace treaties. The indispensable role of the "persuader/diplomat" emerged, navigating the delicate balance of power.

Diplomacy played a pivotal role in Ancient China, establishing peaceful relations with neighboring states and upholding order and stability within the empire. Key features of diplomacy in Ancient China included:

- **The Tribute system**: A hallmark of Chinese diplomacy, this system required neighboring states to acknowledge the Chinese emperor's supremacy and pay tribute. In exchange, they gained trade and diplomatic relations, projecting Chinese power and influence across the region.

- **Marriage alliances**: Chinese emperors skillfully employed marriage alliances to foster peaceful relations with neighboring states. Strategic marriages between ruling families-built bonds of kinship and mutual obligation.

- **Diplomatic missions**: Envoys and ambassadors were dispatched to neighboring states to negotiate treaties, alliances, and trade agreements. These skilled negotiators deftly navigated the complexities of regional politics.

- **Military alliances**: Recognizing the strength in unity, the Chinese formed military alliances with neighboring states to safeguard against shared threats. They collaborated in battles and provided military aid in exchange for support.

- **Cultural diplomacy**: Valuing Chinese culture and civilization, emperors used cultural diplomacy to promote their influence. Scholars, artists, and emissaries were sent to neighboring states to spread Chinese culture and forge amicable relations.

Ancient China's diplomacy was a blend of hard and soft power strategies, utilizing the tribute system and military alliances to project their strength and influence. Through these intricate diplomatic maneuvers, Ancient China navigated a complex landscape, leaving a legacy of strategic prowess and international relations acumen.

Unveiling the Diplomatic Marvels of Bharatvarsha

Diplomacy in ancient India weaves a captivating tale of rich history and diverse interactions, where kingdoms and dynasties engaged in diplomatic relations with each other and neighboring lands.

At the heart of ancient Indian diplomacy lies the Arthashastra, a timeless treatise on statecraft and diplomacy attributed to Kautilya, also known as Chanakya. Serving as the principal adviser to Chandragupta Maurya, the founder of the Maurya dynasty, Kautilya's wisdom guided the realm in the third century BC.

Ambassador (Retd) Mahesh Kumar Sachdev, speaking at the Indira Gandhi National Tribal University, illuminates an intriguing concept in Indian history—the Chakravarti Samrat, or "universal emperor." Surrounding kings acknowledged the suzerainty, or zone of protection, of this emperor, akin to the modern-day notion of a superpower, with pacts, doctrines, and areas of influence.

Within the Arthashastra, four methods were advocated for dispute settlement: "Sama" (conciliation), "Dana" (appeasement), "Bheda" (dividing), and "Danda" (use of force) as a last resort. This ancient Indian text on governance, economics, and diplomacy, attributed to the scholarly Kautilya, stands as a profound and timeless classic ahead of its peers, offering objective treatment of foreign policy options and diplomatic practices.

The Mauryan Empire, spanning from around 321 to 185 BCE, boasted a well-established system of diplomacy. Sending emissaries, exchanging gifts, and forming alliances with neighboring states was instrumental in maintaining their influence. Similarly, the Gupta Empire (around 320 to 550 CE) left its indelible mark on diplomacy, renowned for its cultural influence and diplomatic finesse, with neighboring states embracing aspects of Gupta culture and governance.

From ancient treaties to shrewd diplomatic strategies, the saga of diplomacy in ancient India reveals a captivating journey through time, enriching the fabric of global history.

Tracing the Threads of American Diplomacy: Four Worldviews in Perspective

In his groundbreaking book, *Special Providence: American Foreign Policy and How It Changed the World,* historian Walter Russell Mead introduces the concept of four distinct worldviews that have significantly influenced American diplomacy throughout its history.[137] These worldviews emerged from different periods of American history and politics, shaping the nation's approach to foreign affairs.

- **Hamiltonian:** Named after Alexander Hamilton, a Founding Father, Hamiltonians advocate for a strong central government, a powerful military, and active involvement in international trade and commerce. Their foreign policy prioritizes American economic interests and the protection of business abroad.

- **Jeffersonian:** Bearing the name of Thomas Jefferson, another Founding Father, Jeffersonians believe in limited government, individual liberty, and a cautious approach to foreign relations. They prefer a foreign policy that emphasizes diplomacy and trade while avoiding entanglements with other nations.

- **Jacksonian:** Named after Andrew Jackson, the seventh president of the United States, Jacksonians emphasize a strong national defense, the interests of the common people, and a skeptical view of elites and international institutions. Their foreign policy centers on putting American national interests first and being prepared to use military force when necessary.

- **Wilsonian**: Honoring Woodrow Wilson, the twenty-eighth president, Wilsonians support international cooperation, democracy promotion, and the spread of American values and institutions worldwide. Their foreign policy emphasizes diplomacy, multilateralism, and humanitarian intervention.

Throughout history, these four worldviews have vied for influence over American foreign policy, each contributing to the nation's diplomatic success in diverse ways, depending on the prevailing political and historical context.

Exploring Connections: Early Encounters and Complex Relationships

The unveiling of the American continent by Christopher Columbus in 1492 marked the beginning of a new chapter in history. As European explorers sought to colonize this land, they encountered the Native Americans, sparking a series of interactions ranging from cooperation to resistance.

In 1513, Spanish explorer Juan Ponce de León landed in Florida and initiated contact with Native Americans. Later, Pocahontas, the famous Native American woman, played a significant role as a mediator between English colonists and her own people, showcasing early attempts at diplomacy and cultural exchange.

Amid the colonial period, most colonies recognized the benefits of being amicable with the Native Americans. Establishing trade partnerships proved mutually advantageous, as they exchanged gold, furs, food, and other valuable resources. However, the relationship was complex, fraught with conflicting goals and challenges, such as exposure to new diseases and the ever-expanding European population.

Connections and Alliances: The Shifting Dynamics of Diplomacy

As the British and French engaged in the Seven Years' War (1756-1763) in North America, Native American alliances played significant roles, determining the outcomes. The war, also known as the French and Indian War, saw Native American alliances aiding the French against the British.

Through these historical events, one thing becomes apparent: connections and diplomacy have consistently been pivotal in shaping the course of history. The ability to forge alliances and navigate intricate relationships proved decisive in the outcomes of conflicts and the pursuit of shared goals.

Uniting Europe: The Congress of Vienna

The Congress of Vienna, held between September 1814 and June 1815 in Vienna, Austria, was a landmark series of meetings aimed at reshaping Europe after the tumultuous Napoleonic Wars. Representatives from major European powers, including Austria, Prussia, Russia, and Great Britain, as well as smaller states, gathered to restore stability to the continent.

Led by influential figures such as Prince Klemens von Metternich of Austria, Tsar Alexander I of Russia, and Lord Castlereagh of Great Britain, the Congress succeeded in redrawing the map of Europe and establishing a new balance of power among the nations. By fostering a system of collective security and cooperation, the Congress aimed to prevent future conflicts and laid the groundwork for international law and diplomacy, shaping the conduct of international relations for decades to come.

The significance of the Congress of Vienna cannot be overstated—it marked the dawn of a new era characterized by peace and stability after years of war and upheaval. The Great Powers, including Russia, Great Britain, Austria, Prussia, and France, shared the broad goal of creating a new political order in Europe. The Congress System functioned until 1823, when regular meetings among the Great Powers ceased.

The Congress of Vienna, a diplomatic conference convened after the fall of Napoleon Bonaparte, aimed to restore the European political order. Chaired by Austrian statesman Klemens von Metternich and held in Vienna, the Congress pursued four major objectives: establishing a balance of power, supporting conservative regimes, containing France, and promoting cooperation for lasting peace. Each of the major players, including Russia, Great Britain, Austria, Prussia, and France, pursued its individual agenda.

The primary mission of the Congress of Vienna was to introduce unity and equilibrium among European nations. It also aimed to hold Napoleon accountable for his actions and to strengthen the influence of the Catholic Church while unifying Europe under a single ruler. Notably, this gathering was the first instance of pan-European cooperation to control political affairs, and it was hailed as a resounding success in achieving its goals.

Connecting America: A Tale of Diplomacy, Religious Tolerance, and Information

Meanwhile, in America, the country consisted of eighteen states, and James Madison served as the president. With the defeat and exile of Napoleon in April 1814, Britain had the opportunity to redirect its troops and ships to continue its war with America. The unfortunate consequence was the "burning of Washington," which resulted from the ongoing conflict between Britain and France, with neutral American ships becoming targets as both nations tried to weaken each other's trade.

In the face of such challenges, it becomes evident how crucial connections can be. History tells us that being connected can have far-reaching implications for nations and their citizens.

George Washington, the revered leader of the young nation, embodied the values of religious liberty and tolerance. In 1790, in response to a letter from the Touro Synagogue in Newport, Rhode Island, congratulating him on his election, Washington wrote back, emphasizing that Americans only owed an explanation of their religious beliefs to God. This letter became a powerful symbol of American values, reaffirming the ideal of religious freedom that connects us all.

Washington's commitment to religious freedom was a promise that defined a righteous path for the United States. He understood the importance of respecting diverse religious beliefs and advocated for an America where every individual could find safety and security under their own "vine and fig tree."

As America grew, the need for effective communication became apparent to George Washington and the Founding Fathers. They recognized that an informed citizenry was vital for a successful democracy. The mail system was established to allow every citizen to have a direct line of communication with their government, fostering a sense of connection and engagement. The Declaration of Independence and the Constitution were circulated through the mail as broadsides to inform all the colonies of the developments in Philadelphia.

To further promote informed citizenship, subsidized rates for newspapers were authorized, leading to a flourishing newspaper industry that reached even those living on the frontier. This generous postage policy played a pivotal role in the development of the nation's press, ensuring that information flowed freely and connected Americans from all corners of the young nation.

Through diplomacy, religious tolerance, and efficient communication, America's interconnectedness shaped its course, laying the foundation for a nation that continues to value freedom, diversity, and the exchange of ideas.

Mastering Diplomacy: Benjamin Franklin's Remarkable Legacy

Benjamin Franklin, a brilliant figure in American history, earned his reputation as one of the most prominent diplomats of the eighteenth century. His remarkable skills in negotiation and persuasion played a pivotal role in shaping the destiny of the United States on the world stage.

Franklin's diplomatic odyssey began in 1757 when he embarked on a mission to London, representing the Pennsylvania colonial assembly in a taxation dispute with King George II's government. This early experience laid the foundation for his future diplomatic endeavors, as he honed his expertise in navigating complex international relations.

When the American Revolution unfolded, Franklin's diplomatic acumen became a vital asset for the Continental Congress. In 1776, he was sent to France as a commissioner for the Colonies, and by 1778, he held the prestigious title of minister plenipotentiary, a modern equivalent to an ambassador. His mission was to secure support and recognition for the fledgling United States.

Franklin's skillful negotiations led to a significant turning point when France signed the Treaty of Alliance with the United States in 1778. This landmark treaty granted the newly formed republic international acceptance and provided invaluable military, financial, and political assistance. With France's backing, the American colonies gained the strength to defeat the British in their quest for independence.

Not content with just one diplomatic achievement, Franklin also served as the minister plenipotentiary to Sweden. In this capacity, he successfully negotiated a treaty with the Swedish government, further bolstering the United States' diplomatic standing in Europe.

In a defining moment for American diplomacy, Franklin acted as the signatory for the United States in the Treaty of Paris of 1783.[138] This historic agreement severed the colonial bonds with England and formally recognized the United States as an independent nation.

Benjamin Franklin's legacy as a master diplomat endures to this day. His contributions laid the groundwork for American foreign policy and established a framework for international relations that has guided the nation for centuries. Through his exceptional diplomatic prowess, Franklin not only secured the future of the United States but also left an indelible mark on the world of diplomacy.

John Adams and the XYZ Affair: A Diplomatic Triumph

During John Adams's presidency in the late 1790s, a significant political and diplomatic incident unfolded between the United States and France known as the XYZ Affair. The affair arose from disputes over commerce, trade, and the seizure of American ships by the French Navy.

In response to the escalating tensions, Adams took a decisive step and dispatched a delegation of three men to France to negotiate a settlement. However, the French foreign minister, Charles-Maurice de Talleyrand, made outrageous demands, including a bribe, which the Americans firmly rejected. President Adams stood resolute in his commitment to defend American sovereignty and dignity, refusing to bow to French aggression.

Upon the delegation's return, Adams revealed the XYZ Affair to Congress, leading to a public outcry in the United States. Despite the controversy and political backlash, Adams's handling of the situation was ultimately regarded as a diplomatic success. By avoiding a full-scale war with France, Adams protected American interests and fostered a foundation for future diplomatic endeavors.

The XYZ Affair also played a significant role in shaping American foreign policy and bolstering the US Navy. It heightened tensions between political factions and influenced the passage of the Alien and Sedition Acts, aimed at addressing political dissent and immigration concerns.

Pioneering the West: America's Journey of Expansion

As America expanded westward, explorers like Meriwether Lewis and William Clark embarked on a journey to explore unknown territories. They found an asset in Sacagawea, a Native American woman who became an indispensable translator and guide for their expedition. With her help, they successfully explored the territory of the Louisiana Purchase, an achievement that shaped the nation's understanding of its vast lands and diverse cultures.

Sherman's Brilliant Leadership: Understanding the Impact of War and Societies

During the Civil War, General Sherman emerged as a brilliant leader who understood the impact of war on soldiers and societies. He sought a peaceful resolution through the preservation of the Union, a conviction that guided his actions as a US Army lieutenant general. While Sherman recognized the cost of war, he also understood the need to protect settlers moving westward, leading to complex and often difficult decisions.

Sherman's strategic approach to war emphasized destructive and psychological warfare, seeking to persuade Southerners that their government could not defend them effectively. He believed that weakening the Confederacy's resolve would help bring about an end to the conflict and ultimately promote peace.

In the face of challenging circumstances, John Adams, the explorers Lewis and Clark, and General Sherman demonstrated exceptional leadership and diplomatic prowess. Their actions and decisions continue to resonate as crucial chapters in American diplomatic history.

Lincoln's Diplomacy and the Challenges of a Globalizing America[139]

Abraham Lincoln, the sixteenth president of the United States, confronted various diplomatic challenges during his tenure, notably during the American Civil War. In a rapidly globalizing world, Lincoln's diplomatic approach was guided by his commitment to preserving the Union, ending slavery, and nurturing positive relationships with other nations.

Amid the American Civil War, one of Lincoln's most significant diplomatic triumphs was the successful resolution of the Trent Affair in 1861. This incident involved the interception of the British ship, the Trent, by a US Navy vessel, resulting in the removal of two Confederate diplomats. The event sparked tensions between the US and Britain, with fears of escalating into a potential war. However, Lincoln adeptly defused the crisis by releasing the diplomats and issuing a public apology, satisfying the British government, and avoiding armed conflict.

Another noteworthy example of Lincoln's diplomatic prowess was his handling of relations with France during the Civil War. Despite France's sympathy toward the Confederacy and its prior recognition as a belligerent power, Lincoln's administration worked diligently to maintain amicable ties. Lincoln even dispatched an envoy, Charles Francis Adams, to Paris for negotiations, preventing France from officially recognizing the Confederacy and providing substantial aid. Through skillful diplomacy and negotiation, Lincoln secured France's neutrality during the war, an essential strategic move in a globalized context.

Lincoln's diplomatic approach during the Civil War demonstrated his commitment to nurturing positive international relationships while prioritizing the preservation of the Union and the abolition of slavery. His adept handling of diplomatic crises and negotiations resulted in crucial victories for the Union, establishing him as a skilled diplomat and statesman on the world stage.

Lincoln's significance as a leader extends beyond the realm of diplomacy. He marked the creation of the American republic not with the writing of the Constitution in 1787 but with the signing of the Declaration of Independence in 1776. The Declaration's principle that "all men were created equal" became the driving force for the Civil War, according to Lincoln. He envisioned a united nation with a robust central government founded on popular sovereignty—"a government of the people, by the people, for the people"—as the means to achieve "a new birth of freedom" in America.

In the context of a globalizing world, the Gettysburg Address held immense importance.[140] In 1863, America stood as a significant democracy amid a world dominated by power and hierarchy, where liberty and equality were often overshadowed. However, the idea of equal citizens had two inherent weaknesses: the tolerance of slavery, which contradicted the principle of equality, and the question of authority in a democratic society. Majority rule, essential in a democracy, could potentially lead to resistance and civil war when citizens refused to accept decisions contrary to their opinions.

Lincoln pondered whether there was a flaw in popular government that condemned it to disintegrate. As the world embraced globalization and interconnectedness, the challenges of democracy became increasingly complex. However, Lincoln's unwavering commitment to equality and unity, along with his diplomatic prowess, served as a guiding light for America during a transformative era in its history. His vision for a nation united by a shared commitment to liberty and equality continues to resonate as the United States navigates the complexities of a globalized world.

International relations and diplomacy stand as a potent force capable of shaping destinies and rewriting the course of history. With skilled negotiators and adept diplomats at the helm, diplomacy can bridge the gaps between nations, dissolve conflicts, and build alliances that unite the globe. From historic peace treaties that have ended centuries-long wars to groundbreaking international agreements that address pressing global challenges, the power of diplomacy knows no bounds.

As we delve into our next chapter, we will enter a thrilling journey through world events that exemplify the transformative impact of diplomacy. From high-stake diplomatic summits that have defused tensions to awe-inspiring sporting events that unite nations under a common banner, we will witness firsthand how diplomacy has the potential to change the world, unraveling a kaleidoscope of possibilities for a more harmonious and interconnected future.

> "Diplomacy is not only a necessary evil,
> but it is also an indispensable tool of government."[141]
> Winston Churchill

Timeless Talks: Leaders Feasting on Ideas and Insights

As they enjoy their beans and vegetables, the leaders begin to discuss the potential of diplomacy in shaping the world for the better.

George Washington "Gentlemen, as we stand on the brink of a new era of progress and innovation, it is vital that we comprehend the significance of this newfangled technology of broadband access in our increasingly interconnected world."

Abraham Lincoln "Forgive me, but I am not entirely familiar with this concept of broadband access. Pray, can you elaborate further on its meaning?"

Mahatma Gandhi "Indeed, broadband access refers to the availability and quality of high-speed internet connections. In this day and age, as more and more of our lives are conducted online, 'tis of the utmost importance for connecting the world and revolutionizing access to education, health care, and the delivery of critical human needs."

Nelson Mandela "I see, thank you for enlightening me. I understand the importance of connections in fostering understanding and cooperation, but I am not entirely certain how broadband access fits into that."

Winston Churchill "Gentlemen, broadband access is crucial for the next wave of innovation, economic growth, productivity enhancement, educational advancements, and social change. With broadband access, we can connect more people and communities than ever before, breaking down barriers and promoting understanding and cooperation on a global scale."

George Washington "I concur, this technology will aid us in bridging the gap between nations and cultures, and with the power of connections, we can make a positive impact on the world. I remember during the American Revolution, we had to navigate diplomatic relations with foreign nations. It was not easy, but through cultural exchange and understanding, we were able to form alliances and treaties that benefited both sides."

Nelson Mandela "I, too, have seen the power of cultural diplomacy in my own experiences. During my struggle against apartheid in South Africa, I emphasized the importance of understanding and appreciating different cultures to promote unity and reconciliation. I remember how we used sports to connect with the world, it was a powerful tool to break down barriers and bring people together."

Winston Churchill "As a leader during World War II, I understand the importance of cultural diplomacy in navigating international relations. I remember the importance of understanding and appreciating the cultures of our allies to effectively communicate and cooperate with them to defeat the Axis powers.

George Washington "Gentlemen, as leaders of our respective nations, we must recognize the importance of diplomacy in shaping the course of international relations. By building relationships and understanding with other nations, we can work toward common goals and create a more peaceful and harmonious world."

Mahatma Gandhi interjects "I agree that diplomacy is important, but I must remind us that it should be accessible to all people, not just the rich and powerful. We must ensure that the voices and needs of the poor and marginalized are also heard in diplomatic discourse."

Nelson Mandela "I agree with Mr. Gandhi. Diplomacy should be inclusive and strive to address the needs of all people, not just the privileged few. It should be a tool for promoting equality and justice, not just for the benefit of a select few."

Winston Churchill "I agree with all of you. Diplomacy should be inclusive and accessible to all people, regardless of their socioeconomic status. It should be a tool for promoting peace, understanding and cooperation between nations."

George Washington "I couldn't agree more, my fellow leaders. Diplomacy has the power to bring people from different cultures and backgrounds together and to promote understanding and cooperation between nations. It can also be a powerful force for promoting equality and justice for all."

SIX

WORLD EVENTS THAT CONNECT US

STEP BY STEP IN CONNECTING HISTORY TO PRESENT DAY DIPLOMACY

"THE ABILITY TO CONNECT WITH OTHERS AND TO UNDERSTAND THEIR CULTURES IS THE FOUNDATION OF TRUE DIPLOMACY."
- WINSTON CHURCHILL

Chapter 6

WORLD EVENTS THAT CONNECT US

"Diplomacy is not a mere convenience of protocol; it is an art of utilizing the means, opportunities, and circumstances in hand for the attainment of a definite object. It is not the manifestation of a timid or an uncertain spirit. It is not the instrument of suppressive policies or of a desire to exploit. It is a mode of dealing with our fellow men with a view to serve a common purpose. It implies a readiness to adjust our own claims and aspirations of others, a spirit of compromise and accommodation."[142]
Mathatma Gandhi

IN A WORLD pulsating with excitement and boundless possibilities, dynamic world events beckon us to partake in a thrilling global dance of diplomacy and connection. From dazzling international conferences that gather visionaries from diverse cultures to electrifying sports tournaments that unite nations in friendly competition, these extraordinary gatherings bring a sense of camaraderie and shared purpose. Whether it's witnessing historic peace accords being signed or collaborating on groundbreaking initiatives to address pressing global challenges, these events showcase the immense power of diplomacy in establishing meaningful connections between nations and individuals. As we come together to celebrate culture, knowledge, and progress, the spirit of unity prevails, transcending borders and language barriers. In these exhilarating moments, we realize that our shared humanity binds us as one, inspiring us to shape a brighter future together through the transformative force of diplomacy.

World events serve as blending together the destinies of nations and individuals alike. From awe-inspiring moon landings that united humanity under the banner of exploration, to exhilarating sports tournaments that ignite a global passion for competition, these moments resonate with us all, transcending borders and languages. Gripping headlines about breakthrough scientific discoveries and medical advancements remind us of the boundless potential of human ingenuity and cooperation. Likewise, when faced with adversity, such as natural disasters or humanitarian crises, the outpouring of international aid and support showcases the strength of our interconnectedness. These world events are not merely stories for the history books; they are living testimonies of our collective journey as a global community. Each step, be it a triumph or a challenge, reminds us that we are part of something grander than ourselves, fostering a shared sense of purpose and belonging. As we witness these world events unfold, we stand united in a thrilling narrative that connects us, transcending time, and space, and shaping the course of our shared human story.

A myriad of captivating examples showcases the profound impact of world events that connect us across borders and cultures. First and foremost, global sporting extravaganzas like the Olympic Games, the World Cup, and the Commonwealth Games serve as grand stages where athletes and fans from every corner of the world unite, creating an unparalleled sense of shared experience and camaraderie. Moreover, cultural festivals and events, such as mesmerizing music festivals, enchanting art showcases, and delightful food celebrations, bring together people from diverse backgrounds, fostering mutual understanding and deep appreciation for each other's traditions and customs. Finally, the grandeur of international conferences and summits, exemplified by the United Nations General Assembly, brings together visionary leaders and representatives from far-flung nations, engaging in thoughtful dialogue to address global challenges and forge collaborative solutions for a better world. In these moments of connection and diplomacy, the world is bound together by the unyielding power of shared humanity.

So, what if the world made new friends and added exciting memories? What if we had a large-scale multicultural event that would showcase different countries around the world. These world events[143] would be informative and an exciting "trip around the globe" for attendees to learn about the world, showcasing the multiculturalism of another country representing food, drinks, music, and games from that area of the world. These events already exist and are connecting us around the world.

Grab Your Passport and Experience the World at Play

There are many world events that can connect people from different parts of the world.[144] Presented below is a compilation of global events meticulously gathered by the United Nations.[145]

Globe in Motion: A Compilation of Global Events

- **The Masters, Augusta, Georgia**
  The Masters is an iconic golf tournament held annually in Augusta, Georgia, USA. It is one of the most prestigious events in the world of golf and attracts top players from around the globe.

- **Kentucky Derby, Louisville, Kentucky**
  Known as "The Most Exciting Two Minutes in Sports," the Kentucky Derby brings together the finest thoroughbred horses and skilled jockeys to compete for the iconic garland of roses.

- **The US Open, New York, New York**
  One of the most anticipated tennis tournaments in the world and one of the four Grand Slam events, the US Open attracts top tennis players from around the globe to compete for the coveted title.

- **FIFA World Cup**
  International football captivates the globe with its electrifying spectacle of skill, passion, and national pride. Held every four years, in different host countries around the world. Bringing together teams from around the world, competing for the coveted title of world champion. With a history dating back to 1930, the World Cup has become a symbol of unity and camaraderie, transcending borders, and uniting nations in the spirit of friendly competition.

- **Mardi Gras Festival, New Orleans, Lousiana**
  The Mardi Gras Festival, held annually in the vibrant city of New Orleans, Louisiana, is a celebration of culture, music, and revelry.

Known for its colorful parades, elaborate costumes, and lively street parties, Mardi Gras draws millions of visitors from around the world.

- **Chinese New Year, Shanghai, China**
  One of the most important traditional festivals in Chinese culture, Chinese New Year marks the beginning of the lunar new year and is a time for family reunions, feasting, and cultural festivities.

- **Oktoberfest, Munich, Germany**
  A world-renowned beer festival held annually in Munich, Germany. This iconic event attracts millions of visitors from around the globe.

- **Sapporo Snow Festival, Sapporo, Japan**
  Every February in Sapporo, Japan. This spectacular winter celebration draws visitors from all over the world who come to witness the city transformed into a snowy wonderland.

- **St. Patrick's Day, Dublin, Ireland**
  Held annually on March 17th, this lively festival honors Saint Patrick, the patron saint of Ireland. Parades featuring colorful floats, traditional music, and dance groups.

- **Running of the Bulls, Pamplona, Spain**
  The running of the bills takes place in Pamplona, Spain, during the annual San Fermín festival. Held between July 6th and July 14th, this centuries-old tradition attracts daring participants and enthusiastic spectators from around the world.

- **Albuquerque International Balloon Fiesta, Albuquerque, New Mexico**
  Held in early October, this world-renowned hot air Balloon Fiesta event attracts balloon enthusiasts, thrill-seekers, and families from all corners of the globe.

WORLD EVENTS THAT CONNECT US

- **Tōrō Nagashi, Sasebo, Japan**
  The festival centers around floating lanterns, or tōrō, which are released into the serene waters. Each lantern carries heartfelt wishes and prayers, guiding the spirits of the departed on their journey to the afterlife.

- **Cooper Hill's Cheese Rolling Festival, Gloucester, UK**
  Attracts participants and spectators from around the world every year as people gather on Cooper's Hill, a steep grassy slope, to take part in the exhilarating tradition of chasing a wheel of cheese down the hill.

- **Winterlude, Ottawa & Quebec, Canada**
  Majestic ice sculptures showcasing sculptors from around the world, embracing the rich cultural heritage of Canada.

- **Burning Man, Black Rock City, Nevada**
  People come from all over the world to attend this annual event. Burning Man is the massive wooden effigy, known as "the Man," which stands tall before being ceremoniously set ablaze during the event's climax. This ritualistic burning symbolizes the liberation of creative energies and the release of what no longer serves, leaving space for new possibilities and transformation.

- **Lantern Festival in Hawaii, Honolulu, Hawaii**
  Symbolizing the transition from darkness to light, as lanterns of various shapes and sizes, with intricate designs and heartfelt messages, are released into the sky, creating a mesmerizing display of floating lights where people come from all over the world attend.

- **The Hajj Pilgrimage**
  Each year, during the Islamic month of Dhu al-Hijjah, the Hajj pilgrimage draws Muslims from all corners of the globe, coming together as one united community to fulfill their spiritual duties, a journey of devotion, self-discovery, and unity.

- **Henley Royal Regatta, Henley-on-Thames, England**
  The regatta's revered history and stunning spectacle of rowing races in traditional wooden rowing boats. Attending are members of the royal family and people from all over the world.

- **Carnival of Venice**
  Dating back to the Middle Ages, this iconic festival epitomizes the Venetian spirit of revelry, opulence, and artistic expression. The heart of the Carnival lies in its elaborate masks, including concerts, and theater productions, with people attending from all over the world.

- **Dragon Boat Carnival, Hong Kong**
  This ancient tradition, dating back over 2,000 years, honors the memory of the legendary Chinese poet Qu Yuan and has evolved into a thrilling celebration of unity, teamwork, and community spirit. Dragon boats race through the waters and spectators come from all over.

- **Cannes Film Festival, Cannes, France**
  The International Film Festival (Festival International du Film) and known in English as the Cannes Film Festival, held annually with its glamorous red-carpet events, prestigious film screenings, and star-studded gatherings, the festival exudes an aura of elegance and artistic excellence. Attended by people all over the world.

- **Royal Ascot Races, Berkshire, UK**
  An iconic celebration of equestrian excellence, fashion, and regal traditions dating back to 1711. Each year, this prestigious horse racing event attracts an elegant and diverse audience, including members of the royal family, high society, and racing enthusiasts from around the world.

- **Cervia International Kite Festival, Cervia, Italy**
  The festival brings together kite enthusiasts and artists from around the world, showcasing their remarkable creations and innovative designs. The event's open and inclusive atmosphere encourages visitors of all ages to participate.

- **Cherry Blossom Festival, Kyoto, Japan**
  Every spring, when the cherry trees burst into a magnificent display of pink and white blossoms, the city of Kyoto transforms into a magical wonderland, attracting visitors from all over the world.

- **Wimbledon, London, UK**
  Dating back to 1877 and known as the oldest tennis tournament in the world, Wimbledon has been captivating audiences for over a century with its storied history and unparalleled traditions.

- **Le Tour de France**
  The world's most prestigious cycling race takes cyclists and spectators on an exhilarating journey through the picturesque landscapes of France. Founded in 1903.

- **Cork Jazz Festival, Cork City, Ireland**
  A celebration of music and culture, established in 1978. This iconic festival has evolved into one of the most significant jazz events in Europe, drawing music enthusiasts and jazz aficionados from around the world.

- **Carnival, Rio de Janeiro, Brazil**
  Dating back to the eighteenth century, this iconic event has evolved into one of the largest and most famous carnivals on the planet, attracting millions of visitors from every corner of the globe. is an electrifying explosion of color, music, and culture that captivates the world.

- **Snow & Ice Festival, Harbin, China**
  A mesmerizing winter wonderland that showcases the breathtaking beauty of ice and snow sculptures in an enchanting display of artistry and imagination, held annually.

- **Mardi Gras Festival, New Orleans, Louisiana**
  A vibrant and exuberant celebration that brings together people from all walks of life to revel in the spirit of joy and merriment. Held annually in the weeks leading up to Lent.,

- **Chinese New Year, Shanghai, China**
  Traditional red lanterns adorn every corner, symbolizing good luck and prosperity. Elaborate dragon and lion dance performances captivate the crowds, driving away evil spirits and ushering in good fortune.

- **Austin City Limits, Austin, Texas**
  A legendary music festival that brings together music lovers from all corners of the globe for an unforgettable experience.

- **Daytona 500, Daytona Beach, Florida**
  A celebration of speed, adrenaline, and automotive excellence. As one of the most prestigious and anticipated events in motorsports, the Daytona 500 attracts racing enthusiasts from around the globe.

- **Venice Biennale, Venice, Italy**
  A beacon of artistic brilliance and cultural exchange. Renowned as one of the world's most prestigious art events, the Venice Biennale brings together artists, curators, and art enthusiasts from every corner of the globe for a mesmerizing celebration of contemporary art.

- **Coachella Music Festival, Indio, California**
  Renowned as one of the world's most iconic music events, Coachella brings together music lovers, artists, and festival goers from all walks of life for an unforgettable experience that transcends genres and unites people through the power of music.

- **The French Open, Paris, France**
  Held annually in the enchanting city of Paris, France, stands as one of the most prestigious and celebrated tennis tournaments in the world. It has a rich history dating back to 1891.

- **Bonnaroo Music Festival, Manchester, Tennesee**
  Bonnaroo fosters a spirit of unity and inclusivity, creating a vast and interconnected community that embraces diversity and celebrates individuality. With a commitment to sustainability and environmental

consciousness, the festival provides an enriching space where people can connect with nature, art installations, and like-minded souls.

- **The Summer Games**
  An international sporting extravaganza held quadrennially stands as a glorious testament to the spirit of competition and global unity. As athletes from diverse nations gather on the world stage, the Summer Games become a vibrant celebration of athleticism, sportsmanship, and cultural exchange.

- **Bregenz Festival, Bregenz, Austria**
  A captivating celebration of music and theater. Each year, this renowned festival lures art enthusiasts and visitors from around the globe to revel in its enchanting performances and unique open-air stage.

- **Italian Grand Prix, Monza, Italy**
  With a history spanning over a century, this prestigious race attracts motorsport enthusiasts and racing aficionados from all corners of the world.

- **FIS Alpine World Ski Championships**
  Showcases the pinnacle of alpine ski racing on the global stage. Held at iconic ski resorts around the world, this prestigious event brings together the finest ski racers from different nations to compete for the coveted title of world champion.

- **Rugby World Cup**
  Brings together nations from around the globe in a fierce battle for rugby supremacy. This prestigious tournament, held every four years, showcases the finest rugby talent as they compete for the ultimate prize—the Webb Ellis Cup.

- **Monaco Grand Prix, Monaco**
  The crown of motorsport takes center stage on the dazzling streets of Monaco, one of the most glamorous destinations in the world. This

prestigious Formula 1 race is a thrilling showcase of speed, skill, and precision, capturing the hearts of racing enthusiasts and spectators alike.

- **Tomorrowland, Boom, Belgium**
  A music festival with a sense of camaraderie among the festival goers, which creates an atmosphere of unity and positivity that is truly unmatched.

- **Melt Festival, Gräfenhainichen, Germany**
  More than just a celebration of music; it's a celebration of culture and community. From the diverse crowd of festival goers to the array of interactive art installations, the spirit of togetherness and acceptance permeates every corner of the event.

- **North Sea Jazz Festival, Rotterdam, Netherlands**
  A celebration of cultural exchange and artistic diversity. People from all walks of life come together in harmony to share their love for music and to celebrate the beauty of unity.

- **Hermanus Whale Festival, Cape Town, South Africa**
  Celebration of marine life, and majesty of the ocean's gentle giants.

- **Comic-Con, San Diego, California**
  A festival of screenings of upcoming movies and TV shows, and sneak peeks of highly anticipated releases.

- **The Invictus Games, Worldwide**
  A global celebration of resilience, courage, and determination that spans across nations, uniting wounded, injured, and sick servicemen and women from around the world. Originating from the vision of Prince Harry, the Invictus Games have grown into an international phenomenon, showcasing the indomitable spirit of military personnel who have faced life-altering challenges.

- **Yi Peng Lantern Festival, Chiang Mai, Thailand**
  A mesmerizing celebration of lights and wishes that illuminates the night sky in Chiang Mai, Thailand. Steeped in centuries of tradition and cultural significance, the Yi Peng Lantern Festival draws visitors from across the globe to witness its awe-inspiring beauty.

- **Al Dhafra Festival, Abu Dhabi, United Arab Emirates**
  The festival is not just about camels; it's a celebration of Emirati arts, crafts, and culinary delights. Local artisans display their exquisite craftsmanship, from weaving intricate carpets and crafting intricate pottery to fashioning ornate jewelry adorned with traditional motifs.

- **The International Industry Baking Expo, Las Vegas, Nevada**
  Bakers, pastry chefs, and industry professionals from around the globe gather to showcase their culinary masterpieces and cutting-edge innovations. People come from all over to participate.

The Global Impact of Sports and the Olympics

> "Courage is the first of humans qualities because it is the quality that guarantees all the others."[146]
> Winston Churchill

In our interconnected world, where conflicts and discord persist, we often seek solace and distraction from the hardships by immersing ourselves in a digital realm of cute pet photos and funny videos. However, every four years, a truly global event emerges, transcending boundaries and uniting countries like never before—the Olympics.

When the 2016 Olympics commenced in Rio, the world witnessed a spectacular display of cultural unity through art and dance. The depiction of the rainforest during the opening ceremony was particularly captivating, showcasing the rich tapestry of Brazil's heritage. As the parade of nations unfolded, the palpable joy and camaraderie among the participants, especially those from war-torn countries, were truly inspiring. The Olympics served as a powerful reminder of the potential for positive outcomes when nations put aside their differences and come together in the spirit of kindness and cooperation.

An especially poignant moment in the 2016 Olympics was the introduction of a refugee team. Comprising athletes who had fled conflict in their home countries, this team brought hope and inspiration to millions worldwide. These individuals, once living in fear, now stood proudly on the Olympic stage, realizing their dreams, and symbolizing the resilience of the human spirit.

The Olympics serve as a beacon of hope for a better, more unified future. While the dream of a world without war may seem distant, this global event proves that humanity can unite in times of adversity. It is a testament to our capacity to come together as a global community, transcending borders, and differences, and celebrating the best of what humanity has to offer.

Beyond the Olympics, the festive season also presents an opportunity for countries across the globe to unite through holiday events. From wintry skies adorned with stars to majestic Christmas trees and traditional cuisines, nations come together to celebrate the spirit of togetherness and joy. Germany, England, Dubai, Denmark, Hungary, Austria, Chile, Hong Kong, Italy, and countless others from diverse cultures and traditions, intertwining through these festivities and supporting a global gathering that knows no borders.

Amidst the tumultuous landscape of our world, the Olympics and holiday events emerge as exhilarating beacons of possibility and hope. They ignite a spark within us, showcasing the incredible power of embracing our shared humanity. As the world gathers to witness these grand spectacles, they serve as a vivid reminder that despite our diverse backgrounds and challenges, we possess the ability to unite in celebration. With hearts ablaze, we come together, embracing the richness of our cultures and traditions, intertwining in a harmonious dance of global connection. These moments resonate deep within us, kindling the flames of understanding, cooperation, and respect that bind us together as a resilient global community. Each Olympic triumph and holiday joyousness paves a path toward a brighter tomorrow, where the unyielding spirit of unity transforms our world into shared dreams and aspirations.

Get ready to enter the next chapter of our riveting adventure. From untangling intricate connections to exploring its profound impacts, we'll fearlessly delve into the enigma of Globalization: a cause for concern. Uncovering mysteries and confronting challenges, we'll shed light on the complex web of this global phenomenon. So, fasten your seatbelts and brace yourself for an exhilarating journey of discovery, navigating the twists and turns of globalization's influence on our ever-changing world.

> "A house divided against itself cannot stand."[147]
> Abraham Lincoln

Timeless Talks: Leaders Feasting on Ideas and Insights

Amidst the flickering candlelight casting a warm glow upon the table, the leaders gather, their attentive gaze fixed upon the unfolding current events that serve as a common thread binding us all together. Meanwhile, the crackling fire adds a comforting ambiance to the atmosphere.

> **George Washington** "I must admit, I am skeptical of this notion of global interconnectedness. In my time, diplomacy was primarily focused on forming alliances and treaties with neighboring nations, not on events happening across the ocean."
>
> **Abraham Lincoln** "While I understand your reservations, George, I believe that the world has always been interconnected. With advancements in technology and communication, we are now more aware of events happening in distant places. And so, it is more important than ever that we understand and take into account the global impact of our actions."
>
> **Mahatma Gandhi** "I believe that as a global community, we must strive for nonviolence and mutual respect in all of our actions. The actions of one nation can have ripple effects across the world, and so it is our responsibility to consider the impact of our decisions on all peoples, both rich and poor."
>
> **Nelson Mandela** "We must take into account the impact of our actions on all nations and peoples. Diplomacy must be inclusive, and all voices must be heard to build a more peaceful and just world."

Winston Churchill "I agree with all of you. The world is more interconnected than ever before, and we must work together to understand and address the complex issues facing us today. We must remember that an action in one corner of the world can affect us all, and so we must work together to build a more peaceful and united world for all."

George Washington "I am not convinced; it seems hard to fathom that events happening on the other side of the world could have any bearing on us here."

Abraham Lincoln "Indeed, it is a difficult concept to grasp, but as the world grows more interconnected, we must recognize that events in one country can have effects for all people across the globe."

Nelson Mandela "Just as with cultural diplomacy, we must understand that we are all part of a global community, and the actions of one country can impact us all."

Mahatma Gandhi "I agree with my fellow leaders. It is essential that we recognize our interconnectedness and work toward solutions that will benefit all people, regardless of their station in life."

Winston Churchill "Most importantly, we must also understand the interconnectedness of world events."

George Washington "I see your point, but it seems a difficult concept to grasp, that events happening across the ocean could affect us here in the colonies."

Nelson Mandela "Indeed, the world is more connected than ever before, and it is important that we recognize and understand these connections. Just as with cultural diplomacy, the actions and decisions of one nation can have ripple effects across the globe."

Mahatma Gandhi "We must see ourselves as part of a global community and understand that the actions and decisions of one country can have an impact on all nations. I also want to stress that we must ensure that diplomacy is accessible to all people, regardless of their economic status."

Abraham Lincoln "I concur. The world is more interconnected than ever before, and that means that we must work together to understand the complex issues facing us today and find solutions that will benefit us all. And I agree with Gandhi; we must ensure that diplomacy is accessible to all people, not just the wealthy and powerful."

Winston Churchill "Gentlemen, I have fought many political battles in my time, and as leaders of our respective nations, we must recognize the importance of diplomacy in today's interconnected world. It is crucial that we work together to build a better, more peaceful and united world for all and ensure that diplomacy is accessible to all, regardless of their economic status."

Nelson Mandela "I understand the importance of inclusivity in diplomacy, having spent many years in prison. We must consider the impact of our actions on all nations and peoples. Diplomacy must be inclusive, and all voices must be heard to build a more peaceful and just world."

George Washington "I agree, we must ensure that all voices are heard, not just the voices of the powerful. Diplomacy must serve the interests of all, not just the interests of a select few."

Abraham Lincoln "While I understand your reservations, George, I believe that the world has always been interconnected. I have faced a divided nation and indeed, we must strive for diplomacy that is inclusive, equitable and just for all. Only then can we truly build a more peaceful and united world, so, it is more important than ever that we understand and consider the global impact of our action.

Mahatma Gandhi "I agree. Diplomacy must be inclusive and serve the interests of all, not just the powerful. We must strive for a world where all people, regardless of their background or circumstances, have access to diplomacy and the ability to shape their own destinies."

Chapter 7

GLOBALIZATION: A CAUSE FOR CONCERN

"The world is a dangerous place to live, not because of the people who are evil, because of the people who do not do anything about it."[148]
Winston Churchill

EMBRACE THE PULSE-POUNDING excitement of this chapter, where we plunge headfirst into the heart of Globalization and its concerns. Prepare to be captivated as we unravel the intricate threads of this global phenomenon, exploring its far-reaching impacts and unforeseen consequences. The world is on the brink of transformation, and with adrenaline-pumping anticipation, we'll navigate the twists and turns that lie ahead. Armed with courage and curiosity, we'll confront the challenges and mysteries, unearthing the secrets that make globalization a riveting enigma. So, gear up for discovery, as we boldly navigate the complexities of globalization's influence on our ever-evolving world. Brace yourself for a thrill ride like no other!

Understanding the Roots of Fear Toward Other Countries

There are numerous reasons behind the fear that some individuals harbor toward other countries. One significant factor is a lack of understanding or familiarity with the diverse cultures, values, and practices of those nations. When people encounter the unfamiliar, it can evoke feelings of apprehension and uncertainty.

Moreover, mistrust plays a pivotal role in nurturing fear. The belief that another country may have conflicting interests or goals can lead to a fear of potential harm or detrimental actions directed at one's own nation. This sense of suspicion can create a barrier to building meaningful relationships and collaborations between countries.

Past conflicts or historical tensions can also contribute to fear. Lingering animosity and distrust resulting from previous confrontations can shape a negative perception of the other country, fostering a sense of apprehension even in the absence of current conflicts.

Language and communication can also be a source of fear. Misunderstandings due to differences in life experiences and language usage can lead to misinterpretations and unintentional conflicts.

Negative portrayals in the media can further amplify these fears. Biased or one-sided depictions of other countries can perpetuate stereotypes and misconceptions, heightening apprehension, and mistrust.

The fear of globalization is an additional concern that some individuals harbor. They may view globalization as a threat to cultural diversity, fearing that it could erode traditions, languages, and local economies. This fear of change can generate resistance toward embracing a more interconnected world.

In many cases, society has been conditioned to perceive differences as threats, and an instinctive fear of the unknown can take root. To overcome these barriers, it is essential to acknowledge and challenge these fears and seek out accurate and balanced information about other countries. Embracing cultural diversity and fostering open-mindedness can pave the way for a more connected and cooperative global community.

There are two basic motivating forces: fear and love. When we are afraid, we pull back from life. When we are in love, we are open to all that life has to offer with passion, excitement, and acceptance. We need to learn to love ourselves first, in all our glory and our imperfections. If we cannot love ourselves, we cannot fully open to our ability to love others or our potential to create. Evolution and all hope for a better world rest in the fearlessness and open-hearted vision of people who embrace life."[149]

John Lennon

Unraveling the Opposition: Understanding Globalization's Critics

The opposition to globalization is a complex and multifaceted phenomenon, stemming from various perspectives and reasons. While globalization has facilitated numerous benefits like increased trade, economic growth, and cultural exchange, it has faced criticism from diverse segments of society. Economic inequality is a significant concern, as globalization has widened the wealth gap and left marginalized communities and workers behind. Job displacement and outsourcing also raise worries about economic insecurity and social unrest in developed countries. Additionally, opponents of globalization voice concerns about cultural homogenization, environmental consequences, loss of national sovereignty, labor standards, and human rights abuses, and financial instability. Fear of losing cultural identity fuels resistance and preservation of traditional customs. It's crucial to recognize that opposition to globalization varies across regions and communities. Some advocate for reforming the global economic system, while others favor cautious approaches or partial retreats. Globalization advances an emerging global consciousness, blending ideas, lifestyles, and cultures worldwide. While it can bring about positive changes like increased economic opportunities and cultural exchange, it can also lead to the spread of negative ideas and fears, such as xenophobia and discrimination. However, it is essential to acknowledge that fear and anxiety have complex causes beyond globalization alone. It's worth noting that despite understandable fears, globalization has also been a catalyst for positive changes, including economic growth and the spread of knowledge and ideas. Understanding the multifaceted impacts of globalization is crucial for addressing legitimate concerns while harnessing its positive aspects for the collective benefit of humanity. Striking a balance between promoting global cooperation and addressing challenges remains a critical task for shaping the future of our interconnected world. Anti-globalization sentiment arises from diverse origins. In developing nations, this reaction emerges as a response to the perceived threat to traditional values brought about by the influx of foreign products and ideas.

Holidays: The Paradox of Connection and Disconnection

Consider the case of Valentine's Day[150] as an illustration. Initially, Saint Valentine, who lived from 226 to 278 CE in Italy, remained relatively obscure among the vast pantheon of over 10,000 Catholic saints. However, in the 1850s, American entrepreneurs commenced the commercialization of this day by selling greeting cards. Notably, it was not until the mid-twentieth century that Valentine's Day gained recognition beyond the borders of the United States and Britain.

Presently, on every February 14th, bustling crowds fill malls in Asian cities, reservations overflow at restaurants and shows, as individuals loosely commemorate a near-mythical figure from centuries ago and a continent away. The global embrace of this tradition demonstrates the far-reaching influence of globalization, even extending to cultural celebrations deeply rooted in distant histories.

A lot of people in Asian countries believe a holiday like Valentine's Day is an example of foreign practices which erodes traditional culture.

Holidays, with their diverse cultural and religious origins, showcase the paradoxical interplay of connection and disconnection on a global scale. These festive occasions bring people together, creating a sense of unity and shared celebration across borders. Yet, simultaneously, they reveal the disparities and challenges that persist in our interconnected world.

The global nature of holidays transcends geographical boundaries, bringing people from different corners of the earth together in shared festivities. As individuals of various backgrounds come together to celebrate common traditions, a sense of belonging to a global community is nurtured. The exchange of greetings, customs, and rituals creates a thread of connection that spans continents, uniting people in the joy of celebration.

During holidays, acts of generosity and compassion transcend national borders. Charitable endeavors and humanitarian efforts become global undertakings, as people extend their support and care to those in need across the world. The spirit of giving and the recognition of shared humanity bind us in a collective endeavor to uplift and support one another.

However, despite the spirit of connection, holidays can also accentuate disconnections and disparities that persist on a global scale. Economic inequalities become evident as some communities indulge in lavish celebrations while others struggle to meet their basic needs. Cultural differences may lead to misunderstandings and misinterpretations, creating barriers to understanding and acceptance.

In regions experiencing conflict or political unrest, holidays may be marked by discord and disunity. Different cultural practices or religious beliefs can be misunderstood or met with resistance, furthering divisions, and disconnections among diverse communities.

Moreover, the commercialization and consumerism associated with holidays can distract from their true essence. The emphasis on materialism may overshadow the spiritual and cultural significance of these occasions, leading to a superficial experience that leaves some feeling disconnected from the true spirit of celebration.

To address the paradox of connection and disconnection during holidays in the world, guiding cultural exchange and understanding is crucial. Welcoming the diversity of global celebrations allows us to appreciate and respect each other's traditions, creating a more inclusive and harmonious global community.

Holidays also provide an opportunity for collective reflection on pressing global issues. Acknowledging the challenges faced by different communities and countries can inspire empathy and solidarity in addressing common problems such as poverty, environmental concerns, and social injustices.

Holidays epitomize the duality of connection and disconnection in our globalized world. While they unite people in shared celebration and acts of compassion, they also expose the disparities and cultural barriers that persist. By recognizing and embracing the diversity of global celebrations and engaging in collective efforts to address global challenges, we can strive to bridge the gaps.

Globalization Unveiled: Unraveling Causes for Concern

In richer nations, laid-off workers in the rust belts of Ohio, for example, blame globalization for misfortunes, job losses, and economic stagnation.

Although the reality does exist, politicians overstate diagnoses by blaming international trade, offshoring of production, and immigrants taking jobs.

According to the Information Technology and Innovation Foundation (ITIF),[151] a non-profit think tank based in Washington, DC, in 2019, the report, titled *The Myth of the Manufacturing Jobs Renaissance,* analyzes the reasons behind the decline in US manufacturing jobs and the role played by automation, trade, and other factors. And for every one US job lost through international trade from 1980 to 2016, researchers conclude that about four jobs have been lost because of automation, robotics, information technology, and other productivity boosters.[152]

Consumers who pay lower prices, managers who earn higher salaries, and shareholders enriched by dividends and equity growth have benefitted from automation and international trade.[153]

So international trade has, of course, resulted in some job losses, but far fewer than from automation. On the upside, international trade does create millions of new jobs.

Sometimes humans can be manipulated, for example, in an unfortunate belief of anti-globalization. In the context of the 2016 US presidential election and the European Brexit vote, as well as regions with limited immigrant populations like Wyoming or Lincolnshire, residents often become susceptible targets of fear-based tactics, leading to increased support for nativist politicians. Conversely, metropolitan areas, characterized by greater prosperity and a higher concentration of educated residents, tend to be less threatened by multicultural ideas and diverse ethnicities.

The selling of products and political platforms is often driven by fear. In the year 2000, the American population predominantly obtained their news from trusted sources like The New York Times, while the British public relied on the BBC and the Times of London for their information.

Digital Connections: The Soaring Popularity of social media

The concept of social media began to gain popularity and recognition in the early 2000s. Websites like Friendster (launched in 2002) and MySpace (launched in 2003) played pivotal roles in introducing the idea of connecting and interacting with others online. However, the widespread belief and adoption of social media as a significant communication and networking tool began to solidify around 2004-2006 with the emergence of platforms like Facebook, which rapidly gained millions of users. Social media is relied on by many, believing their information is accurate.[154]

Social media refers to websites and applications that enable users to create and share content or participate in social networking. Social media platforms typically allow users to connect with others, share photos, videos, and messages, and engage in real-time conversations through chat or comments.[155]

Prominent social media platforms include Facebook, Twitter, Threads, Instagram, LinkedIn, TikTok, Snapchat, and more. Each platform boasts distinct features and user demographics, yet they all facilitate online interaction and connection. The advent of social media has profoundly reshaped society, revolutionizing communication, information sharing, and relationship formation. While it has ushered in positive changes, such as expanded access to information and enhanced social networking opportunities, it has also been linked to negative consequences like cyberbullying, addictive behaviors, and the propagation of misinformation. As the evolution of social media persists, its impact on society remains a subject of ongoing discourse and deliberation. Social media platforms employ algorithms that tailor content to individual preferences, inadvertently creating echo chambers that reinforce pre-existing beliefs. This phenomenon can be concerning as it fosters polarization and limits exposure to diverse perspectives, resulting in a skewed perception of facts.

Being better connected is not an end itself; it's a great new beginning filled with boundless opportunities to promote the well-being of humanity throughout the world through mutual understanding, trust, and respect.

Helping people comprehend that embracing a new culture doesn't necessitate relinquishing their own is imperative. The coexistence of cultures can be mutually enriching rather than exclusive.

So, what makes diplomacy valuable? Despite the indifference shown by certain politicians and leaders toward democracy and human rights on the global stage, neglecting these fundamental aspects of America's international engagement risks compromising the legitimacy and effectiveness of military intervention. Sustainable solutions demand diplomatic efforts and sustained backing for the establishment of stable, peaceful societies.

Globalization often elicits fear, with concerns about its impact on cultural diversity. People worry that traditions, languages, and local economies may undergo transformation. However, when we view ourselves as interconnected rather than isolated, we can establish connections based on our shared humanity, diminishing adversarial perceptions, and supporting a sense of global unity.

Certain regions remain resistant to change, resisting the transition toward liberal democracy due to the potential challenge it poses to their leaders' authority. However, the world should strive toward an evolution that leads to the establishment of free and democratic societies, as this path holds the potential for a more equitable global future.

About That Cave!

Are you choosing to stay within your comfort zone or venturing out to engage with our interconnected world?

When we set a goal for ourselves, it often demands that we step outside our familiar boundaries and embrace growth. However, our primitive brain tends to resist such exploration and challenges due to its inherent fear of the unknown.

Imagine leaving the safety of your well-known "cave" to face new challenges and acquire unfamiliar knowledge. In response, your primitive brain triggers a protective response, urging you to revert to a defensive mode and avoid engagement. It loudly warns you to retreat to your haven and avoid the risks of the unfamiliar.

This instinct explains why many individuals experience fear and anxiety when confronted with novel situations, especially those involving people from different cultures. Our primitive brain tends to favor familiarity and similarity, encouraging us to stick with our own "pack" – people of the same religion, political background, or shared identity.

While it might sometimes feel tempting to remain disconnected from the unfamiliar, this choice ultimately deepens the gap between us and others. Refusing to explore new horizons and maintaining a closed mindset hampers our personal growth and restricts us within the confines of our comfort zones.

> **"Alone we can do so little, together we can do so much!"**[156]
> **Helen Keller**

Unlocking Global Connectivity: Embracing Positive Changes in a Globalized World

In today's era of globalization, it's essential to recognize the myriad positive changes that this phenomenon has brought to our world. The pathways to global connection are abundant and diverse, offering us the opportunity to engage with different cultures, communities, and perspectives. With the surge of technology, we stand at the threshold of unprecedented connectivity, with a multitude of ways to bridge geographical boundaries and connect with individuals from every corner of the globe.

- **Social media**: has revolutionized our ability to communicate and interact with people across nations and continents. Social media platforms such as Facebook, Threads, Twitter, Instagram, and LinkedIn serve as powerful mediums for fostering connections that transcend borders. These platforms enable us to engage, share, and collaborate with a diverse array of individuals, enriching our global network of relationships.

- **Email**: In an instant, emails traverse oceans, reaching recipients in far-flung locations. Email communication has emerged as a simple yet efficient channel to connect with people residing in different parts of the world. Through this mode, we exchange ideas, thoughts, and sentiments, creating bridges of understanding that span the globe.

- **Instant messaging apps**: Apps like WhatsApp, Telegram, and Signal have become conduits for real-time conversations that span continents. These instant messaging platforms empower users to send text messages, voice recordings, and video calls, connecting us to individuals with diverse backgrounds and stories.

- **Video conferencing**: Video conferencing platforms like Zoom, Skype, and Google Meet transcend geographical limitations, allowing us to hold virtual meetings with individuals located in various corners of the world. These tools enable face-to-face interactions that facilitate collaboration, knowledge sharing, and relationship-building.

- **Online forums**: Online forums and message boards create virtual spaces where like-minded individuals can connect, share insights, and engage in discussions about a myriad of topics. These platforms foster connections among individuals who share common interests, regardless of their geographic location.

- **Online gaming**: Online gaming has evolved into a global phenomenon, where players from different countries come together to compete, collaborate, and communicate within virtual worlds. Platforms like Xbox Live and PlayStation Network not only entertain but also unite gamers across cultures.

- **Blogging and vlogging**: Blogging and vlogging empower individuals to share their experiences, perspectives, and stories with a global audience. Through these digital mediums, we invite others into our lives, bringing connections and understanding that extend beyond borders.

- **Friendships** Across continents forming friendships with individuals from diverse cultures within our own communities can create meaningful connections that transcend borders. Initiating interactions, such as becoming pen pals or sharing experiences with those from different backgrounds, cultivates bonds that enrich our understanding of the world.

- **Learning a language**: Acquiring a new language opens doors to connecting with people from different countries and immersing oneself in their cultures. By speaking a common language, we create a shared space for understanding and communication.

- **Exploring the world**: Traveling to different countries provides firsthand exposure to new cultures, customs, and traditions. Through such exploration, we establish connections with the people and places we encounter, broadening our global outlook.

- **Teaching your language**: A two-way connection teaching your native language, such as English, to individuals from other countries facilitates cross-cultural connections. Language exchange programs further deepen these connections by promoting mutual learning and understanding.

- **Staying informed**: Reading newspapers or magazines from different countries offers insight into the current events, perspectives, and issues that shape global societies. This practice cultivates a sense of connectedness with the world at large.

- **Volunteering**: Impacting Lives, globally participating in volunteer and charity initiatives creates opportunities to connect with people from diverse backgrounds while contributing to positive change on a global scale. These endeavors stimulate relationships built on shared values and aspirations.

- **Television**: International television shows, news programs, and documentaries offer a window into the lives, cultures, and experiences of people from around the world. Through television, we gain exposure to diverse perspectives that expand our understanding.

In a world that continues to shrink due to technological advancements and interconnectedness, embracing these avenues of connection enables us to build bridges of understanding, empathy, and collaboration. The positive changes brought about by globalization pave the way for a more connected, informed, and global community.

Embracing Connection: Enriching Lives Through Unity and Diversity

Connection serves as the steadfast anchor supporting us on life's remarkable journey. Its impact is profound, not only transforming the lives of others but also enriching our own, regardless of our geographical location. As we forge connections and refine our communication skills, we intricately weave the fabric of profound relationships.

Naturally, we find solace in discovering common ground with those who share our perspectives, fostering a sense of belonging and ease. Yet, the true essence of connection is illuminated when we summon the courage to extend ourselves to those whose experiences differ vastly from our own. While this might appear daunting, the ability to engage with individuals from diverse cultures and viewpoints is a vital asset.

By embracing these connections, we swing open the doors to novel worlds and enriching encounters. Immersing ourselves in the lives of those with unique ways of existence widens our horizons, granting us invaluable insights into the intricate tapestry of humanity. In doing so, we nurture empathy and comprehension, shattering the barriers that could otherwise divide us.

Our capacity to connect intertwines into a powerful strand, knitting us together as an intricately woven global community. Let us celebrate the beauty of these interwoven connections and embrace the boundless richness that blossoms from embracing diversity. Through these profound bonds, we embark on a collective journey toward a radiant and united world.

Forging Connections with New Encounters: Valuable Tips for Any Situation and Location

- **Make eye contact:**
  Do not check your phone or scan the room when someone's talking to you; it appears that you're not listening, and you destroy the conversation.

- **Listen:**
  When someone is talking to you, listen, period. When you don't listen, it makes the other person feel like you don't care.

- **Get to know the other person:**
  In every conversation, ask questions. Try to focus on getting to know the other person. People love to talk about themselves. When we ask

- **Our name is our identity:**
  Remembering who you're talking to is a key to making the person feel important and a great way to connect with them.

- **Care about others:**
  Always care about those around you. Be encouraging, positive, uplifting, and supportive. People love feeling appreciated and cared about.

- **Smile at the friends in the room:**
  Greet people as if they are your friends. We all have something in common, so find that "something" and smile. This will decrease the intimidation factor and the "front" people sometimes put up as a defense.

Phil Rosenthal, creator of the *Everyone Loves Raymond*[157] TV show said it best: "There's a lot of value in getting to know people from different cultures and different countries. It enriches your life and opens your mind to new ideas and new ways of doing things."

Universal Communication: Bridging the Language Divide

In a world boasting a staggering 7,117 distinct languages,[158] the challenge of connecting with other countries becomes apparent—how can meaningful communication transcend linguistic barriers?

The exact count of languages spoken worldwide is challenging to ascertain due to the nuanced distinction between a "language" and a dialect or variation. Additionally, many endangered languages remain undocumented, adding complexity to the tally.

Communication serves as a bridge, sharing our movies, literature, and other forms of media with different countries. Learning other languages becomes crucial in fostering understanding among diverse communities. These efforts hold the potential to catalyze political, cultural, and commercial relationships, promoting collaboration on a global scale.

Envisioning a universal means of human communication raises intriguing possibilities. While technological advancements might hold the promise of a universal mode of communication, we still have a journey ahead. Communication manifests in myriad forms, both familiar and emerging, shaping the ways we connect and exchange information.

- **Verbal communication**: This involves using spoken or written words to convey a message. It can be done face-to-face, over the phone, or through written documents such as letters, emails, or text messages.

- **Nonverbal communication**: This includes body language, facial expressions, gestures, and tone of voice. It can convey meaning without using words.

- **Visual communication**: This involves using images, graphics, charts, diagrams, and videos to convey a message. It can be used to clarify complex concepts or to make a presentation more engaging.

- **Audio communication**: This includes using sound or music to convey a message. It can be used in various forms such as radio, podcasts, or music.

- **Digital communication**: This involves using technology such as computers, smartphones, or social media to communicate with others. It includes email, instant messaging, video conferencing, and social networking.

- **Written communication**: This involves using written words to convey a message. It includes books, newspapers, magazines, and other forms of print media.

- **Gestural communication**: This involves using hand gestures and sign language to convey a message. It is often used by people with hearing impairments or in situations where verbal communication is not possible.

A few examples of the many different forms of communication in the world include[159]:

- **Facial Expressions**: Facial expressions serve as a primal form of communication, allowing humans to convey emotions universally across many cultures. The recognition of these expressions is not limited to humans alone; Charles Darwin, the renowned naturalist, acknowledged their significance. In his book "The Expression of the Emotions in Man and Animals," Darwin suggests that certain key emotions can even be discerned in animals. For instance, chimpanzees exhibit laughter when tickled, even as infants, and can display smiles. They are also capable of interpreting our facial expressions of pleasure and disgust.

- **Gestures**: Gestures complement facial expressions and enhance communication when distance or other factors hinder verbal interaction. In an episode of the TV show "Monk," the protagonist uses gestures to communicate vital information to his assistant through a window. Gestures can convey directions, suggest movements, or indicate areas of interest. However, it is crucial to consider that gestures can vary significantly across cultures. For instance, in Japanese culture, pointing is considered impolite, while Western cultures place importance on eye contact as a cornerstone of polite conversation.

- **Emoticons**: Emoticons are contemporary counterparts of the universally recognized hobo signs. Initially starting with facial emotions, they have expanded to include gestures and common visual representations of various concepts. Emojis, a type of emoticon, have become a visual form of commonly used vocabulary, ranging from smiley faces to symbols representing love, birthday, food, animals, sports, and more. Emojis provide a simplified and easily understandable means of communication, allowing a picture to convey meaning equivalent to a thousand words.

- **Sign Language:** Sign language has a rich history and serves as a form of communication for the deaf and hard of hearing. Benedictine monks used to sign during their vows of silence in the 1500s, and Pedro Ponce de León, a monk, is considered the father of education for the deaf, having invented the first manual alphabet for fingerspelling. Helen Keller, who was blind and deaf, is one of the most famous individuals associated with finger spelling. French Sign Language, developed in the late 1700s, ultimately led to the widely used American Sign Language (ASL). ASL enables fluent communication between English-speaking and French-speaking signers, facilitating everyday interactions such as air travel, ordering from a menu, and asking questions.

- **Music:** Music serves as a universal language that transcends words and expresses complex feelings and moods. Rhythm, a fundamental aspect of music, is a shared element across cultures, allowing for communication through dance and music-making instruments. The brain responds to different combinations of notes, enabling us to distinguish between peaceful and frenetic music or identify happy and sad tones. Music has been extensively used in movies to heighten emotional responses and signal impending action. While musical preferences may vary between cultures, the emotional responses and physiological reactions to music remain consistent among individuals from diverse backgrounds. As Henry Wadsworth Longfellow famously stated, "Music is the universal language of all mankind," a sentiment supported by scientific research.

English, Chinese, Hindi, Arabic, Spanish: The Big Five Languages

Ethnologue, known as the reference publication *Languages of the World,* has been providing statistics and comprehensive information on the world's living languages since its publication in 1951. Widely recognized and authoritative, *Ethnologue* serves as a valuable resource, primarily dedicated to cataloging and documenting the languages spoken across the globe.[160]

According to *Ethnologue,* the Earth is home to over 7,000 languages, but many of them have limited speaker populations. Only eight languages have more than 100 million native speakers, while nearly 4,000 languages have fewer than

10,000 speakers. Some languages face the risk of extinction, with 692 having fewer than 100 speakers.

Among the languages that have gained global prominence are Chinese (1.2 billion speakers), Spanish (400 million), English (360 million), Hindi (350 million), and Arabic (250 million). English stands out as a potential universal language for several reasons. It is relatively easy to learn, uses the widely recognized Latin script, and has long been associated with social mobility. The number of non-native English speakers further boosts its global reach, potentially surpassing 2 billion people. English's influence is bolstered by its prevalence in business, science, technology, and entertainment, with English-language cinema and music enjoying worldwide popularity.

It's worth noting that population trends suggest the rise of languages like French and Chinese. China's emergence as a global leader has led to an increased interest in learning Chinese, particularly in the fields of technology and groundbreaking science. This shift in influence could potentially shape the future of a global language.

While the language of mathematics can be considered a universal language, its verbal expression varies across cultures. Mathematical concepts, from basic arithmetic to advanced calculus, remain consistent, but the linguistic representation differs. Numeric systems, such as Arabic numerals in the Western world, Chinese pictograms, or Hindi's Devanagari script, pose mutual unintelligibility in terms of number representation.

Programming languages, used to communicate with computers and perform complex computations, are predominantly based on the language of logic and mathematics. While there are thousands of programming languages, many originated in English-speaking countries or were designed by non-native English speakers to encourage widespread adoption. They employ vocabulary and syntax like natural languages, with keywords and symbols organizing logic and actions. For example, in the Java programming language, the command to display a message on the screen is written as "print," understood universally among Java programmers.

Although there are programming languages in non-English languages, they are less prevalent and understood by a smaller fraction of the global population. The future may bring advancements in universal translator software, created by individuals familiar with various human languages, to bridge linguistic barriers and foster global unity.

Morse Code

There are still other ways to communicate and connect globally and one of these is Morse Code.

Even in the digital age, Morse code remains a globally recognized and utilized method of communication. This system of dots and dashes continues to serve as a valuable means of relaying messages, particularly in situations where modern technology may fail or in emergencies.

To effectively use Morse code, it is essential to understand the meaning of the basic signals. The code consists of two distinct signal units: dots and dashes. Dots resemble simple periods, while dashes are represented by long horizontal lines akin to hyphens. These two signals, in combination, can represent every character in the English language. In Morse code terminology, dots are referred to as "dits," pronounced with a short "i" sound and a silent "t." On the other hand, dashes are formally known as "dahs," pronounced with a short "a" sound.

By familiarizing oneself with Morse code, individuals can tap into a reliable and versatile method of communication that transcends barriers and has stood the test of time.

The World of CRYPTO

The world of cryptocurrency has revolutionized finance by introducing digital or virtual currencies supported by cryptographic systems.[161] These currencies enable secure online payments without intermediaries, enhancing transaction efficiency and reducing costs.

The term "crypto" refers to the encryption algorithms and cryptographic techniques that protect these digital assets. Cryptocurrencies can be obtained through specialized platforms called cryptocurrency exchanges.

One of the main reasons why cryptocurrencies are appealing is their independence from central authorities, making them resistant to government interference. Unlike traditional currencies controlled by central banks, cryptocurrencies operate on decentralized networks, granting individuals greater control over their financial transactions.

The impact of cryptocurrencies extends beyond monetary transactions. They offer the advantage of global payments without the need for intermediaries like banks. This simplifies cross-border payments and promotes financial inclusion, particularly in regions with limited access to traditional banking services. This advancement fosters inclusive and connected societies, bringing the unbanked population into the market.

With the use of cell phones and crypto accounts, people worldwide can securely hold their wealth. For countries in Africa and regions in the Middle East, this opens opportunities for a significant portion of the population to enter the market. Collectively, these individuals contribute to raising the global economy by increasing spending and fostering free markets. Cryptocurrencies have unlocked new possibilities for individuals across the globe, contributing to the development of more inclusive and interconnected societies.

Zoom Virtual World[162]

Before 1918, the world experienced relatively isolated pandemics, with limited global impact. However, in 1918, during the height of World War I, as soldiers returned home, a deadly flu known as the "Great Influenza of 1918" spread worldwide, becoming the deadliest plague in history until 2020. This pandemic claimed the lives of a hundred million people, coinciding with the early stages of globalization.

During the 1918 pandemic, the lack of resources and communication channels exacerbated its devastating effects. There were no modern tools like TV, phones, internet, or websites to access information, and transportation and food supply were severely restricted. Moreover, essential communication tools like Zoom, which became a lifeline in 2020, were nonexistent during that time.

Fast forward to 2020, the COVID-19 pandemic forced office closures, event cancellations, and travel restrictions. In this modern era of globalization, Zoom emerged as a crucial connector for the world, providing a virtual avenue for communication and sustaining connections when in-person interactions were not possible. It liberated us to connect from the safety of our homes, and "Zoom" became synonymous with video conferencing.

Despite the challenges, the power of modern technology and globalization allowed us to stay connected in ways that were unimaginable in 1918. Zoom became a lifeline, enabling us to check on loved ones, communicate with friends worldwide, and support each other during these unprecedented times. This experience underscores the immense importance of globalization and its role in maintaining connections and solidarity across borders, transcending the barriers of distance and circumstance.

Qualities of Countries that Lead and Connect!

Globalized TV Shows Connecting Cultures Worldwide

Step into the enchanting world of IMDb's TV series, where glamour and exotic designs from global marketplaces take center stage. In a recent episode, the journey of elegance began with a captivating bracelet from Japan, followed by a mesmerizing necklace from Malaysia, and stunning earrings from India. The storyline echoes the sentiment of "Capture the glamour and exotic designs found in marketplaces around the world with gemstones set in sterling silver and pieces crafted in lustrous 18k gold over silver and brass." As the show's tagline suggests, "Travel the world via JTV's Global Destinations jewelry collection" and immerse yourself in a treasure trove of artistry and culture.

But the global adventures don't end there, as another popular show on IMDb beckons us to explore the delights of cuisine. Join Chef Essie Bartels in her TV series "Global Gourmet," where viewers embark on a tantalizing journey around the world, savoring flavors, and aromas from diverse culinary landscapes.

Behind these captivating shows lies a team of skilled professionals, including Food Technologists, Microbiologists, and Chefs, who are passionate about creating a world of epicurean delights. They keenly observe market trends, attentively listen to consumer feedback, and diligently research through various food channels to gain profound knowledge about what people eat. Their mission is clear: to make the Epicurean experience an unforgettable and ever-evolving adventure.

As these shows captivate audiences worldwide, they beautifully illustrate the interconnectedness of our global community. Amazing presentations from the USA, Canada, UK, France, Denmark, Norway, Sweden, Finland, Australia, Thailand, and India showcase the beauty of cultures coming together.

And speaking of celebrations, what better way to rejoice in the unity of our world than through food specials during holidays? The Vermont Country Store has crafted a delightful offering of "Come Together for the Holidays" specialties, bringing flavors from America, Germany, England, Scotland, Ireland, France, Italy, India, Switzerland, Sweden, Holland, Japan, and Spain to your table. So, let's raise our glasses and savor the delightful symphony of tastes from every corner of the globe, celebrating the rich tapestry of our global connections.

And what about ketchup? Heinz Ketchup[163] conducted an intriguing experiment, reaching out to people worldwide with a simple request: "Draw ketchup." The outcome? In a fascinating display of unanimous recognition, participants from every corner of the globe drew the iconic Heinz ketchup, solidifying its place as a universally known and beloved condiment.

Globalization: Uniting Humanity through Interconnectedness

Farok J. Contractor, a professor in the Management and Global Business Department at Rutgers Business School, emphasizes that despite certain trends like slowing trade growth, globalization remains an unstoppable force.[164] While increasing nationalism may lead to protectionist measures for certain product categories and immigration may level off in some countries, the acceptance of foreign investment continues to be embraced by nations.

In essence, globalization is a testament to the advancement of human connections and progress, supporting prosperity along the way, even though it can also bring about its fair share of challenges and frustrations in the process.

Geopolitics: An Exploration of Power, Geography, and Diplomacy

Geopolitics[165] is a multifaceted field of study that explores the intricate connections between geography, politics, and power within the international arena. It examines how physical and human geography influence international relations, including the dynamics between nations, resource distribution, and the formation of strategic alliances and rivalries. By analyzing factors such as natural resources, climate, population, terrain, culture, and significant geopolitical events like wars, treaties, and alliances, geopolitics seeks to comprehend the complexities of global affairs.

It examines the ways in which geographical features and resources can affect political power, international relations, and military strategy. Geopolitics also considers how economic, cultural, and historical factors interact with geographical factors to shape political outcomes. It is often used to analyze issues such as international conflict, regional alliances, and the distribution of resources and power on a global scale.

Global Politics: Embracing the Age of Interconnected Nations and Transnational Challenges.

The dawn of a new age has emerged—the era of global politics. Global politics is a field of study that delves into the political relations and interactions among various actors on the global stage. These actors encompass nation-states, international organizations, as well as non-state entities like multinational corporations, advocacy groups, and transnational social movements.

Global politics encompasses the analysis of a diverse array of issues, spanning from international conflict and security to economic development and trade, environmental policy, human rights, and global governance. It thrives on the ever-growing interconnectedness of actors and matters across national boundaries, alongside the burgeoning influence of non-state actors in global decision-making processes. Moreover, it's influenced by a spectrum of theoretical perspectives including realism, liberalism, constructivism, and critical theory. Each perspective lends a unique vantage point to the nature of global politics, as well as the prospects for international cooperation and conflict resolution.

So, how did global politics integrate itself into our world? Globalization and geopolitics represent contrasting facets of global evolution following the end of the Cold War. While globalization fosters interdependence, transnational flows, and erases state frontiers, geopolitics conjures images of grand power gamesmanship and power politics.

The defining characteristic of global politics is the growing interconnectedness of actors and issues across national borders. Non-state actors have gained significant influence in global decision-making processes, challenging the traditional power dynamics dominated by nation-states. This interconnectedness brings with it new opportunities for cooperation and understanding, but it also raises new challenges that require innovative approaches to address effectively.

Interwoven Horizons: The Dynamic Intersection of Globalization, Geopolitics, and Global Politics

Globalization, Global politics, and Geopolitics are closely connected and influence each other in various ways. Global politics refers to the study and analysis of political interactions, decision-making processes, and power dynamics that occur on an international or global scale. Global politics encompasses a wide range of issues, including diplomacy, international relations, security, human rights, trade, environmental concerns, global governance, and more. It examines how countries interact with one another, cooperate, or compete for resources and influence, and address shared challenges and conflicts. Geopolitics refers to the study of how geography, resources, and power dynamics shape the interactions between states and other actors on the international stage. On the other hand, globalization is the process of increased interconnectedness and interdependence among countries and people, driven by advancements in technology, communication, and transportation.

Interwoven Realms: The Nexus of Global Politics, Geopolitics, and Globalization Shaping Modern Dynamics and Challenges

- **Diplomatic relations**: Global politics involve diplomatic interactions and negotiations between countries on a wide range of issues, such as trade, security, and climate change. Geopolitical considerations influence diplomatic strategies and alliances, while globalization facilitates communication and coordination among nations, allowing for more extensive diplomatic networks.

- **Economic interdependence**: Globalization fosters economic interdependence among countries, leading to a globalized economy where trade, investment, and supply chains span across borders. Geopolitics plays a role in shaping economic relations, with countries pursuing strategic economic interests to gain influence on the global stage.

- **Security and conflict**: Geopolitics and global politics intersect in matters of security and conflict. Geopolitical considerations, such as strategic locations or access to resources, often play a role in shaping military alliances and conflicts. Global politics involves efforts to address security challenges on an international scale, such as countering terrorism or managing nuclear proliferation.

- **Cultural exchange**: Globalization has led to increased cultural exchange among countries, promoting the spread of ideas, languages, and traditions across borders. Geopolitical dynamics influence cultural interactions and can either facilitate or hinder cultural exchange between nations.

- **Environmental concerns**: Global politics and geopolitics have a significant impact on environmental issues. As environmental challenges like climate change are global in nature, countries need to cooperate through global politics to address these problems effectively. Geopolitics can influence how countries prioritize environmental concerns based on their strategic interests and resource dependencies.

- **Migration and refugees**: Globalization has facilitated the movement of people across borders, leading to increased international migration and refugee flows. Geopolitical factors, such as conflicts and economic disparities, drive migration patterns. Global politics comes into play when addressing the humanitarian and political implications of migration and refugee issues.

- **Technological advancements**: Globalization and geopolitics are closely linked to technological advancements. The spread of information and communication technologies enables global political interactions and shapes geopolitical power structures. Technological developments also impact economic competitiveness and national security strategies.

- **International organizations**: Global politics and geopolitics influence the role and effectiveness of international organizations such as the United Nations, World Trade Organization, and International Monetary Fund. These organizations serve as platforms for addressing global challenges and conflicts while reflecting the power dynamics among nations.

In essence, global politics, geopolitics, and globalization are intricately connected, with each impacting and molding the other in the ever-changing global panorama. Grasping these interconnections is vital for comprehending the intricacies and possibilities of the contemporary world.

FOR, IN THE FINAL ANALYSIS, OUR MOST BASIC COMMON LINK IS THAT WE ALL INHABIT THIS SMALL PLANET. WE ALL BREATHE THE SAME AIR. WE ALL CHERISH OUR CHILDREN'S FUTURE. AND WE ARE ALL MORTAL.
-JFK, American University Speech.
June 10, 1963.

Cultural diplomacy can be an effective tool for building relationships and promoting understanding between nations. It allows people from different cultures to learn about and appreciate one another's traditions and values and can help to build mutual respect and cooperation.

Unveiling the Social Media Paradox: Connecting and Disconnecting in a Digital World

Social Media Disconnection encompasses a range of phenomena tied to the adverse impacts of social media on mental well-being, interpersonal connections, and self-esteem.

For some, immersing themselves in the digital world leads to a detachment from genuine human interactions and emotions. Conversely, others struggle with feelings of detachment from their own identity and self-worth as they measure themselves against their peers on social platforms. The paradox emerges when considering that, while designed to foster connections, social media has paradoxically fostered division and disrupted relationships.

The scarcity of comprehensive information often fuels impulsive reactions driven by fragmentary knowledge. Amidst an era characterized by uncertainty, fear, and anxiety, these interconnected influences evoke diverse responses from individuals. The intricate nature of these interactions raises inquiries into how the digital landscape shapes human behavior and emotions in intricate and unpredictable ways.

Fear: False Evidence Appearing Real

Archie Bunker was a character played by actor Carroll O'Connor on the TV show *All in the Family*,[166] which ran from 1971 to 1979. The show was a groundbreaking sitcom that tackled social and political issues of the time through the interactions of the working-class Bunker family and their neighbors. Archie Bunker was known for his narrow-minded and bigoted views, particularly toward people who were different from him in terms of race, ethnicity, and gender. He was often blunt, and often used offensive language, but over the course of the show, he also showed moments of growth and empathy as he learned to see the world from different perspectives.

His character reflected the attitudes and beliefs of a certain segment of American society at the time, who were resistant to the changing social and cultural norms. As the world around him was evolving and becoming more diverse, Archie Bunker's fear and discomfort were a common reaction for some who felt threatened by the changes.

It's important to note that while Archie Bunker's views were widely criticized, the character's portrayal also helped to challenge and dismantle some of the harmful stereotypes and biases of the time. The show tackled issues such as race relations, gender roles, and LGBTQ rights in a way that was groundbreaking for its time.

Overall, Archie Bunker's character serves as a reminder of the importance of acknowledging and addressing our own biases and fears when faced with change and diversity. It is only by confronting these challenges that we can move toward greater understanding and acceptance of one another.

The legacy of *All in the Family* can be seen in the many shows that followed that also tackled controversial social issues and the more open and accepting attitudes that have come to characterize American society. While there is still work to be done to address issues of racism, sexism, and other forms of discrimination, shows like *All in the Family* helped to pave the way for a more inclusive and accepting society. TV diplomacy!

From a Global Perspective: Embracing Unity through Respect and Understanding"

In the past, our interactions were limited, and we lived in a more insular world where we primarily focused on the country, we lived in. However, as we've grown, evolved, and progressed, we've come to realize the significance of global connections and the need to engage with the rest of the world.

While fear may have the potential to divide us, there are fundamental aspects that unite all human beings. Beneath the sky, which is blue above all of us, lie our shared basic needs for shelter, food, water, clothing, sanitation, education, and healthcare. These necessities transcend borders and cultural differences, forming a common thread that binds us together as a global community.

Throughout history, people have sometimes become apprehensive and confused by the presence of differences, fearing the unknown or the "new." However, the path to understanding begins when we open ourselves up to connecting with those who are different from us—people from other countries, diverse cultures, and languages. Through these interactions, we gain fresh perspectives that broaden our understanding of the world.

Diplomacy and Globalization in Action

When we engage in conversations with individuals from different backgrounds, we discover that there is no absolute right or wrong. Rather, there is a spectrum of perspectives and experiences that deserve respect and consideration. Embracing this realization allows us to foster an environment of respect, where we recognize the value of diverse viewpoints and cultures.

In our journey from a confined mindset to a global perspective, we learn to appreciate the richness of diversity, breaking down barriers of misunderstanding and prejudice. By embracing unity through respect and understanding, we can build a more harmonious and interconnected world, where our collective strength lies in our shared humanity.

Promoting a Culture of Respect and Kindness: Building Stronger Connections

At the onset of the pandemic, when discussions about the coronavirus were prevalent, an incident unfolded in a nearby affluent neighborhood that soon became widely shared on social media. The incident revolved around a family of Chinese descent who had recently moved into the neighborhood, sparking apprehensive conversations and speculations regarding their potential association with the virus. Unfortunately, a few weeks later, their house fell victim to acts of vandalism, including egging, toilet-papering, and other malicious acts. The community quickly learned about the incident through a Facebook post that gained significant attention.

Witnessing the distressing aftermath, compassionate neighbors rushed to the scene, where they found the woman of the family in tears and the man pacing anxiously in their front yard. Moved by empathy, the neighbors extended their support and reassurance, letting the family know they were not alone. "It's okay, we will help you," they consoled. Together, they embarked on the cleanup process, displaying their solidarity by posting uplifting pictures on the community Facebook page with a heartfelt caption: "NEIGHBORS, they wrote, and FRIENDS!"

The impact of this incident went beyond the immediate response. The once hesitant neighbors, prompted by a shared sense of compassion, began actively engaging with the affected family, leading to the formation of unexpected friendships. Despite the perpetrators remaining unidentified, their deplorable actions inadvertently served as a catalyst for strengthening the bond within the community. Overwhelmed by remorse, the wrongdoers retreated into seclusion, burdened by their shameful deeds. While the incident itself was undeniably appalling, it ultimately reinforced the unity and solidarity among the community members, encouraging a renewed sense of togetherness.

It really takes someone to stand up to a wrong situation. Be a strong person and connect with what you know is kindness.

India's Diplomatic Footprint

In India, Chendamangalam is a place located in the Ernakulam district of the southern Indian state of Kerala, known for its historic significance and cultural diversity.[167] The town is situated on the banks of the Periyar River and has a rich history dating back to ancient times.

Chendamangalam stands out due to its remarkable characteristic of being home to religious sites representing four different faiths–Hinduism, Christianity,

Judaism, and Islam. What makes it truly exceptional is the harmonious coexistence that has prevailed among these faiths for centuries. Nearby, the town hosts a Hindu temple, a Christian church, a Jewish synagogue (particularly the renowned Paradesi Synagogue), and a Muslim Mosque.

The Paradesi Synagogue, located in Chendamangalam, is widely recognized as one of the oldest functioning synagogues within the Commonwealth of Nations. Similarly, the Kottayil Kovilakam St. George Orthodox Church, an ancient structure with a rich historical background, serves as the Christian place of worship in the town.

This unique amalgamation of religions and cultures has bestowed upon Chendamangalam a distinct identity, drawing visitors from various corners of the globe who are eager to witness this exceptional testament to religious harmony and peaceful coexistence. Despite the significant differences in their beliefs, the people of Chendamangalam have consistently demonstrated respect for one another, instilling an environment where conflicts based on religious differences are virtually non-existent.

It is both intriguing and refreshing to witness how the town of Chendamangalam serves as a remarkable example of harmonious coexistence, where individuals from four distinct religions and diverse backgrounds live in proximity, supporting an environment of tolerance, mutual respect, and cultural diversity.

Japan: An Exemplar for Diplomacy

Japan is indeed known for being one of the world's most successful democracies and having one of the largest economies.[168] The country is renowned for its advanced technology, cultural heritage, and strong work ethic.

The US-Japan Alliance is a strategic partnership that has been in place since the end of World War II, and it remains one of the most important relationships in Asia. The alliance is built on a foundation of shared values, mutual interests, and a commitment to promoting peace, stability, and prosperity in the region.

One of the unique features of Japanese culture is the emphasis on respect for others. Japanese society places a great value on politeness, humility, and deference to authority, which is evident in the way people interact with each other in daily life. This emphasis on respect is reflected in the language, customs, and social norms of the country.

For example, Japanese people are known for their bowing as a sign of respect when greeting others, showing gratitude, or apologizing. The language itself has different levels of formality.

The culture of respect holds a significant place in Japanese society, contributing to the country's renowned reputation for orderliness, safety, and stability. Visitors often marvel at the abundant politeness and respect they encounter in their interactions with the locals during their stay in Japan.

The Japanese culture, characterized by acceptance and respect for one another, their occupations, is remarkable.

The Art of Connecting in an Interconnected World

Now, let's delve into the concept of "to connect." This term generally refers to the act of joining or linking two or more things together, either in a physical or metaphorical sense. In the realm of technology and communication, "to connect" involves establishing links or communication between devices, computers, or networks, such as connecting to the internet, a Wi-Fi network, or a Bluetooth device.

On a social level, "to connect" signifies the establishment of bonds or relationships with others, whether it's an emotional, intellectual, or personal connection. In the context of transportation and travel, making connections between different modes of transportation, like connecting flights, trains, or buses, is essential.

Furthermore, in the business world, "to connect" takes on the meaning of establishing relationships or networks with other professionals or organizations in the same field. This could involve connecting with potential clients, industry experts, or colleagues.

Overall, "to connect" is a broad and versatile term that encompasses various ways of linking, joining, or establishing relationships between different things or people.

Now, why do we sometimes feel disconnected? Is it a defensive mechanism? Or is it our way of promoting peace in the world?

The answer lies in diplomacy and better international relations. Achieving meaningful connections with others from diverse cultures requires a sincere commitment to understanding and appreciating their way of life. Embracing dialogue and shared values becomes crucial in fostering mutual understanding, cooperation, and harmony among nations. By actively engaging in cultural diplomacy, we can bridge the gaps that often lead to disconnection and build a world where diverse societies come together for a more united and peaceful future.

Untangling Disconnection: Exploring the Multifaceted Causes

There are many reasons why people or groups may find themselves disconnected from each other. Differences in culture, language, beliefs, or values can often create barriers to understanding and collaboration.

Nonetheless, one effective approach to bridge these divides and create a closer bond among people is through the promotion of cultural diplomacy and better international relations. Cultural diplomacy entails utilizing cultural exchanges, arts, and various forms of expression to nurture mutual understanding, respect, and cooperation between diverse countries and communities.

Through cultural diplomacy, individuals can gain insight into and develop an appreciation for each other's cultures, traditions, and values. This process helps break down stereotypes and misconceptions, paving the way for more profound and meaningful relationships between people from varying backgrounds.

Furthermore, the promotion of better international relations holds the potential to address global challenges and advance peace and security. By forming coalitions and identifying common ground, nations can collaborate in tackling pressing issues such as climate change, poverty, terrorism, and human rights abuses.

Embracing cultural diplomacy and nurturing stronger international relations are vital steps toward uniting people, overcoming differences, and collectively addressing the critical problems that affect our interconnected world.

Working across the aisle and finding ways to connect and collaborate with others can be a powerful tool for promoting positive change and improving the world we live in. It requires a willingness to listen, learn, and compromise, as well as a commitment to building trust and understanding.

While our concerns may be real, they serve as a catalyst for unlocking a world brimming with boundless opportunities. Amid challenges, we'll discover the pathways to a brighter future, where new horizons beckon and adventures await. As we dare to dream big and seize the chances that globalization presents, remember; the world is our playground, and together, we'll conquer the unknown and shape a better, more interconnected tomorrow.

Step into the next chapter where we talk about the art of thriving in a globalized world. Discover the strategies and skills that pave the way for success in an interconnected and dynamic global landscape.

> "The preeminence of free government will be exemplified by all the attributes which can win the affections of its citizens and command the respect of the world."[169]
> George Washington

Timeless Talks: Leaders Feasting on Ideas and Insights

While breaking bread together, the leaders initiated a conversation, delving into the profound impact of globalization on the global landscape and engaging in a discourse about the significance of Bitcoin in the digital economy.

As the five great leaders discuss the impacts of globalization and their concerns, Winston Churchill turns to the others with a question: "Gentlemen, I must ask, what are your thoughts on Bitcoin and the role it plays in our digital economy?"

George Washington "I must admit, I am not familiar with this 'Bitcoin.' Can you explain it to me?"

Abraham Lincoln "I, too, have heard of it, but I am not entirely sure how it functions or could impact our economy."

Mahatma Gandhi "I believe that as leaders, we must always be open to new and innovative ideas but also be mindful of their potential impacts and effects on our economy and society."

Nelson Mandela "Yes, it is important to understand the implications of new technologies such as Bitcoin and consider how they can be used for the greater good and to promote economic stability and progress."

Winston Churchill "I understand that it is a digital currency. It could be a revolutionary concept for the future economy, but it is important to evaluate it closely, its security, and its potential impact on the economy."

Mahatma Gandhi "Bitcoin is not rich or poor. This is every person's opportunity, and we've never had this before."

Abraham Lincoln remarks "The Internet will connect us, but the problem that we are not on the Gold Standard is still troublesome."

Nelson Mandela "In the midst of chaos, there is opportunity,' like Sun Tzu said. The greatest risk is not taking one."

George Washington "I know the Romans used to cut the edge off the coins so there was less gold in each coin and then blend them with silver and copper.

Winston Churchill "Governments get themselves excessively into debt, which devalues the money."

George Washington "But it is the democratization of information, and crypto will be the fastest adoption of technology in history."

Winston Churchill "Yes, the internet grew at 63 percent a year and mobile phones in the 1990s–2010, which allows for this technology of this Bitcoin."

Nelson Mandela "I like the idea that it could be available to everyone in the world; after all, banks are not always available to everyone."

Mahatma Gandhi "I like that crypto is growing at 113 percent a year peacefully around the world, and everyone has the opportunity. This is not just money; it is the entire exchange transfer and storage of value for the internet."

Abraham Lincoln "It's actually an entirely parallel financial system and business structure for the world!"

Nelson Mandela "It's being adopted faster than anything we can ever imagine. It has grown as an asset and gone up 2 million percent since inception. And no other asset in recorded history has ever done this for the world."

George Washington "I am still hesitant as I have to think how America will prosper from this."

Abraham Lincoln "The union of opportunity for all is exciting. Plus, believing that the government's job is to do what a community of people cannot do for themselves, this Bitcoin will almost allow people to do things for themselves."

Winston Churchill "There is nothing government can give you that it hasn't taken from you in the first place." He adds: "The positive thinker sees the invisible, feels the intangible, and achieves the impossible."

The five great leaders continue the conversation on Bitcoin, discussing its potential as an opportunity for everyone, regardless of wealth and its potential to democratize access to financial services. They acknowledge the rapid growth and adoption of crypto and the positive implications for our world.

Chapter 8

SURVIVING IN A GLOBALIZED WORLD

"Am I not destroying my enemies when I make friends of them?" [170]
Abraham Lincoln

STEP INTO A world pulsating with possibilities, where survival in a globalized landscape demands courage, resilience, and adaptability. In this exhilarating chapter, we'll uncover the secrets to not just surviving but thriving amidst the whirlwind of globalization. Brace yourself for an awe-inspiring adventure as we unravel the intricacies of interconnected economies, cultures, and technologies. From navigating the labyrinth of cross-border trade to embracing the melting pot of diversity, we'll equip you with the tools needed to conquer the challenges and seize the abundant opportunities that await. We'll emerge as triumphant trailblazers in the unstoppable tide of globalization. Get ready to embark on a thrilling odyssey of discovery and empowerment, where survival is just the beginning of an extraordinary voyage!

Survival Strategies: Embracing Global Interdependence

Surviving in a globalized world is of paramount importance due to the interconnected nature of today's challenges and opportunities. Many pressing issues, such as climate change, pandemics, and economic instability, transcend borders and demand international cooperation to find effective solutions. In this context, embracing international connections becomes essential for countries to thrive and prosper.

Countries engaging in mutual trade and investments create a conducive environment for economic growth and development. Embracing global connections opens access to new markets, cutting-edge technologies, and valuable resources, propelling nations toward prosperous economic expansion. In an interconnected world, economic success is closely linked to how well countries integrate into the global market and collaborate with others.

Moreover, cultivating diplomatic bonds with other nations nurtures greater understanding and cooperation, paving the way for peace and stability on a global scale. By reducing tensions and promoting harmonious relations, these connections become a pillar of support for a more peaceful world. Peace and stability are prerequisites for sustainable development and provide the foundation for addressing global challenges effectively.

Amidst the complexities and uncertainties of the present, seeking solace in the past through nostalgia becomes a way to find stability and reassurance. Nostalgia acts as an emotional anchor, reminding us of our roots and the moments that have shaped our identities. It allows us to hold onto a sense of continuity, a reminder that the essence of who we are remains connected to the experiences that have shaped us. In a world where rapid changes are commonplace, holding onto our shared cultural heritage and past experiences can provide a sense of grounding and direction.

In essence, surviving in a globalized world is about embracing both the challenges and benefits of interconnectedness. Through international cooperation, countries can effectively address global challenges like climate change and pandemics, while also leveraging opportunities for economic growth and development. Simultaneously, cherishing our shared human experiences through nostalgia helps us understand where we came from and gives us a sense of purpose in navigating the complexities of the present and the uncertainties of the future.

The exploration of nostalgia and its profound impact on our lives can be connected to globalization. As the world becomes increasingly interconnected, the exchange of cultural experiences and memories transcends borders, contributing to a shared global nostalgia. Through the power of technology and communication, people from different corners of the world can connect and reminisce about similar moments from their past, creating a sense of unity and belonging.

Moreover, globalization has facilitated the preservation and dissemination of cultural heritage. Old photographs, vintage toys, and nostalgic music are not confined to specific regions or communities anymore. They can be shared and appreciated on a global scale, encouraging cross-cultural understanding and appreciation.

In this context, nostalgia becomes a shared human experience that links individuals and communities across continents. As we celebrate and cherish our individual and collective histories, we also embrace the interconnectedness of human experience.

Capturing the Essence of Nostalgia

Heidi Marler lives in England with a pink Barbie house and said, "My home is my happy place."[171] Heidi has decorated her house in pink "Barbiecore" and "Barbiecore" brings her back to a time of peacefulness, security, and happiness. There is even a 1960s-time capsule home in New Jersey, and as you walk inside, you'll find an entryway that'll make you feel like you walked through a machine that took you back fifty years. Everything from the walls to the front door to the stairs is covered in avocado green. This color is even carried over to the living room and dining room but with additional touches of pale pink and navy.

It's a blast from the past when you walk into the all-American eatery themed like Mom's Kitchen at Disney World. The Prime-Time Café[172] which is a classic American comfort food fifties kitchen and a good old-fashioned family gathering. People can even take a seat at a retro TV table and enjoy black-and-white clips from popular prime time shows circa 1955. All of this takes you back to a bygone era.

When faced with anxiety in our rapidly changing world, it's natural to yearn for the comfort of familiar times. We long for an era where the rules were clear, and life seemed more straightforward. However, younger generations, unburdened by the same preconceived notions, are eager to embrace the future with open minds. Though it may seem daunting, the world perpetually moves forward, bringing both opportunities and challenges along the way.

The world is undergoing rapid transformation, neither inherently positive nor negative, compelling us to recognize the necessity of forging connections with one another. In this era of accessible and affordable global access, we are swiftly evolving into a cohesive global society that profoundly impacts every individual. Remarkably, we have never been more equipped to confront the allenges at hand, armed with an abundance of collective knowledge, advanced technology, and vast resources unprecedented in history.

Given these circumstances, the time has come to develop new friendships and establish meaningful connections. It is essential to cultivate a deeper connection with ourselves, fostering self-awareness and personal growth. Equally significant is connecting with our immediate communities, nurturing bonds that strengthen social cohesion, support systems, and shared goals. Moreover, it is imperative to extend our connections to the broader world, recognizing our interconnectedness and engaging in global conversations and collaborations.

Ray Dalio founder of Bridgewater Associates and author of *The Changing World Order*, has said, "The only thing that really matters is the way people are with each other."[173]

By embracing these connections on multiple levels, we can navigate the changing landscape together, drawing upon the vast potential that arises from our collective unity and understanding. In doing so, we can foster a more inclusive, empathetic, and collaborative global society that embraces the challenges and opportunities of our time.

President Abraham Lincoln of America played a pivotal role in uniting a fractured and divided country, marked by conflicts over power, race, identity, and economics. Amidst the division and polarization, Lincoln's lessons continue to resonate. He worked tirelessly to preserve the American experiment, emphasizing the question in his inaugural address, "Is there any better, or equal hope, in the world?"[174] The very essence of connection that he sought to establish remains crucial in today's world.

With the rapid pace of globalization, the need for connection extends to the global community. Back in 1858, Lincoln emphasized, "The task of democracy is to guide enough individuals to share a moral vision concerning power, liberty, justice, security, and opportunity, with the aspiration of bringing people and nations closer to the ideals of goodness."[175] His words from 1861, "We are not enemies, but friends,"[176] still stand as a profound reminder of the importance of unity and understanding.

Beyond Economics: The Multi-Dimensional Scope of Globalization

Globalization encompasses more than just economic aspects; it extends to the political, cultural, military, and environmental domains. Moreover, globalization is not a recent development, as interdependence among nations across continents was already taking shape long before the First World War. Technological advancements such as the invention of the steam engine and the introduction of the telegraph played a significant role in reducing transportation and communication costs during that time.

Remember the old saying, "More heads are better than one"? Connecting with other countries is the same. What was found in the 1990s is that countries that had global economies grew an average of 5 percent more than a country that was less globalized.[177] Cultural outlook has increased by information that is available on the internet and helped to grow the people's strength to challenge human rights. We can see how connecting with other countries can lessen the chance of disagreements as being connected entails communication.

However, forging connections can also yield negative consequences. When we establish friendly ties with other nations, we inadvertently open the door for them to connect in ways that might lead to negative outcomes. This underscores the importance of maintaining connections, as it allows us to actively contribute to generating positive resolutions.

Of course, terrible situations can occur. For example, climate change can disrupt everything from extreme weather, lack of water, flooding, and loss of lives. Cybersecurity problems can cause major disruptions across the world, disrupting e-commerce, shutting down major businesses, disrupting our supply chains, and airline chaos.

"In 2004, the global cybersecurity market was worth just $3.5 billion," says Steve Morgan,[178] founder of Cybersecurity Ventures, "and now it's one of the largest and fastest growing sectors in the information economy." Fast forward to 2021, and David Braue reports that "Cybersecurity spending is to exceed $1.75 trillion from 2021-2025, due to the computer hacks theft/ransomware/etc. around the world."[179]

The necessity for global connectivity has reached a pivotal juncture, particularly considering recent inclinations toward isolationism and protectionism, exemplified by concepts like 'America First.' Such approaches might inadvertently foster an 'America Only' mindset, potentially disregarding the significance of establishing connections with other nations. In contrast, the imperative of embracing globalization, cultivating unity, and propelling international cooperation becomes increasingly apparent. It is worth noting that numerous global challenges can only find effective resolutions when countries unite as a cohesive force."

The pandemic served as a stark reminder that no nation is immune to world events. Issues like disease outbreaks, environmental threats, terrorism, and weapons of mass destruction require a united, international effort to find solutions. As British Prime Minister Tony Blair asserted after the September 11 attacks, "We are all internationalists now."[180]

And yet another esteemed individual, Joseph Nye delving into the intricacies of "The Paradox of American Power, "eloquently illustrates the distribution of power among countries as a three-dimensional chess game."[181] Each dimension represents unique characteristics and dynamics: military power leading to a unipolar distribution, economic influence more evenly shared among the United States, Europe, and Japan, and transnational relations where power disperses beyond government control.

Unforeseen Consequences: The Perils of Overlooking International Connection and Cooperation

Neglecting the importance of connecting and cooperating with other nations can lead to unforeseen problems. When assistance is not evenly distributed, and one country bears a disproportionate burden, it can create imbalances and strain relationships. America has often felt the weight of carrying the responsibility for various global challenges, leading to concerns about its role and the need for a collective effort.

In their book *American Foreign Policy for a New Century*,[182] Ivo H. Daalder and James M. Lindsay delve into this subject, underscoring that both Americanists and Globalists offer valid perspectives. While the landscape of globalization continues to shape the world, the role of power remains paramount in international politics.

Significantly, American, and allied initiatives have successfully transformed certain regions into havens of peace. Nevertheless, the impact of military power remains influential in other parts of the world. Even in the absence of a singular geostrategic threat comparable to Germany or the Soviet Union, challenges of a lesser magnitude persist. This demands the use of military and economic prowess to either mitigate or resolve them.

The commitment to maintaining the rule of law goes beyond mere establishment; it requires both the capacity and determination to enforce these regulations. However, a dilemma arises in collective action scenarios where costs are high, and benefits are distributed across nations. This is precisely where overwhelming power and the capacity to provide global public goods become crucial. The preeminence of strong leadership plays a pivotal role in upholding the rule of law on a global scale, advocating for principles of justice and order.

Madeleine Albright often said, "The United States is exactly what it is—the indispensable nation that makes it possible to mobilize the world into effective action."[183]

The foundational elements of relationships can serve as connectors between countries, dispersing the costs of actions and enabling collective achievements. This collaborative approach allows for greater capacity, ensuring that collective endeavors yield more substantial results. It can also prevent the scenario of various groups forming alliances against specific others, mitigating the risk of disproportionate power dynamics.

Championing a Global Framework: Upholding Democracy, Human Rights, and Free Enterprise

While establishing connections with influential entities is important, it alone doesn't suffice to achieve mutually beneficial objectives. Most countries share common aspirations, including safeguarding their liberty, security, and prosperity. The most effective route to attain these aspirations involves endorsing an international order grounded in principles of democracy, human rights, and free enterprise.

Cultivating an international order that extends freedom and prosperity to a larger populace holds intrinsic benefits for the global community. Embracing market democracies worldwide ushers in a host of advantages, including elevated financial well-being, heightened stability, and enhanced security for all stakeholders involved.

Africa is a great example. China invested more than $200 billion in the power and transportation sectors across Africa between 2000 and 2017 according to the Aid Data initiative at William and Mary, the Virginia college.[184] The money went to ports, railways, highways, and airports. These Chinese loans have enabled African cities to refurbish their infrastructure, making transportation easier and cheaper for people and goods.

The Center for Global Development in Washington has said, "The US struggles to outline a positive vision of what the world should be. The easiest way they've found is through comparison to enemies: 'We are free, China is not; we are helping, China is extorting.'"[185]

And according to a Washington Post article on Nov. 25, 2021, titled "Unrivaled Growth, 5 cities at the Fore," many Africans have responded with skepticism regarding Chinese intentions, "What is the problem with getting help to attain the same level of development others have?"[186]

One substantial reason for bolstering connections is the inevitability of new challenges arising. Globalization equips us to respond to urgent situations that can impact us all, such as the ongoing pandemic crisis. To tackle such issues effectively, it's crucial to maintain an international system for reporting and monitoring research, especially in perilous circumstances. This system would serve as an early warning system, should biotechnologists accidentally or intentionally create harmful pathogens.

Strengthening our global ties is paramount because there will always be groups aiming to cause harm and violence. The essence of global politics lies not in expecting everyone to share our values, but in cultivating respect for each other while championing positive virtues. By acting as role models for other nations and consistently emphasizing respect, we can cultivate positive, healthy connections.

Following World War II, the United States engaged with other nations, setting the stage for a constructive geopolitical world. This experience underscores that the connections we share are vital for all, as we coexist in this global landscape.

Navigating the World: Embracing Internet Diplomacy

The Internet was introduced to the public to facilitate communication and information sharing between researchers and institutions. During the 1960s, the US

Department of Defense developed a computer network called the ARPANET (Advanced Research Projects Agency Network) to allow researchers to share data and collaborate on projects. Over time, the ARPANET evolved and expanded, eventually becoming what we now know as the internet.[187]

The Internet: A Catalyst for Diplomacy and Human Connections

The Internet has become an indispensable aspect of modern life, providing people with seamless access to information, communication tools, entertainment, and facilitating global commerce and trade. It has revolutionized how individuals communicate and interact with each other, leaving a profound impact on diplomacy as well.

In essence, the Internet can be seen as a form of digital diplomacy, enabling nations and other actors to communicate and exchange information and ideas in a direct and accessible manner. Its influence extends beyond mere connectivity, playing a crucial role in diplomatic efforts at various levels.

Governments benefit from the Internet's capabilities as it facilitates effective communication, information sharing, and negotiation of agreements between nations. At the same time, individuals and non-government organizations find greater ease in engaging in diplomatic endeavors, advocating for human rights, and advancing cross-cultural understanding. It has paved the way for public diplomacy by providing direct channels for governments and organizations to connect with citizens and stakeholders across borders, bypassing traditional media and intermediaries. Furthermore, it cultivates a deeper understanding and cooperation among nations and cultures, thereby contributing to enhanced harmony on the global stage.

In this context, video conferencing tools like Zoom and FaceTime have emerged as powerful facilitators of human connections. Particularly during the COVID-19 pandemic, they played a pivotal role in bridging physical distances, enabling virtual meetings, online classes, and maintaining emotional connections with loved ones despite restrictions.

The significance of these tools extends to cultural diplomacy, as they enable cross-cultural exchanges and encourage discussions and debates among individuals from diverse backgrounds. This rich interaction promotes mutual understanding and cooperation, thereby strengthening the ties that bind us as a global community.

However, as the Internet revolutionizes diplomacy, it also presents new challenges and risks. Cyberattacks, misinformation, and digital manipulation are pressing concerns that demand strategic responses from governments, organizations, and individuals to safeguard against potential disruptions.

Agreeably, the Internet has emerged as a powerful catalyst for diplomacy, playing a pivotal role in fostering human connections and promoting cross-cultural understanding. It has brought the world closer together, transcending geographical barriers, and opening new avenues for collaboration and cooperation. Yet, as we embrace the benefits, we must remain vigilant in navigating the risks and complexities to ensure that diplomacy in the digital age thrives with transparency, security, and genuine dialogue.

Unraveling the Web of Connectivity: The Impact of the Internet on Human Connections

The impact of the Internet on human connections is complex and multi-faceted. On one hand, the Internet has made it easier for people to connect with each other, regardless of distance and time zones. People can now communicate and collaborate with one another in real-time, participate in online communities, and form relationships with people they may never have met in person.

Additionally, the Internet has also been criticized for disconnecting people from each other and from their own emotions, thoughts, and experiences. The constant barrage of stimuli from screens and devices can be overwhelming, and people may find themselves feeling more isolated and disconnected as a result. Additionally, people can become addicted to the Internet, spending more and more time online at the expense of face-to-face interactions and real-world experiences.

The Internet has connected and disconnected people from each other and from themselves. While it provides many benefits and opportunities for connection, it is also important to be mindful of its potential to disconnect us and take steps to maintain a healthy balance between our online and offline lives.

However, not all nations in the world have equal access to the Internet. In some parts of the world, access to the Internet is widespread, and infrastructure is well-developed, while in other parts of the world, access to the Internet is limited or non-existent. While the Internet has become an essential tool for communication and information access, there are still many parts of the world where access to the Internet is limited.

Some of the factors that contribute to limited Internet access include poverty, lack of infrastructure, low levels of education, and government restrictions. In many rural and remote areas, there may not be the necessary infrastructure in place to provide reliable Internet access, while in other areas, high costs or lack of technology can make access difficult. In some countries, government censorship and restrictions on Internet use can limit access to information and prevent people from exercising their right to free speech.

Factors that impact access to the Internet include income, geography, and political factors. In low-income countries, for example, the cost of accessing the Internet and the lack of infrastructure can be significant barriers to adoption. In rural areas, the lack of access to high-speed broadband can make it difficult for people to take advantage of the opportunities the Internet provides.

Some governments restrict access to the Internet or limit the flow of information online. These restrictions can be motivated by political or social concerns or can be aimed at controlling dissent and preserving the power of the state.

Uniting Across the Internet Divide

Efforts are underway to bridge the digital divide and bring the internet to people and communities that currently lack access. For example, initiatives like Google's Loon project aim to bring the internet to remote and underserved communities by using high-altitude balloons.

These efforts are being made to increase internet access globally, particularly in developing countries, initiatives such as the "Digital Transformation of the African Continent" aim to increase access to the internet and bridge the digital divide in Africa.[188] Other initiatives are focused on building infrastructure and improving the affordability of access.

The rapid improvement in Internet accessibility over the past few decades has undoubtedly brought significant benefits to many parts of the world. However, it is crucial to acknowledge that there are still regions where Internet access remains limited or unavailable, and bridging this digital divide should be a priority to ensure that everyone can reap the advantages of connectivity.

The importance of universal Internet access goes beyond mere convenience; it has far-reaching implications for education, economic development, and social progress. Access to the Internet opens doors to a wealth of knowledge and resources, empowering individuals with opportunities for personal growth and skill development. It serves as a catalyst for economic growth, fostering entrepreneurship, and enabling participation in the global marketplace.

In the realm of cultural diplomacy, the role of the Internet cannot be overstated. It serves as a powerful medium for shaping people's perceptions of different cultures and nurturing cross-cultural understanding and cooperation. By providing a gateway to diverse perspectives, online platforms enable individuals to engage with people from various backgrounds, participate in meaningful discussions, and challenge stereotypes and prejudices. Through these interactions, a greater sense of understanding, tolerance, and respect can flourish, fostering an environment conducive to cultural diplomacy.

Nevertheless, we must be mindful that limited access to the Internet can inadvertently hinder the exchange of cultural perspectives. In such cases, individuals may be exposed to only a narrow range of viewpoints, leading to potential misunderstandings, and perpetuating preconceived notions about other cultures. This underscores the urgency of expanding Internet access to ensure that everyone has equal opportunities to explore and engage with diverse cultural perspectives.

The interconnected world we live in has undoubtedly brought many benefits, but it also comes with its share of challenges. By prioritizing universal Internet access and nurturing a diverse and inclusive online space, we can promote greater cross-cultural understanding, support cultural diplomacy efforts, and build a more harmonious global community. In doing so, we embrace the power of connectivity to create a world that thrives on mutual respect, collaboration, and shared knowledge.

Let's Explore the Multifaceted Nature of Our Interconnected World and Delve into Some Key Points That Exemplify This Reality:

- **Global news**: The advancements in technology and instant communication have revolutionized how we access news from around the world. While this has allowed us to stay informed about both positive and negative events occurring in distant locations, it's important to note that the immediacy of reporting can sometimes overshadow the positive news with unfortunate incidents, conflicts, or natural disasters.

- **Economic interdependence**: The forces of globalization and interconnected economies have brought about increased economic interdependence. Undoubtedly, this has resulted in numerous benefits such as economic growth, expanded trade opportunities, and access to a wider range of goods and services. However, it's also vital to recognize that economic downturns, financial crises, or recessions in one part of the world can ripple across the globe, impacting economies on an international scale.

- **Social and cultural interactions**: The interconnectedness of our world has facilitated cultural exchange, travel, and migration, enabling people from diverse backgrounds to interact and learn from one another. While this has enriched our collective cultural experiences, it also presents challenges such as cultural clashes and conflicts stemming from differing values or ideologies. Navigating these complexities requires understanding, empathy, and open dialogue.

- **Environmental concerns**: Our global connectivity has heightened awareness of pressing environmental issues and challenges. The impact of climate change, deforestation, pollution, and other ecological concerns can no longer be confined to individual regions; they resonate on a global scale. This serves as a reminder of the urgent need for collaborative efforts and collective action to address these pressing challenges.

Maintaining a balanced perspective is crucial. Embracing the interconnectedness of our world is acknowledging the progress and opportunities it offers while also being mindful of the challenges and negative aspects. By being informed about both positive and negative news, we gain a deeper understanding of the complexities we face as a global community. Such awareness empowers us to work together toward collective solutions, fostering a world where interconnectedness thrives alongside responsible stewardship and genuine cooperation.

Globalization's Transformative Influence on the Modern World

In today's interconnected world, the lessons we can learn from history are more relevant than ever. Drawing inspiration from Abraham Lincoln's efforts to unite a divided nation, we can seek to connect with others who hold different values and perspectives. Lincoln's vision of a united and interconnected nation is exactly what we need to navigate the complexities of the global landscape and address contemporary challenges together.

Globalization, with its advancements in technology and communication, is a powerful force that connects us like never before. However, it also presents us with both positive and negative outcomes. On one hand, the internet facilitates instant communication and access to news from around the world, enabling us to stay informed and engaged on global issues. Moreover, cultural exchanges and interactions have become more accessible, creating cross-cultural understanding and cooperation.

Navigating the Pitfalls of Internet Negativity

On the other hand, the internet's influence can also lead to misinformation, cyberattacks, and digital manipulation, challenging the integrity of diplomacy and international relations. Additionally, not all nations have equal access to the internet, creating a digital divide that must be addressed to ensure everyone benefits from the opportunities that connectivity offers.

Global challenges, such as inflation, have become a shared concern that transcends national borders. The interconnected nature of the global economy means that disruptions in one part of the world can have far-reaching consequences. Addressing such challenges requires international cooperation and collective action.

To build a resilient and interconnected world, promoting unity and understanding among nations is paramount. Embracing the diversity of perspectives and cultures will enable us to solve global problems more effectively. As we navigate the complexities of the interconnected world, the building blocks of relationships are crucial in sharing the costs of action and fostering collaboration.

In our pursuit of connectivity and unity, it is essential to promote an international order based on democracy, human rights, and free enterprise. Embracing market democracies worldwide not only leads to economic prosperity but also enhances stability and security on a global scale.

Connecting with the world is vital as new challenges will inevitably arise. Issues like pandemics, environmental crises, terrorism, and weapons of mass destruction require collective action and international cooperation. No single nation can address these challenges alone; it takes a community, a global effort.

As we embrace connectivity and unity, it is crucial to be aware that globalization has its complexities. We must strive to maintain a healthy balance between our online and offline lives, ensuring that the internet connects rather than disconnects us from ourselves and others.

Navigating the world in the era of global politics requires recognizing the transformative power of interconnectedness. Embracing unity, collaboration, and cultural exchange will empower us to address shared challenges, build resilient economies, and support a world of understanding, respect, and cooperation. By connecting with one another and promoting international cooperation, we can truly create a world that thrives on mutual respect and shared values.

> "Let us not seek to fix the blame for the past. Let us accept our own responsibility for the future."
> —John F. Kennedy[189]

Societies and the Imperative of Interconnection

According to Sociologist Shmuel Eisenstadt, in the year 1500, some of the most powerful and largest cities in the world existed in China, India, and Turkey, and in the year 1000 BC, many of the mightiest cities were in Peru, Iraq, and Central

Asia. In the year 500 BC, they could be found in central Mexico, Italy, and China. In 2500 BCE, the most formidable rulers lived in Iraq, Egypt, and Pakistan.

Societal collapse seldom occurs if collapse is taken to mean "the complete end of those political systems and their accompanying civilizational framework." [190] In the book, *The Collapse of Complex Societies*, by Joseph A. Tainter,[191] he explains that political collapse carries lessons not just for the study of ancient societies, but for the members of all complex societies in the present and future.

Dr. Tainter's exploration comprises almost two dozen instances of collapse and encompasses a review spanning over 2000 years of explanations. In his intricate portrayal of humanity's narrative, he weaves a tale characterized by the threads of survival and rebirth. Through his insightful analysis, he reveals that although crises have undeniably shaped history and political structures have undergone metamorphosis, the occurrence of societies collapsing in an ultimate sense remains uncommon. This concept resembles the recurring refrain of a familiar tune: 'Welcome back, well the names have all changed since you hung around, the people may change but those dreams have remained, and they've turned around.' Hence, societies indeed undergo transformation, yet they endure rather than dissipate. This underscores the crux of our interdependence, highlighting the profound significance of our mutual reliance.

The Significance of Play in Cultivating Global Connections

The profound significance of play in connecting our world becomes evident when we recognize its impact on both childhood and adulthood. In the realm of childhood, play takes center stage as the primary means for learning, nurturing children's physical, social, and emotional well-being. Through play, children develop invaluable skills like resilience, enabling them to navigate life's challenges with confidence.

As children engage in play, they learn the art of interacting with the world, honing essential social and communication skills such as teamwork, sharing, negotiation, conflict resolution, and self-advocacy. Moreover, play serves as a gateway for children to explore and understand shapes, colors, cause and effect, and their own selves. It empowers them to conquer fears, make decisions, delve into personal interests, and interact harmoniously with peers.

As individuals transition into adulthood, the significance of play remains undiminished. Embracing the importance of play in the lives of adults cultivates environments that foster personal growth, well-being, creativity, and collaboration. Playful and creative adults bring fresh perspectives and innovative ideas to their work, contributing to enhanced productivity and forward-thinking solutions. Engaging in playful activities that involve group interactions further enhances crucial skills like teamwork, effective communication, and collaboration – all vital in a globalized world.

Intriguingly, play intertwines with cultural expression, acting as a vehicle for preserving cherished traditions and promoting intercultural understanding and appreciation. Embracing play throughout life offers a powerful conduit for connecting diverse communities, bridging cultures, and fostering a sense of unity amidst diversity.

The importance of play knows no bounds. It shapes childhood experiences, equipping children with the skills they need to flourish, and continues to resonate through adulthood, empowering individuals to thrive creatively, collaborate effectively, and bridge the gaps that divide us.

"Playmate, Come Out and Play with Me"[192] is a traditional nursery rhyme and singing game that has been passed down through generations. The author of the rhyme is unknown, but it is believed to have originated in the United States in the nineteenth century. The lyrics go as follows:

"Playmate, come out and play with me, and bring your dollies three, climb up my apple tree, slide down my rainbow, into my cellar door, and we'll be jolly friends, Forevermore, one, two, three!"

Forging Connections through Play: Strengthening Bonds and Bridging Cultures

Inviting someone to join in play and shared activities holds the power to create lasting connections and build meaningful relationships. Regardless of age, engaging in play enables individuals to establish strong bonds and develop essential interpersonal skills such as empathy, effective communication, and cooperation.

In the context of group play, teamwork and collaboration come to the forefront, fostering skills that are vital in our globally interconnected world. Working together in diverse teams, people can achieve common objectives, cultivate cooperation, and navigate the complexities of our interconnected society.

Play also serves as a platform for cultural expression and preservation. Adults can explore and celebrate their heritage through playful activities, ensuring that traditions are upheld and passed down to future generations. Furthermore, play facilitates intercultural exchange, sparking understanding, appreciation, and dialogue among diverse communities.

In many ways, connecting through play echoes the principles of diplomacy. Just as diplomacy involves negotiation, communication, and understanding, play promotes cooperation and conflict resolution among individuals and groups.

Recognizing the profound significance of play and embracing it throughout life contributes to a vibrant, resilient, and interconnected world. Beyond bringing joy, play nurtures personal growth, well-being, creativity, and collaboration. Moreover, it plays a pivotal role in promoting understanding, communication, and cooperation, fostering stronger connections among individuals and communities alike.

A Movie That Strikes a Chord: Connecting in Times of Adversity

The movie "The Day After Tomorrow" (2004) delivers a powerful message through the president's speech. It highlights the consequences of our actions on the planet's resources and the need for unity amidst global challenges. Though fictional, it reminds us that life constantly evolves, presenting new challenges.

"For years, we operated under the belief. that we could continue... ...consuming our planet's natural resources. without consequence. We were wrong. I was wrong. The fact that my first address to you comes from a consulate on foreign soil... ...is a testament to our changed reality. Not only Americans... ...but people all around the globe are now guests in the nations... ...we once called The Third World. In our time of need, they have taken us in and sheltered us. And I am deeply grateful. for their hospitality."[193]

We must recognize the importance of connection and communication with other countries during tough times, relying on each other for support and hospitality. As we navigate changing realities, fostering meaningful relationships with nations around the world becomes increasingly crucial.

As we conclude our thrilling expedition through the intricacies of Surviving in a Globalized World, we stand enlightened and empowered. The journey has revealed the challenges and opportunities that arise in this interconnected realm, forging us into resilient global citizens. Armed with newfound knowledge and strategies, we embark on the path ahead with confidence, knowing that while the concerns for globalization are noteworthy, they also open doors to a better world filled with boundless opportunities. Let us embrace this dynamic era with open minds, proactive attitudes, and a shared commitment to shaping a brighter, more harmonious future for all.

In the next chapter, we'll navigate the thrilling intersection of these two dynamic forces, exploring how they intertwine to shape the course of history and forge the future of our interconnected world. Get ready to immerse yourself in the art of diplomacy and the power of politics as they converge, paving the way for a captivating narrative that unravels the mysteries of global governance and international relations. Don't miss this chance to unravel the secrets of how connections form the backbone of diplomacy and politics in our ever-changing world!

"Courageous people do not fear forgiving, for the sake of peace." [194]
Nelson Mandela

Timeless Talks: Leaders Feasting on Ideas and Insights

As they warm up by the fire, the topic of navigating the complexities of a globalized world comes up.

Winston Churchill "Gentlemen, I was thinking about how the world is constantly changing through globalization; what if we discuss surviving in a globalized world?"

Nelson Mandela "I see the implications of a globalized world; it brings both opportunities and challenges. I am worried about how it could affect our economy, our culture, and the way we interact with other nations."

George Washington "I understand your concerns, Nelson. It is important that we adapt and find ways to survive in this new world but also be mindful of the potential negative effects it could have on our society."

Abraham Lincoln "I agree. It's important to be aware of the potential impacts of globalization and address them head on. But it's also important to keep in mind that not all aspects of globalization are negative; it can bring prosperity and progress as well."

Mahatma Gandhi "I believe that as leaders, it is important to recognize that not all of us will see eye to eye on every aspect of globalization. But it is important to have open and honest discussions, even if we agree to disagree sometimes."

Winston Churchill "Indeed, it is important to approach this complex topic with an open mind and strive to find ways to mitigate the negative effects while reaping the benefits of globalization. Together, we can work to find solutions that will help us survive and thrive in this globalized world."

George Washington "In my time, the world was not as interconnected as it is now. Trade and communication were limited to our neighboring nations and colonies. But now, we are facing a world where economies, cultures, and societies are interwoven in ways we never thought possible."

Abraham Lincoln "Indeed, the world is changing rapidly, and we must adapt to survive. We must find ways to navigate this newly globalized world and ensure that our nation remains competitive and prosperous."

Mahatma Gandhi "I believe that as leaders, it is our responsibility to ensure that the benefits of globalization are shared by all, not just the wealthy and powerful. We must work toward solutions that uplift and empower the poor and marginalized."

Nelson Mandela "I agree with Gandhi. We must work toward solutions that uplift and empower the poor and marginalized and also find ways to protect our culture and heritage while embracing the opportunities and progress brought by globalization."

Winston Churchill "I understand the concerns of my colleagues. In my time, I have seen how globalization can bring prosperity and challenges. But I believe that if we approach this complex issue with open minds and a willingness to work together, we can find solutions that will help us survive and thrive in this globalized world."

George Washington "I see your point, and I believe it is important to find a balance between preserving our culture and heritage and embracing the opportunities brought by globalization. We must find a way to navigate this new world and ensure that our nation remains strong and competitive."

Nelson Mandela "I agree. As leaders, it is our responsibility to ensure that the benefits of globalization are shared by all and that we find ways to protect our culture and heritage while also embracing the opportunities and progress brought by globalization."

Abraham Lincoln "I concur, it is important to find a balance between preserving our culture and heritage and embracing the opportunities brought by globalization. We must work toward solutions that uplift and empower all people and ensure that our nation remains strong and competitive in this globalized world."

Chapter 9

DIPLOMACY AND POLITICS: THE INTERSECTION OF CONNECTING

> "Diplomacy is the art of telling people to go to hell in such a way that they ask for directions."[195]
> Winston Churchill

WELCOME TO THE captivating realm where Diplomacy and Politics converge, unveiling the extraordinary intersection of connecting that fuels the very heart of our global landscape. Brace yourself for an exhilarating exploration of the dynamic forces that shape nations and weave the intricate mural of international relations. From high-stakes negotiations to strategic maneuvers that ripple across borders, we'll delve into the thrilling world of diplomacy, where alliances are developed, and bridges of understanding span the horizon. As we navigate the twists and turns of political landscapes, prepare to be invigorated by the electrifying dance of diplomacy, where the power of connection stands as a force of transformation and progress. Get ready to witness the artistry of dialogue, the composition of negotiation, and the symposium of ideas that will forever alter the way you perceive the grand stage of global affairs. So, step into this riveting chapter and be swept away by the exhilarating overture of diplomacy and politics: The intersection of connecting.

Politics can significantly impact the process of engaging with other countries, leading to various outcomes. For instance:

- **Foreign policy**: Foreign policy refers to a country's actions and relationships with other countries. The goals of a country's foreign policy can shape its approach to connecting with other countries and influence the ways in which it engages with the international community.

- **International organizations**: International organizations, such as the United Nations and the European Union, can play a role in connecting countries by infusing cooperation and collaboration on global challenges. Countries can become members of these organizations and participate in their activities as a means of connecting with other countries.

Additionally, politics can play a significant role in the process of connecting with other countries, as it shapes the ways in which countries interact with one another and work toward common goals.

John F. Kennedy practiced a sense of statecraft as "the art of the possible,"[196] which can be seen here from his remarks at Amherst College in October 1963:

> "I look forward to an America which will reward achievement in the arts as we reward achievement in business or statecraft. I look forward to an America which will steadily raise the standards of artistic accomplishment, and which will steadily enlarge cultural opportunities for all our citizens. And I look forward to an America which commands respect throughout the world not only for its strength but for its civilization as well. And I look forward to a world which will be safe not only for democracy and diversity but also for personal distinction."

Cultural Diplomacy Disregarded: Unraveling the Apathy

There could be various reasons. Some of the possible reasons include:

- **Lack of awareness**: Some people may not be aware of the significance of cultural diplomacy and how it affects their daily lives and the world at large.

- **Disinterest in cultural matters**: Some individuals may not be interested in cultural matters and may view them as unimportant.

- **Political and ideological differences**: People may have different political beliefs and ideologies, which can impact their views on cultural diplomacy.

- **Misunderstanding the concept**: Some individuals may have a misunderstanding of what cultural diplomacy is and its purpose, leading to a lack of appreciation for its importance.

- **Nationalistic tendencies**: People with strong nationalistic tendencies may view cultural diplomacy as a threat to their own cultural identity.

- **Economic considerations**: In some cases, people may prioritize economic considerations over cultural diplomacy, as they see it as less important for their personal and national interests.

It is important to understand that cultural diplomacy can play a crucial role in establishing cross-cultural understanding and promoting peace, stability, and mutual respect.

Critics of America's Involvement in Cultural Diplomacy Have Various Concerns, Including:

- **Ineffectiveness**: Some people argue that cultural diplomacy is not an effective means of promoting a country's image and values, and that it has limited impact on foreign relations.

- **Wasteful spending**: Cultural diplomacy often requires significant financial resources, and some people believe that this money could be better spent on other initiatives.

- **Insensitivity**: Cultural diplomacy initiatives can sometimes be seen as insensitive or inappropriate, especially if they are perceived as promoting a specific cultural group or set of values at the expense of others.

- **Lack of tangible results**: Some people may feel that cultural diplomacy does not result in any tangible outcomes and therefore question its value.

- **Political bias**: Political considerations can sometimes influence cultural diplomacy, leading to accusations of bias or propaganda.

- **Lack of awareness**: People may simply not be aware of cultural diplomacy and its purpose, leading them to view it as unimportant.

- **Self-absorption**: In today's fast-paced and individualistic society, some people may be more focused on their own lives and interests and less concerned with international affairs.

- **Fear or mistrust**: Negative experiences, stereotypes, or misinformation about other cultures can lead to fear or mistrust of other nations and their values, reducing the importance of cultural diplomacy.

- **Education**: Lack of education about cultural diplomacy, foreign affairs, and other cultures can also lead to a lack of understanding and appreciation for this field.

- **Media influence**: The media can also play a role in shaping people's views of cultural diplomacy, and negative media coverage can contribute to a perception that cultural diplomacy is unimportant or ineffective.

Kindling Interest: Paving the Path to Cultivate Concern

It is important to emphasize the positive impact that cultural diplomacy can have on developing international understanding and improving relationships between nations.

- **Show tangible results**: By highlighting specific examples of successful cultural diplomacy initiatives and their tangible outcomes, it can help to demonstrate the value of this approach.

- **Address criticisms**: By acknowledging and addressing some of the common criticisms of cultural diplomacy, it can help to build a more informed and nuanced understanding of this field.

- **Guiding participation**: Encouraging people to get involved in cultural diplomacy initiatives and events can help to build support and raise awareness of the value of this approach.

- **Ensure transparency and accountability**: By being transparent about the goals and objectives of cultural diplomacy initiatives, as well as the processes and outcomes, it can help to build trust and increase support.

- **Promote diversity and inclusivity**: Ensuring that cultural diplomacy initiatives encompass a broad spectrum of perspectives, nurturing support and enhancing the effectiveness of these initiatives.

By implementing these strategies, we can build greater support for cultural diplomacy and raise awareness of its significance and value. However, it's essential to acknowledge that some individuals may hold pessimistic views about cultural diplomacy due to factors like mistrust, political differences, or historical conflicts. Some may even question its effectiveness compared to other forms of diplomacy, perceiving it as a means of spreading influence or propaganda instead of promoting genuine cultural exchange.

Unveiling the Hidden Effects of Cultural Diplomacy

We must recognize that cultural diplomacy is a multifaceted field with complexities that make measuring its impact challenging. The true effects of cultural diplomacy efforts may not be immediately evident, requiring a long-term perspective for assessment.

Despite these challenges and controversies, many advocates believe cultural diplomacy is pivotal in promoting cross-cultural understanding, forging connections between nations, and contributing to global peace and stability. Success may be more likely when there is pre-existing trust and a shared interest in cultural exchange and collaboration. However, cultural diplomacy can also play a critical role in building relationships and guiding understanding between previously unreceptive nations.

Making the decision to pursue cultural diplomacy with a specific country necessitates careful consideration of potential risks and benefits. It requires in-depth analyses of the political, cultural, and social context between the two nations. When executed thoughtfully and strategically, cultural diplomacy can effectively promote cross-cultural understanding, bridge gaps between nations, and contribute positively to worldwide harmony.

In the spirit of unity, the Disney song "It's a Small World" aptly celebrates the idea of an interconnected world, reminding us that embracing cultural diversity and promoting mutual understanding can bring us all closer together.

Sahle-Work Zewde, Ethiopia's president of Africa said in 2020, "It's the People-To-People connections that make a lasting impact."[197]

United by Shared Interests, Connected by Celebrating Differences

Cultural differences possess the dual ability to both unite and divide us. On one hand, these differences present invaluable opportunities for mutual learning, exchanging ideas, and gaining a profound appreciation for diverse ways of life. However, they can also pave the way for misunderstandings, conflicts, and a lack of trust.

In the realm of cultural diplomacy, the key lies in recognizing and respecting these differences while actively seeking common ground to foster understanding and connection. This can be achieved through promoting cultural exchange, encouraging collaboration, and dispelling stereotypes and misconceptions.

The goal of cultural diplomacy is to nurture cross-cultural understanding and forge meaningful bridges between nations and people, transcending their differences. By doing so, cultural diplomacy becomes a potent force in crafting a more peaceful and stable world, where individuals from various cultures work in harmony to address shared challenges and create a brighter future for all.

Indeed, differences have the power to bring us together, enabling cultural exchange and collaboration that enriches our perspectives and deepens our appreciation for the richness of human diversity. However, it is essential to approach these differences with sensitivity and respect, addressing any potential conflicts or misunderstandings through open dialogue and understanding.

In the realm of cultural diplomacy, these efforts are instrumental in cherishing a world where nations and individuals can unite harmoniously, working toward a more peaceful and stable future.

Embracing Diversity: The Unifying Power of Differences

While seemingly elegant in theory, globalization suffers in practice. These are the lessons of Brexit and the rise of Donald Trump, explains Yale University and former chairman of Morgan Stanley, and Stephen S. Roach,[198] author of *Unbalanced: The Codependency of America and China.*

David Ricardo a British political economist and member of the Parliament of Great Britain and Ireland in the early nineteenth century believed if a country simply produces in accordance with its comparative advantage (in terms of resource endowments and workers' skills), presto, it will gain through increased cross-border trade. Trade liberalization – the elixir of globalization – promises benefits for all".[199]

However, Stephen Roach presents a differing viewpoint, suggesting that globalization has lost its political support due to various factors. One reason is the significant changes in the global trade landscape, with countries like China emerging as low-wage imitators, altering the dynamics of international trade. Additionally, political resistance to globalization has also played a role in its decline.

Historically, during times of war such as World War I and the Great Depression, globalization experienced a sharp decline of around 60 percent. Major economies turned inward and implemented protective trade policies, exemplified by the Smoot-Hawley Tariff Act of 1930 in the United States.[200] This act increased tariffs, putting strain on struggling nations, particularly those indebted to the US, and prompting retaliatory measures from other countries. Consequently, international trade suffered a significant decline.

While differences among nations exist, it is crucial to focus on our shared values as the foundation for genuine and equitable global cooperation. Recognizing and bridging these differences can help overcome frustrations and disappointments, stimulating a path toward a united and prosperous future.

Global Leadership and Our Connection to Great Britain

America's President Joe Biden put into words: "In a world of constant change, Queen Elizabeth was a steadying presence and a source of comfort and pride for generations of Britons."[201]

As Americans, we connected through Queen Elizabeth. "Americans love the queen,"[202] CNN announced in 2012 on the eve of Elizabeth's sixtieth anniversary on the throne, with new poll numbers showing US public approval of her at 82 percent. Heritage Foundation scholar Nile Gardiner asked the UK Telegraph: "if perhaps she, not the US president, should really be considered the "leader of the free world."[203] In 2013, The New Yorker discussed, "The queen just seems exotic and foreign to us, from another time."[204] Twenty-three million Americans watched the 2011 "royal wedding" between Prince William and Princess Catherine of Wales. [205]

A partisan head of government just can't rise above the politics of the age the way the queen has. In America, he or she couldn't even come close. "Why do Americans love the British Royal Family?"[206] *The New York Times* asked a panel in 2012. Revolution-era Americans "may have been fed up with royal politics, but most were anything but tired of royal pomp and circumstance,"[207] answered a Boston University professor.

In America, there is no equivalent of the queen —no nonpartisan figure who can serve as a unifying symbol of the country. Having a head of government who is also a head of state means Americans will never have a unifying figure like the queen.

The process of prime ministers seeking the royal blessing to unite the country during times of transition is a highly effective ritual that brings together the parliament harmoniously. Queen Elizabeth reigned for seventy years. She was a unifying figure who brought stability and cultural inheritance to a world of uncertainty.

The *Washington Post*'s September 18, 2022 article about Queen Elizabeth interviewed Andrew Ross, twenty-seven, of Cambridge, who explained that "the queen united families": "As a monarch over us for 70 years, me, my parents, my grandparents, my great-grandparents, we all experience the same feeling. She's the world's queen,"[208] he added. "She's incredibly special not only our small, wee country, but to the entire world." he added. Perhaps, as Andrew Ross suggested, "her appeal was related to her inscrutable politics — that no one really knew what the queen thought. She was a connector, a uniter, and that is what we all loved."[209]

"None of us has a monopoly of wisdom, and we must always be ready to listen."[210] Elizabeth II

This was a classic example of Elizabethan diplomacy. She did not lobby; she did not advocate; she just shook a hand.

She was better informed than perhaps anyone else in the world, the only person in the modern era ever to have read secret intelligence assessments every week for seventy years. That age, that experience, and that knowledge meant the Queen had the authority and credibility to convene the right people and ask the right questions. She was a walking, talking instrument of soft power. Queen Elizabeth shared, "Although you'll face many obstacles, and it may seem overwhelming at times, there are always answers and solutions."[211] She symbolized unity, constancy, and human decency. She did connect us all.

Exploring the Modern Tools of Diplomacy in Today's World

Uber and Lyft bring cultures together! Through commercial interactions, they help to break down walls between cultures and replace them with bonds of communication.

If you want to encounter a world free from prejudice, step into an Uber or Lyft. You'll meet individuals from diverse corners of the globe, hear their stories, learn about their home countries, and celebrate their dreams of being in a new place, wherever that may be. Uber and Lyft provide a unique platform that allows passengers to engage in conversations with drivers and hear their personal stories. During these rides, passengers can learn about their drivers' families, share their experiences, and connect on an emotional level. It becomes a space where drivers can open up, express their joys and sorrows, and share their journey of moving to a new country. By actively listening and engaging in these conversations, passengers can witness the drivers' emotional moments, empathize with their struggles, and rejoice in their happiness. It creates a shared experience that transcends a simple ride, fostering connections and understanding between people from diverse backgrounds.

These are just some of the countries representing the diverse range of people that can be encountered during rides using Uber and Lyft: Cameroon, Nigeria, Singapore, Nepal, Santa Domingo, United States, Germany, Russia, Togo, Egypt, Ireland, India, China, Mexico, Brazil, Azerbaijan, Turkey, Estonia, Jamaica, Venezuela, Ivory Coast, Bahrain, Belize, Algeria, Columbia, Honduras, India, Ecuador, Burkina Faso, Ghana, Washington DC, Sierra Leone, South Korea, Ukraine, Taiwan, Pakistan, Gambia, Haiti, Cuba, Mongolia, Cape Verde, Ethiopia, Syria, Congo, Sri Lanka.

The enjoyment in hearing the drivers' stories, sharing in their happiness, and witnessing their experiences come to life during their encounters with drivers from all over the world through Uber and Lyft rides. They embody the essence of their dream by working, sending money back to their home countries, learning the language, and assimilating into their new way of life.

Uber[212] was founded in 2009 as Uber Cab by Garrett Camp, a computer programmer, and the co-founder of StumbleUpon, and Travis Kalanick, who had sold his Red Swoosh startup for $19 million in 2007. He realized that sharing the cost with people could make it affordable, and his idea morphed into Uber.

Lyft[213] was founded in 2012, and (originally founded in 2007 as Zimride, offering long-distance rides). The change from Zimride to Lyft was the result of the lack of the same service for short-distance journeys.

Uber first launched almost three years before Lyft came into existence. Lyft, however, was the first to launch "rideshare" as an offering. Zimride was initially launched in 2007 in a few cities across the US.[214]

Everyone should partake in this eye-opening experience of a ride with Lyft or Uber, as it transcends being a mere "ride" and becomes an opportunity to gain insights about people from diverse countries. During one of the rides, a driver shared the heart-wrenching story of his brother's tragic death, a result of his profession as a policeman in their home country. Another driver described the constant fear experienced in their country, where random shootings were a distressing reality.

Throughout the rides, individuals can learn about various countries, such as Cameroon in Africa, and gain an understanding of the prejudice they face, their support for families back home, and even how some had never seen "snow" before.

It becomes evident that our world thrives on diversity, acting as a melting pot that necessitates the inclusion and unification of all people. Individuals like Guy, Delroy, Francisco, Yuniel, Abimbola, Gagandeep, Andrei, Kim, Kokou, David, Emmanuel, Jairo, Momcilo, Khalid, Abdul, William, Yaroslav, Hildy, Momodou, James, Rohit, Kadafy, Alusine, Antwane, Abdou, Yuying, Zeyla, Abid, Rajendra, and Krystal, who serve as a poignant reminder of the wonderful world shared by everyone. These individuals as they drive people in Uber and Lyft serve as teachers, offering invaluable insights into their own countries and creating connections across the globe.

Amazon's Role as a Hero During the Pandemic

During the pandemic, Amazon kept 99 percent of Americans going. [215]

You couldn't always go physically to the store, so Amazon gave you the opportunity to shop any time you wanted, in your pajamas while ordering from China or making dinner while talking to a company in Australia. Just about any product you needed was available; yes, even toilet paper.

One day during the pandemic a person on social media mentioned he had to go to the post office. While waiting at a traffic light, he noticed the Amazon distribution center located nearby, and around seventy-five Amazon trucks emerged and lined up in front of them. What struck him was the sense of excitement that spread among everyone in the now elongated line of vehicles. People started honking their horns and waving with enthusiasm. He found himself joining in, smiling, and waving as fervently as he could. In those uncertain and fearful times, they all felt reassured by the presence of the Amazon trucks.

He clarifies that he is not attempting to create an Amazon commercial or claim that the company is flawless. However, during the pandemic, Amazon was a dependable and vital service that people relied on. In his neighborhood, which comprises 400 homes, four Amazon trucks pass through daily. Interestingly, whenever they encounter an Amazon truck, he and others in the neighborhood continue to smile and wave, even doing so with other delivery trucks they notice. It's like recognizing a dependable friend always there for them, and the drivers also wave back, reinforcing that sense of connection and camaraderie.

Understanding the Dynamics of Connection and Disconnection

In the realm of diplomacy and politics, the dynamics of connection and disconnection are equally vital. When nations or political entities attempt to isolate themselves from the global stage to assert their independence, they might inadvertently find themselves losing influence and becoming detached from the international community. The pursuit of absolute sovereignty can lead to a diminished voice in global affairs.

Just like individuals, countries too are social actors in the world arena. Meaningful interactions and diplomatic relationships with other nations are essential for achieving shared goals and addressing global challenges. Isolating oneself from diplomatic engagements and international partnerships can hinder progress and diminish a nation's standing on the world stage.

Diplomacy thrives on the art of building bridges, cooperation, and forging alliances. It involves striking a delicate balance between safeguarding national interests and recognizing the interdependence and interconnectedness of the global community. Embracing diplomacy and active engagement with other nations can open doors to new opportunities, strengthen national interests, and contribute positively to a nation's growth and influence.

Take the United Gymnastics Conference,[216] for instance. Born out of dissatisfaction with the gymnastics governing body's inherent bias in the 1980s, it serves as a model of informal connections that fostered bonds of friendship, fairness, and sportsmanship among participants and schools. This connection paved the way for an equitable environment.

Similarly, NATO[217] operates on analogous principles. It emerges as a defender against inequity, standing up for those treated unfairly. While it's true that not every member fulfills their financial commitments, the alliance remains a symbol of collective effort. As someone once said, "NATO lasts because it is in the national interest of each member."[218]

Magnus Petersson, head of the Centre for Transatlantic Studies at the Norwegian Institute for Defence Studies, highlights that while debates continue over defense spending distribution, experts unanimously agree that the advantages of active U.S. involvement in NATO outweigh the costs. Petersson emphatically asserts that reducing participation in NATO would result in far greater expenses—both financially and in terms of security. He firmly believes that this course of action would be counterproductive to U.S. interests, potentially leading to tumultuous scenarios that directly threaten the United States. Consequently, disengagement could force the U.S. into future interventions, incurring significantly higher costs than maintaining active engagement.[219]

The Power of Openness and Collaborative Endeavors

The achievements of Rome and the all-encompassing ethos of Athens did not stem from diminished military might or the constriction of Roman and Athenian citizenship. Contrarily, both ancient civilizations flourished due to their adeptness in embracing diversity and expanding their influence through diverse avenues.

In contemporary times, the recurrence of the phrase "America First" seems to resonate with sentiments reminiscent of a 1930s isolationist movement. This movement not only championed isolation but also carried an undertone of anti-Semitic sentiments.

The underlying notion here is that historical instances, such as those of Rome and Athens, underscore that strength and prosperity can arise through openness, inclusiveness, and collaboration with others. In contrast, recent rhetoric invoking isolationist concepts raises concerns about the potential repercussions of withdrawing inward and sidelining global cooperation.

While countries that share language, civilization, and temperament tend to build better relations, this comfort is situational. However, when faced with adversity, as seen in World War II, the imperative to unite friends becomes evident. This need for unity was instrumental in the formation of NATO, a collective defense mechanism that underscores the significance of international collaboration.

Harry Truman's Diplomatic Legacy: Forging Global Connections

Harry Truman, the thirty-third president of the United States, from 1945 to 1953, was a staunch advocate of international cooperation and alliances, a belief that transcended political party lines. Although a Democrat, Truman collaborated closely with internationalist Republicans in Congress to endorse and commit the United States to several crucial international endeavors.

Truman's influence extended to various key initiatives. Firstly, he played a pivotal role in the establishment of the United Nations (UN) in 1945. The UN's founding aimed to advance global peace, security, and collaboration among nations. Serving as a diplomatic platform and mechanism for resolving disputes, the UN sought to forestall conflicts and sustain global order.

Secondly, Truman championed the League of Nations, an intergovernmental organization conceived after World War I with a shared objective of promoting peace and cooperation. Despite the U.S. not joining the League, Truman's endorsement of international institutions underscored his belief in collective security and multilateralism.

Thirdly, Truman fervently supported the Marshall Plan, officially termed the European Recovery Program. Instituted in 1948, this initiative delivered substantial financial aid and resources to assist Europe's war-devastated nations in post-World War II reconstruction. The Marshall Plan aimed at developing stability and economic resurgence across Europe, ultimately benefiting the world by averting further political and economic instability.

Truman's collaboration with internationalist Republicans illuminated a bipartisan dedication to global engagement and the significance of united efforts with other nations to tackle worldwide challenges. The foundations laid by the initiatives he advocated set the stage for the United States' commitment to international alliances and organizations, notably exemplified by NATO.

Established in 1949 under Truman's presidency, the North Atlantic Treaty Organization (NATO).[220] NATO emerged as a defensive military alliance uniting North American and European nations. Its core objective was to counter the Soviet Union's influence and aggression in Cold War-era Europe. Truman's support for international initiatives, such as the UN, the League of Nations (in principle), and the Marshall Plan, reflected his appreciation of the value of collective security and cooperative endeavors to sustain global peace and stability.

This outlook likely influenced America's decision to become a founding member of NATO, reinforcing the conviction that collaborating with other nations for mutual defense is indispensable for worldwide tranquility and security.

Pros of NATO:

- Offers a long-term collective defense of strategically developed countries
- Helps to manage crisis situations around the world
- Works to fight terrorism around the world
- Works with partner countries that are not part of the pact of mutual defense
- Offers a clear command structure
- Provides options for cyber defense within the structure of its treaty
- Offers an open-door policy
- Provides a cost-effective way to provide mutual defense
- Still serves as a deterrent to Russian aggression
- Stops other countries from developing nuclear weapons

Cons of NATO:

- Only five nations fulfill their funding requirements for NATO
- The role of NATO has changed since the collapse of the Warsaw Pact
- The United States has paved the way for NATO over most of its life
- NATO isn't requiring current members to maintain their democratic status

- The expansion of NATO creates more risk for every other member

- NATO members have an over-reliance on the United States

- Article 5 has only been invoked once in the lifetime of the agreement

Globalization and the Rise of Outsourcing: Interconnected Economies

Nurturing our world is intricately interwoven with strands of interconnectedness, and as businesses recognized the advantages of cost-effective labor and abundant materials overseas, the practice of outsourcing gained momentum. This interdependence has cast a profound influence on the global economy, reshaping the interactions between nations and cultivating the growth of cultural diplomacy.

The intricate network of the global economy, propelled by the ascent of outsourcing and globalization, has cast a profound influence on cultural diplomacy. Through shared economic ventures and the consumption of products originating from various corners of the globe, bridges of understanding and appreciation for diverse cultures have been erected. This symbiotic relationship fortifies unity among nations, laying the groundwork for robust diplomatic relationships and a more closely connected world.

- **Cultural diplomacy through trade**: The exchange of goods and services across international borders serves as a conduit for cultural diplomacy. Our engagement with products hailing from diverse countries exposes us to their traditions, values, and heritage. This exchange kindles mutual comprehension and an increased admiration for the multiplicity of cultures, thereby reinforcing diplomatic bonds.

- **Weaving cultural divides**: The decision to outsource manufacturing to foreign shores creates economic links that extend beyond geographical confines. This collaborative spirit encourages individuals from various backgrounds to collaborate, promoting cultural cross-pollination and dismantling cultural barriers.

- **Global supply chains**: The intricate web of global supply chains underscores the mutual reliance of nations. Countries lean on one another for resources, skills, and expertise, nurturing a sense of cooperation and cohesion. As nations collaborate, they nurture relationships rooted in shared interests, further advancing cultural understanding.

- **Shared experiences**: Our daily interactions with products—be it smartphones, clothing, or gadgets—reflect a convergence of cultures from around the world. This shared experience of interacting with goods of varied origins strengthens our sense of interconnectivity and serves as a reminder of our global kinship.

- **Celebrating tolerance and diversity**: The availability of products spanning different nations affords us the opportunity to celebrate diversity and embrace differences. By acknowledging the artistry, craftsmanship, and cultural resonance of these goods, we cultivate a society that is more inclusive and accepting.

- **Encouraging innovation**: Collaborative ventures in manufacturing and technology sow the seeds of innovation and creativity. As distinct nations contribute their expertise to the production process, novel ideas spring forth, enriching economies and enhancing the exchange of cultures.

- **Strengthening diplomatic bonds**: Outsourcing and global trade frequently lead to diplomatic alliances. As countries grow interdependent economically, they are incentivized to maintain harmonious relations and seek resolutions to conflicts through dialogue and negotiation.

Our interconnected world is mirrored in the diverse origins of products we engage with daily. From smartphones and computers originating in Taiwan to sneakers manufactured in China or Vietnam, and cameras showcasing Japan's craftsmanship, we are united by a global mosaic. Computer servers find their origin in India, jeans bear the imprint of Bangladesh, and Shea Butter heralds from Africa. Comfortable cotton shirts come to life in Vietnam, while Lee

Jeans hail from Mexico and Guatemala provides us with bananas. Cinnamon evokes the fragrance of Sri Lanka, while Colombia delights us with coffee. Pinot Noir wine carries the essence of France, and Gruyere Cheese is a gift from Switzerland. Ecco Shoes emerge from Portugal, and the illustrious Samsung Galaxy smartphones are born in Korea. In the realm of cars, Italy, Germany, Sweden, Korea, Japan, and Britain all contribute to our automotive choices. This kaleidoscope of products underscores the global impact of outsourcing and trade, binding us together in an intricate dance of cultural exchange and economic interdependence.

> "Behind a country's wealth and success are the policies that create possibilities, where people drive efforts that shapes the environment and perspective."
> U.S. News 2021[221]

**The study and model used to score and rank countries were developed by BAV Group, a unit of global marketing communications company VMLY&R[222], and The Wharton School University of Pennsylvania, specifically Professor David Reibstein, in consultation with U.S. News & World Report.[223]

According to the 2021 US News report, these are the seventy-eight countries viewed as the most globally connected.[224]

The ranking criterion for countries includes Overall Adventure, Agility, Cultural Influence, Entrepreneurship, Heritage, Movers, Open for Business, Power, Quality of Life, and Social Purpose.

Country	Rank	Country	Rank	Country	Rank
America	#1	Argentina	#32	Australia	#8
Austria	#18	Azerbaijan	#72	Belarus	#65
Belgium	#16	Brazil	#25	Bulgaria	#47
Cambodia	#78	Canada	#6	Chile	#45
China	#9	Colombia	#49	Costa Rica	#53
Croatia	#44	Czechia	#37	Denmark	#19

Dominican Republic	#54	Ecuador	#69	Egypt	#40
El Salvador	#74	Estonia	#59	Finland	#29
France	#2	Germany	#4	Greece	#2
Guatemala	#70	Hungary	#38	India	#24
Indonesia	#42	Iraq	#76	Ireland	#21
Israel	#30	Italy	#5	Japan	#7
Jordan	#64	Kazakhstan	#73	Kenya	#71
Latvia	#62	Lebanon	#66	Lithuania	#57
Malaysia	#35	Mexico	#28	Morocco	#56
Myanmar	#75	Netherlands	#11	New Zealand	#23
Norway	#26	Oman	#67	Panama	#46
Peru	#63	Philippines	#43	Poland	#31
Portugal	#20	Qatar	#41	Romania	#48
Russia	#17	Saudi Arabia	#36	Serbia	#61
Singapore	#14	Slovakia	#51	Slovenia	#55
South Africa	#34	South Korea	#13	Spain	#10
Sri Lanka	#68	Sweden	#15	Switzerland	#12
Thailand	#39	Tunisia	#60	Turkey	#33
Ukraine	#52	United Arab Emirates	#22	United Kingdom	#3
Uruguay	#50	Uzbekistan	#77	Vietnam	

Connecting People and Nations through Globalization and Diplomacy

Globalization can be described not only in terms of loss of jobs through imports and multinational companies but also the transmission and blending of ideas, lifestyles, cultures, and phobias communicated by the internet and social media.

These companies and countries play pivotal roles in connecting people and nations, leveraging globalization, communication, lifestyle, and cost of living factors, all while fostering diplomatic relationships on a global scale.[225]

Work Environments: Unveiling the Ideal Blend of Globalization, Communication, Lifestyle, and Cost of Living

- **South Korea**: South Korea's remarkable economic growth and technological advancements have made it a global leader, fostering connections with nations across the world. Its vibrant lifestyle, rich culture, and efficient communication contribute to its appeal as a great place to work.

- **France**: With its influential cultural heritage and strong diplomatic ties, France plays a vital role in connecting nations through art, literature, and international cooperation. Its diverse lifestyle and favorable cost of living make it an attractive destination for global professionals.

- **Japan**: Japan's commitment to diplomacy and global partnerships has established it as a significant player in international affairs. Its efficient communication networks and unique lifestyle appeal to those seeking enriching work experiences.

- **New Zealand**: Known for its picturesque landscapes and commitment to sustainability, New Zealand actively engages in diplomacy and has strong connections worldwide. Its relaxed lifestyle and pleasant living conditions attract individuals seeking a balanced work-life experience.

- **Canada**: As a nation renowned for its diplomatic efforts and welcoming approach to immigrants, Canada fosters a diverse and interconnected society. Its high-quality communication infrastructure and attractive lifestyle make it an ideal place to work for many.

- **Cambodia**: With a rich cultural history and increasing globalization, Cambodia is becoming a connecting hub in Southeast Asia. Its affordable cost of living and emerging opportunities attracts professionals looking to make an impact on the global stage.

- **Singapore**: Singapore's strategic location and commitment to diplomacy have propelled it as a global financial and business center. Its modern lifestyle and excellent communication systems make it an appealing destination for professionals worldwide.

- **Ecuador**: Ecuador's dedication to fostering international relations and connectivity has enhanced its position in the global community. Its unique lifestyle and reasonable cost of living create a desirable environment for professionals seeking new experiences.

Companies with the Best Globalized Connected Multinational Workplaces:

- **Google**: With a global presence and commitment to innovation, Google connects millions worldwide through its search engine and digital services, promoting international cooperation and diplomacy.

- **Meta** (formerly Facebook): As a leading social media platform, Meta connects individuals from diverse backgrounds, transcending geographical boundaries and fostering diplomatic interactions.

- **IBM**: IBM's multinational workforce and cutting-edge technologies enable global communication and collaboration, fostering connections among diverse teams.

- **Alphabet** (Parent Company of Google): As a conglomerate of technology companies, Alphabet's diverse offerings facilitate international connections, promoting diplomacy in various fields.

- **SAS**: As a multinational software company, SAS's solutions enable businesses worldwide to connect and collaborate effectively, fostering global diplomacy.

- **W.L. Gore**: Known for its innovative approach, W.L. Gore empowers its employees to collaborate and connect across borders, promoting a culture of diplomacy and inclusivity.

- **NetApp**: With a focus on data management solutions, NetApp facilitates the exchange of information on a global scale, contributing to international cooperation.

- **EMC** (Now Part of Dell Technologies): EMC's data storage and management solutions support global connectivity, playing a role in diplomatic exchanges and cross-border cooperation.

- **Microsoft**: Microsoft's software and services enable individuals and organizations to communicate and collaborate worldwide, promoting international diplomacy.

- **Marriott International**: As a global hospitality leader, Marriott fosters connections and cultural understanding through its diverse portfolio of hotels, promoting international diplomacy in the tourism industry.

- **Cisco**: Cisco's networking solutions facilitate global communication, bridging distances and contributing to diplomatic interactions.

- **Diageo**: As a global alcoholic beverages company, Diageo connects people from various cultures, promoting cultural exchange and diplomatic ties.

- **Mars**: With operations worldwide, Mars fosters connections among its global workforce, promoting a culture of diplomacy and collaboration.

- **American Express**: As a global financial services company, American Express supports international transactions and connections, contributing to global economic diplomacy.

- **Belcorp**: A multinational beauty company, Belcorp promotes cultural exchange and connection through its diverse beauty brands.

- **Scotiabank**: As a major international bank, Scotiabank facilitates global financial transactions, contributing to economic diplomacy and cooperation.

- **Hyatt Hotels**: Hyatt's global hospitality network connects travelers from around the world, promoting cultural understanding and diplomatic interactions.

GLOBAL GREATNESS

Globalization is the remarkable system through which things transition from being regional or national to becoming interconnected on a global scale. This phenomenon has had a profound impact on various aspects of our lives, transcending geographical boundaries and fostering connections among people, cultures, and economies worldwide. Below is an illustrative list of various aspects that have experienced globalization, contributing to the concept of global greatness:

- **Trade and commerce**: Globalization has revolutionized the way goods and services are traded across borders. International trade agreements and open markets have facilitated the exchange of products, creating opportunities for businesses to reach consumers worldwide. This interconnectedness has led to economic growth and prosperity for nations involved in global trade.

- **Technology and communication**: Advancements in technology, particularly the internet and telecommunications, have been instrumental in promoting globalization. Instantaneous communication allows people from different corners of the world to connect effortlessly, fostering the exchange of ideas, knowledge, and innovation on a global scale.

- **Cultural exchange**: Globalization has facilitated cultural exchange and appreciation. Through the sharing of music, art, literature, and traditions, diverse cultures can connect and understand one another better.

This intercultural dialogue promotes harmony, tolerance, and mutual respect among nations.

- **Travel and tourism**: The ease of international travel has greatly contributed to globalization. People can explore different countries, experience new cultures, and appreciate the diversity of our world. The tourism industry has thrived as individuals seek to connect with various destinations, fostering cross-cultural interactions.

- **International finance and investment**: Globalization has led to increased international financial flows and investment. Companies can access capital from foreign markets, while investors can diversify their portfolios across the globe. This interconnected financial system promotes economic stability and growth.

- **Education and research**: Globalization has transformed the field of education and research. Students can access educational resources from prestigious institutions around the world, promoting knowledge-sharing and academic collaborations across borders.

- **Migration and diaspora**: People have been on the move throughout history, but globalization has accelerated migration and created global diaspora. The movement of individuals and communities across nations has enriched societies with diverse perspectives, skills, and contributions.

- **Environmental and health challenges**: Globalization has highlighted the interconnectedness of environmental and health challenges. Issues like climate change and pandemics require international cooperation and coordinated efforts to find solutions that benefit the entire planet.

- **Entertainment and media**: The entertainment industry has experienced globalization with the global distribution of movies, television shows, and digital content. Cultural products now reach audiences worldwide, bridging cultural gaps and building a global entertainment community.

- **Humanitarian efforts**: Globalization has enhanced humanitarian efforts, allowing organizations and nations to collaborate in addressing global crises. From disaster relief to fighting poverty, the interconnectedness of the world has amplified the reach and impact of humanitarian initiatives.

A New Epoch of Global Excellence

In essence, globalization has ushered in a new era of global greatness, connecting people, nations, and societies in unprecedented ways. As the world becomes more interconnected, the power of diplomacy and the importance of connecting with each other become even more critical in fostering international cooperation, understanding, and a shared vision for a better future. Embracing the challenges and opportunities of globalization can lead us toward a more inclusive, interconnected, and prosperous global community.

As we draw the curtains on this captivating exploration of diplomacy and politics at the intersection of connecting, we find ourselves enriched with a profound understanding of the world's intricate connection of relationships. Throughout this enthralling journey, we have witnessed how the art of diplomacy brings together nations, cultures, and individuals, establishing bonds of cooperation and understanding. The power of embracing global connections has illuminated the path toward a future where collaboration and unity prevail over division and discord. With each stride forward, we recognize that diplomacy serves as a beacon of hope, guiding us toward a more harmonious and interconnected world. As we bid farewell to this chapter, we carry with us the knowledge that by embracing diplomacy and embracing one another, we hold the key to unlocking a world brimming with possibilities and potential. So, let us continue to tread this path of connection and collaboration, united in our pursuit of a brighter and more equitable future for all.

And now prepare to dive headfirst into the captivating realm of our next chapter, where we unravel the secrets of a world of possibilities through the art of diplomacy and the embrace of global connections. This thrilling adventure will lead us through uncharted territories of innovation and collaboration, as we discover the limitless potential that awaits in our interconnected world. Together, we'll navigate the currents of opportunity, charting a course toward a future filled with boundless promise and transformative change. Join us as we commence on this extraordinary expedition, where the power of diplomacy and global connectivity opens the door to endless possibilities.

> "The art of statesmanship is to foresee the inevitable and to expediate its occurrence."[226]
> **George Washington**

Timeless Talks: Leaders Feasting on Ideas and Insights

The table of five takes a more serious tone as they enter a deep discussion about how important understanding and unity is in politics. The candlelight is flickering, giving the conversation a cozy atmosphere as they bounce ideas and insights off each other about the connection between politics and personal connection.

Mahatma Gandhi "I wonder how diplomacy and politics can help people in our society."

Winston Churchill "Some men change their party for the sake of their principles; for others, their principles for the sake of their party."

Abraham Lincoln "One of my greatest preoccupations as a political thinker is the issue of self-governance and the promise and problems that could arise from it."

Nelson Mandela "As someone who has fought against racism and apartheid, I understand the importance of diplomacy and politics in protecting and uplifting marginalized communities."

George Washington "I have always believed that negotiation is vastly preferable to any other pursuit. I took the leading role in diplomatic relations because I believe it is crucial in shaping society and promoting progress and equality for all."

Abraham Lincoln "Diplomacy helps nations understand, cooperate, and find peace, while connecting with each other goes beyond borders, cultures, and differences, leading to a harmonious and interconnected world."

Mahatma Gandhi "I consider politics to be a work of the heart and not merely of reason. We must always be guided by our principles, not just our political affiliations."

Winston Churchill "I understand your point, Gandhi. But in politics, it is often necessary to make compromises to achieve progress."

Abraham Lincoln "I believe that we must have 'malice toward none' in our political efforts. We must strive to understand and work with those who may have different beliefs and ideologies."

Nelson Mandela "As a strong and purposeful fighter against racism and apartheid, the protector of the oppressed populations of South Africa, I fully agree with both of you. Achieving unity and understanding is crucial in creating a just and equal society."

Winston Churchill "During my time as prime minister, I saw firsthand the importance of diplomacy and politics in the face of war. It was through careful negotiations and alliances that we were able to defeat the enemy and secure victory for our nation."

Mahatma Gandhi "In the struggle for Indian independence, I learned that nonviolence and diplomacy can be powerful weapons in the fight for justice and equality. Through peaceful resistance, we were able to bring about change for the Indian people."

Nelson Mandela "In the fight against apartheid, I saw the importance of diplomacy and politics in creating a more just and equal society for all South Africans. It was through negotiation and dialogue that we were able to bring about change and end the system of racial segregation."

Abraham Lincoln "During the Civil War, I recognized the importance of diplomacy and politics in preserving the Union and abolishing slavery. It was through careful negotiations and persuasive speeches that I was able to keep the border states in the Union and abolish slavery."

George Washington "As the leader of the American Revolution, I saw the crucial role that diplomacy and politics played in securing our independence and establishing our new nation. Through careful negotiation and leadership, I was able to unite the colonies and secure our freedom from Britain."

Winston Churchill "I knew that my speeches had the power to rally the British people during the war. I used my words to build alliances and defeat the enemy. Diplomacy and politics helped me to bring us to victory."

Mahatma Gandhi "My philosophy of nonviolence was not just a personal belief; it was a political weapon. I used it as a powerful diplomatic tool for peace and reconciliation. It helped me to change the course of history."

Nelson Mandela "Negotiating with the apartheid government was a critical aspect of ending the system of racial segregation. Diplomacy and politics played a key role in bringing about change for the people of South Africa."

Abraham Lincoln "I worked hard to keep the Union together. Diplomacy and politics helped me to persuade the border states to stay in the union. It was a tough battle, but we succeeded."

George Washington "Leadership and diplomacy skills were crucial in securing independence from Britain. I used my abilities to unite the colonies and bring them together to fight for our freedom."

Abraham Lincoln "In my opinion, diplomacy and politics are essential in uniting a divided nation and bringing about change for the greater good. It is through careful negotiations, persuasive speeches, and a focus on the common good that we can achieve progress and unity."

Chapter 10

A WORLD OF POSSIBILITIES

> "Education is the most powerful Weapon
> which you can use to Change the World."[227]
> Nelson Mandela

STEP BY STEP, venture into the vast expanse of a world of possibilities, where each stride unveils new horizons of potential. This invigorating chapter takes us on a journey of exploration, where every step we take leads to remarkable discoveries and uncharted territories that await us in the global arena. As we navigate the twists and turns of boundless opportunities, our path becomes a symphony of progress, with diverse perspectives intertwining in perfect harmony. From bustling cities to tranquil landscapes, we uncover the interconnectedness that unites us all. Together, we launch on this exhilarating adventure, where dreams know no boundaries, and the possibilities are infinite. With each stride, we forge a unity that reverberates across continents, uniting us all in the pursuit of a brighter and more promising tomorrow. So, join us as we set forth on this thrilling journey, where the world becomes our canvas, and the steps we take shape a collaborative future filled with endless potential.

What sets our world apart is the relentless spirit of exploration that drives us to uncover uncharted territories and find innovative solutions to global challenges. Diverse perspectives converge and intertwine into a collaborative melody of progress and understanding. Here, unity is celebrated, as individuals and nations unite to create an interconnectedness that transcends borders and embraces the shared human experience, and the unimaginable becomes attainable. Embracing diversity, we form a spirit of global citizenship, propelling us to reach beyond our limits and embrace the transformative power of collaboration.

Our world of possibilities thrives on innovation, where the unique combination of ideas, cultures, and experiences forms intricate patterns of progress.

Embracing Global Connections: Impact in the World

Achieving global greatness may involve several different goals and priorities, depending on the context and specific circumstances of a given situation. Some potential goals that may be pursued in the pursuit of global greatness could include:

- **Promoting peace and stability**: This could involve efforts to reduce tensions and conflicts between countries, as well as efforts to address the root causes of violence and instability.

- **Fostering economic development**: This could involve efforts to promote trade, investment, and economic growth, as well as efforts to address issues such as poverty, inequality, and unemployment.:

- **Protecting the environment**: This could involve efforts to reduce greenhouse gas emissions, protect biodiversity, and address issues such as climate change and pollution.

- **Developing cultural understanding and cooperation**: This could involve efforts to promote cultural exchange and education and address issues such as prejudice and discrimination.

Global Impact: Unraveling the Role in the World

In our unique world, principles like liberty, independence, and self-government shape our collective journey. Embracing diversity, our global community unites people in a profound and impactful way. Through the appreciation of diverse backgrounds, perspectives, and ideas, we foster stronger connections, creating a more inclusive and meaningful society. In a world of vast differences, we embrace and value these distinctions, propelling us forward as a united force. Embracing diversity becomes the catalyst for innovation, enabling us to tackle challenges and achieve remarkable outcomes. The celebration of differences empowers us to address global issues together. Our world thrives on the recognition and honor of unique perspectives, forging connections that transcend boundaries and reinforcing the notion that our diversity is the bedrock of our collective strength. As we continue this awe-inspiring journey, our interconnectedness propels us to navigate challenges and forge a brighter future for all humanity.

After all, our differences don't divide us; they unite us, creating a powerful and purposeful harmony within the group. It is crucial to stay connected to our world, as being part of a community brings a sense of belonging and specialness. When we surround ourselves with others, we experience increased positivity, reduced rudeness, and less stress, leading to a stronger sense of connection with the world around us.

In 1926, Milne and illustrator E.H. Shepard[228] introduced us to Winnie-the-Pooh and his friends, who navigated life's twists and turns with grace and humor, teaching readers to cherish the good and weather the bad. Almost a century later, their wisdom remains just as relevant.

A Give and Take: Our Dynamic Role in the World

Recent times have presented numerous challenges, including rudeness, stress, fear, and a sense of disconnection. The world has grappled with the impacts of the pandemic, uncertain healthcare, economic struggles, political conflicts, and emotional instability, leading to confusion and problems on a global scale.

As individuals, we have the power to provide purpose and make a positive impact. Volunteering, offering a helping hand, and actively participating in meaningful initiatives contribute to a sense of fulfillment and boost morale for us and others. Together, these efforts ripple outward, shaping a world where empathy and compassion thrive.

Unity and diversity go hand in hand, showcasing the beauty of embracing our differences while forging paths toward a shared vision of the future. This journey demands a willingness to listen, compromise, and build bridges instead of walls. Globalization, a multifaceted phenomenon, wields the potential to either unite or divide us. On one hand, it fuels interconnectivity, facilitating the exchange of ideas, goods, and services across borders, fostering collaboration, and understanding among diverse cultures. Yet, the other side reveals its challenges, such as economic inequality and cultural homogenization, eroding local traditions and fostering alienation. The key to harnessing globalization's power lies in effective management and regulation. When guided by principles of fairness, sustainability, and social inclusion, globalization unites us, creating a world of equity and prosperity. Conversely, if driven solely by profit motives and unchecked market forces, it risks exacerbating divisions and nurturing conflict and resentment.

In her article "Thriving Locally in the Global Economy" by Rosabeth Moss Kanter,[229] Professor of Business Administration at Harvard Business School and the founding chair of the Harvard Advanced Leadership Initiative, and a former chief editor of Harvard Business Review, Professor Kanter discusses how opponents of globalization often point to its negative effects on local communities.

Professor Kanter questioned if the effects are always negative and proposed that global forces could be used to support and develop communities rather than tear them down. She found that in the future, success will come to companies that can meet global standards and tap into global networks.

"Ironically, the best way for communities to preserve their local control is to become more competitive globally," states Professor Kanter.[230]

In bygone eras, a company's success hinged on its geographical location, granting dominion over vital resources like capital, labor, and materials. Yet, the landscape has transformed into the global information economy, where supremacy emerges not from a physical location but from the prowess to conceptualize, exhibit competence, and establish meaningful connections. In this new age, foreign companies effortlessly adapt to localize their presence in the global economy, intertwining residents with diverse corners of the world. The shift has dissolved the confines of borders, building a dynamic web of interconnectivity that empowers companies and communities alike to thrive on a global scale.

People in Spartanburg and Greenville connected with foreign companies in their home cities and found that the influence of foreign companies in their area brought successful cultural changes such as the annual International Festival, the Japanese tea garden, and many sister-city relationships. But the real impact had to do with opening minds of the globally relevant skills.[231]

World-class businesses need innovation, production and trade, competence, and connections to help grow global assets that will benefit us all.

Bridging Borders: Global Perspectives on Health Care and Reaching Communities Around the World

In an increasingly interconnected world, the significance of health care transcends national boundaries, calling for a broader understanding of health issues and a collaborative approach to improve global well-being.

Health care is a fundamental human right, yet access and quality vary significantly among different regions and communities. By exploring diverse perspectives on health care from various parts of the world, this initiative seeks to promote dialogue and knowledge-sharing to tackle complex health issues more effectively.

One of the key objectives is to highlight the remarkable efforts of health care professionals and organizations reaching out to underserved communities worldwide. These dedicated individuals and groups are breaking barriers and overcoming geographical, cultural, and economic challenges to deliver life-saving medical services, preventive care, and health education to those in need.

Furthermore, the initiative seeks to emphasize the interconnectedness of global health challenges. Infectious diseases, chronic illnesses, and mental health issues can spread across borders rapidly, impacting people in different corners of the world. By recognizing the shared vulnerabilities and responsibilities, the global community can advance a more cooperative and coordinated response to health crises. And additionally, through promoting cross-cultural understanding, and endeavors to break down stereotypes and misconceptions surrounding health care practices in various regions, create a more inclusive and respectful approach to health care on a global scale.

In a rapidly changing world, technological advancements have revolutionized health care delivery and research. Connecting health care providers, researchers, and policymakers across continents, facilitating the exchange of expertise, best practices, and cutting-edge medical discoveries.

Moreover, this initiative recognizes the vital role of community engagement in building resilient health care systems. By empowering local communities to actively participate in health care decision-making and implementation, we can ensure that health interventions are culturally sensitive, sustainable, and tailored to the unique needs of each community. By working together, we can create a world where every individual has access to quality health care, regardless of their geographical location or socioeconomic status.

Global Disparities in Life Expectancy

Incredibly, our global world is very disconnected. From 2000-2019 overall life expectancy in the United States increased by 2.3 years, but the increase was not consistent among racial and ethnic groups or by geographic area. This is according to a new study funded by the National Institutes of Health that examined trends in life expectancy at the county level.[232]

So, why is this?

Research has shown that the possible reasons for such a gap in life expectancy around the world have included differences in income or education, exposure to environmental risks, and differences in the environment.[233]

Life expectancy has shown varied patterns among different racial and ethnic groups in the United States. While life expectancy for the Black population has witnessed significant improvement, it is still behind that of the white population. At the same time, the white population experienced more moderate gains, and in some areas, even a decline in life expectancy. This study observed that the narrowing of the White-Black life expectancy gap could be attributed to the stagnation and reversal of gains in the White population.

Additionally, the American Indian and Alaska Native populations faced the lowest life expectancy across all groups and experienced a decline in most counties, with some regions having a gap of more than twenty-one years.

On the other hand, the Latino/Hispanic and Asian populations exhibited the longest life expectancy at the national level, although this advantage was not consistently observed in all counties. While these groups maintained longer life expectancy compared to the white population, the advantage diminished in a considerable percentage of counties for the Latino/Hispanic population (42 percent) and in most counties for the Asian population (60.2 percent). Life expectancy at the county level ranged from 58.6 years for the AIAN population to 94.9 years for the Latino/Hispanic population, representing a thirty-six-year difference.

In 2019, life expectancy in years was 85.7 for the Asian population, 82.2 for the Latino population, 78.9 for the White population, 75.3 for the Black population, and 73.1 for the AIAN population.

Between 2000 and 2019, life expectancy increased most significantly for the black population (3.9 years), followed by the Asian population (2.9 years), and the Latino population (2.7 years). In comparison, the white population's increase in life expectancy was more moderate (1.7 years). Notably, there was no improvement in life expectancy for the AIAN populations.

From 2010 to 2019, the Asian, Latino, Black, and White populations experienced only minor improvements in life expectancy.

"The pandemic of 2019 exposed stressors and weaknesses in local and national systems that continuously put our most vulnerable populations at risk. These findings offer county, state, and federal leaders a unique look at the pervasiveness of health disparities in their respective communities," said Laura Dwyer-Lindgren, Ph. D.,[234] lead author and assistant professor of health metrics at the Institute for Health Metrics and Evaluation.

The findings underscore the need for greater attention and action to address health disparities, especially in vulnerable communities. Leaders at the county, state, and federal levels must be aware of the pervasiveness of these disparities to implement targeted interventions and policies for more equitable health outcomes.[235]

Nutrition Disparity: Bridging the Nutrition Gap for Healthier Communities

According to the World Bank,[236] lack of nutrition and malnutrition development costs are enormous, falling hardest on the poor, women, and children. "In 2020, 149 million children under five years old were low height for their age, which indicates not being able to achieve personal genetic potential for height but is also a predictor of many other developmental constraints, including cognitive deficits and future economic opportunities."[237]

The health and food systems disruptions caused by the COVID-19 pandemic has rolled back years of progress on child nutrition. Additionally, the World Bank explains that huge regional differences in the prevalence and the numbers of stunted children persist, with South Asia and Sub-Saharan Africa remaining above the global averages.[238]

The World Bank in September 2023 explained that "the economic costs of undernutrition, in terms of lost national productivity and economic growth, are significant."[239]

Addressing Nutrition Disparity and Bridging the Nutrition Gap for Healthier Communities requires a comprehensive approach that goes beyond immediate interventions. One key aspect of finding long-term solutions is building a more resilient global food system. A resilient food system can withstand shocks and disruptions, ensuring food security and adequate nutrition for all, especially vulnerable populations.

To Achieve a Resilient Food System, Several Key Strategies Can Be Implemented:

- **Sustainable agriculture**: Promoting sustainable farming practices that prioritize soil health, water conservation, and biodiversity can help enhance crop yields and reduce environmental impacts. Agroecological approaches and organic farming can contribute to a more resilient and diverse food supply.

- **Diversifying food sources**: Encouraging a diverse range of crops and food sources can enhance nutritional options and reduce reliance on a limited set of staples. This approach can help prevent food shortages during times of crisis and provide essential nutrients to communities.

- **Investing in food infrastructure**: Strengthening food infrastructure, such as storage facilities, transportation networks, and distribution channels, is crucial for reducing food waste and ensuring that nutritious food reaches communities efficiently.

- **Empowering local food systems**: Supporting local food producers and small-scale farmers can enhance community resilience and food security. Creating opportunities for direct market access and fair-trade practices can benefit both producers and consumers.

- **Enhancing food safety and quality**: Ensuring that food meets safety standards and quality requirements is essential for safeguarding public health. This includes measures to prevent contamination and spoilage of food products.

- **Addressing food insecurity**: Implementing social safety nets and nutrition programs for vulnerable populations, such as school feeding initiatives and cash transfer programs, can help mitigate the immediate impacts of food insecurity.

- **Promoting nutrition education**: Raising awareness about the importance of balanced diets and proper nutrition can empower individuals and communities to make informed food choices.

- **Advocacy and policy support**: Encouraging governments and policymakers to prioritize nutrition and food security issues can lead to the development of evidence-based policies and programs that foster a resilient food system.

- **Global collaboration**: Addressing nutrition disparity and building resilient food systems require international cooperation and partnerships. Collaboration between governments, non-governmental organizations, international agencies, and private sectors can lead to more impactful and sustainable solutions. By adopting a multifaceted approach that combines these strategies, we can create a resilient global food system that ensures food security and adequate nutrition for all. Bridging the nutrition gap is not only critical for the well-being of individuals and communities but also fundamental to achieving sustainable development and a healthier future for our planet.

Sanitation Disparity: Bridging the Gap for Healthier Living Environments

Sanitation disparity refers to the unequal access to adequate sanitation facilities and services, creating significant differences in living conditions and public health outcomes among different communities and regions. The lack of proper sanitation facilities can lead to unsanitary living conditions, compromised hygiene practices, and increased vulnerability to waterborne diseases and other health hazards.

In many parts of the world, especially in developing regions, a sanitation disconnect remains a pressing issue that hinders progress toward better public health and sustainable development goals. Access to clean water, proper sanitation, and safe hygiene practices is a fundamental human right and an essential factor in promoting overall well-being.

Communities lacking access to proper sanitation facilities often resort to open defecation or use unsafe water sources for various needs. This not only poses immediate health risks but also perpetuates a cycle of poverty and underdevelopment, as communities struggle to break free from the burdens of preventable illnesses and reduced productivity.

The impact of inadequate sanitation extends beyond individual health and affects entire communities and economies. The burden of waterborne diseases, such as diarrhea and cholera, places a strain on healthcare systems, reduces workforce productivity, and diverts scarce resources away from education and economic development.

Addressing sanitation disconnect requires a comprehensive approach that involves infrastructure development, education, and community engagement. Investments in sanitation infrastructure, such as the construction of safe toilets and access to clean water sources, are essential for improving living conditions and public health outcomes.

Equally important is raising awareness about proper hygiene practices and the importance of sanitation in preventing diseases. Educational programs can empower communities to adopt and maintain healthier habits, leading to long-term improvements in public health.

In addition, advocating for policies and initiatives that prioritize sanitation and hygiene is crucial for driving change at the regional and national levels. Collaboration between governments, non-governmental organizations, private sectors, and international agencies is essential for developing sustainable solutions and promoting sanitation as a priority in development agendas.

By bridging the sanitation gap and ensuring equitable access to sanitation facilities and services, we can create healthier living environments, reduce the burden of preventable diseases, and pave the way for inclusive and sustainable communities. Prioritizing sanitation is not only a matter of public health but also a fundamental step toward achieving social equity, human dignity, and sustainable development.

Navigating the Knowledge Divide: Educational Disconnect

Educational Disconnect Worldwide refers to the prevailing disparities in access to quality education and educational opportunities across different regions and communities on a global scale. Despite efforts to promote education as a fundamental human right, many individuals and communities continue to face significant barriers that hinder their ability to acquire knowledge and skills necessary for personal growth and societal progress.

One of the primary challenges contributing to the educational disconnect is the lack of adequate infrastructure and resources in certain regions. In developing countries and marginalized communities, schools often suffer from limited funding, outdated facilities, and insufficient teaching materials, making it difficult to provide a conducive learning environment.

Socioeconomic factors also play a crucial role in perpetuating educational disparities. Low-income families may struggle to afford education-related expenses, such as school fees, textbooks, and uniforms, limiting their children's access to quality education. As a result, educational opportunities become skewed, and children from disadvantaged backgrounds may be denied the chance to fulfill their academic potential.

Furthermore, cultural norms and gender biases can influence educational opportunities. In some societies, traditional gender roles may discourage girls from pursuing education or limit their access to certain subjects. Breaking down these barriers and promoting gender equality in education is essential for creating more inclusive and equitable learning environments.

Another aspect of the educational disconnect is the digital divide. In an increasingly technology-driven world, access to digital tools and internet connectivity has become crucial for effective learning. However, not all communities have equal access to digital resources, which can further widen the gap in educational outcomes.

Addressing the educational disconnect worldwide requires a comprehensive and collaborative approach. Governments, policymakers, educators, and international organizations must work together to invest in educational infrastructure, allocate resources equitably, and create inclusive educational policies. Providing scholarships and financial support to underprivileged students can help break the cycle of poverty and open new opportunities for advancement.

Educational institutions must embrace a student-centered approach that recognizes and respects diverse learning styles and cultural backgrounds. Bridging a supportive and inclusive learning environment can empower students to reach their full potential and contribute positively to society.

Addressing the educational disconnect worldwide is crucial for building a more equitable and sustainable future.

Lost in Transmission: The Communication Disconnect

Communication disconnect highlights the prevalent challenges and consequences of ineffective communication that exist across various contexts and settings. Communication is an essential aspect of human interaction, allowing individuals and societies to exchange ideas, share information, and connect with one another. However, in many situations, communication can break down or fail to achieve its intended purpose, leading to misunderstandings, misinterpretations, and missed opportunities for meaningful connections.

In personal relationships, a communication disconnect can lead to conflicts and emotional distance. People may struggle to express their thoughts and feelings clearly, leading to unresolved issues and a breakdown in trust and intimacy. Active listening and effective expression of emotions are crucial for fostering healthy communication within relationships.

In workplaces, miscommunication can lead to inefficiencies, decreased productivity, and conflicts among team members. Clear and transparent communication channels, as well as open dialogue, are vital for promoting collaboration and achieving common goals.

The communication disconnect also extends to cross-cultural interactions. Cultural differences in language, customs, and communication styles can create barriers to effective understanding. Emphasizing cultural sensitivity and practicing active listening can facilitate better cross-cultural communication and close the gaps between diverse communities.

In the realm of technology, the fast-paced and constantly evolving digital landscape can also contribute to a communication disconnect. Misinformation and the spread of rumors through social media platforms can cause confusion and division among individuals. Being critical consumers of information and verifying sources are essential to combating misinformation and promoting accurate communication.

Global issues, such as climate change and social justice, can also suffer from a communication disconnect. Complex challenges may require coordinated efforts from individuals, communities, and governments. Effective communication and advocacy are crucial for raising awareness, promoting action, and mobilizing resources to address these pressing issues.

Overcoming the communication disconnect requires a commitment to active and empathetic communication. Engaging in open dialogues, seeking clarification, and respecting different perspectives are key to a better understanding and collaboration. In addition, cultivating effective communication skills, such as active listening, empathy, and assertiveness, can enhance interpersonal connections and create a productive society.

Recognizing the impact of the communication disconnect is the first step toward improving our communication practices and building stronger connections with one another. By valuing and prioritizing clear, respectful, and empathetic communication, we can bridge the gaps that lead to misunderstandings and work together to address challenges and create a more cohesive and compassionate world.

Roads Untraveled: The Transportation Disconnect

Transportation disconnect refers to the existing disparities and challenges in transportation systems worldwide. Efficient transportation infrastructure is crucial for economic development, accessibility, and connectivity within and between communities. However, in many parts of the world, transportation networks face various issues that hinder their effectiveness and impact on people's lives.

Furthermore, urban centers often struggle with issues such as traffic congestion, pollution, and lack of sustainable transportation options. Overreliance on private vehicles can exacerbate environmental problems and contribute to air pollution and greenhouse gas emissions. Encouraging the use of public transportation and investing in sustainable transport solutions are essential for reducing environmental impact and improving urban mobility.

Additionally, the transportation disconnect also affects marginalized and vulnerable populations. In many communities, low-income individuals may lack access to affordable transportation options, making it challenging to access healthcare facilities, education, and job opportunities. This lack of accessibility perpetuates economic inequality and limits social mobility.

Addressing the transportation disconnect requires a multi-faceted approach that involves collaboration between governments, private sectors, and local communities. Key strategies to improve transportation systems worldwide include:

- **Investing in infrastructure**: Governments should prioritize funding and investing in the construction and maintenance of roads, bridges, and public transit systems to ensure efficient and safe transportation networks.

- **Sustainable mobility**: Encouraging the adoption of sustainable transportation solutions, such as electric vehicles, cycling lanes, and pedestrian-friendly infrastructure, can reduce environmental impact and promote healthier and greener cities.

- **Public-private partnerships**: Collaborating with private sectors can bring innovative solutions and expertise to address transportation challenges effectively.

- **Accessibility and inclusivity**: Ensuring that transportation options are accessible to all individuals, including those with disabilities, can enhance social inclusion and provide equal opportunities for everyone.

- **Technology integration**: Leveraging technology, such as intelligent traffic management systems and ride-sharing applications, can optimize transportation efficiency and enhance user experience.

- **Community engagement**: Engaging with local communities to understand their transportation needs and involving them in decision-making processes can lead to more effective and people-centric transportation solutions.

- **Regional and international cooperation**: Addressing global transportation challenges may require collaboration between countries and international organizations to facilitate the movement of goods and people across borders.

By focusing on improving transportation infrastructure, promoting sustainability, and prioritizing accessibility, the transportation disconnect can be gradually reduced, enhancing connectivity, economic development, and quality of life for people around the world. A well-connected and efficient transportation system is essential for building resilient, equitable, and sustainable communities for generations to come.

Diverse Threads: Unifying and Embracing the Power of Differences

In today's interconnected world, globalization and advanced communication technologies have brought people from diverse backgrounds closer together. As borders become more permeable, cultural exchange and interaction have become commonplace, leading to a richer and more interconnected global tapestry.

Embracing the power of differences begins with recognizing the value of diversity in all its forms–cultural, linguistic, ethnic, religious, and more. By celebrating and respecting our differences, we can foster an inclusive and harmonious global community that thrives on mutual understanding and cooperation.

Cultural diversity serves as a wellspring of creativity, innovation, and knowledge. Each culture brings its own unique perspectives and solutions to global challenges, enriching the collective pool of ideas and approaches.

Diversity also drives economic growth and prosperity. Inclusive economies that embrace diversity tend to be more resilient, adaptive, and competitive in a rapidly changing world. Embracing different perspectives can lead to breakthrough innovations and business strategies that cater to a broader range of consumers and markets.

Furthermore, diversity is at the heart of sustainable development. By engaging diverse communities in decision-making processes, we can ensure that development initiatives are equitable, sensitive to local needs, and aligned with the principles of social justice and environmental stewardship.

However, to truly harness the power of differences, we must actively promote inclusivity and combat discrimination and prejudice. This requires education, awareness, and proactive efforts to dismantle barriers that hinder the full participation of marginalized groups in all aspects of society.

Global collaborations and partnerships are also essential in embracing the power of differences. By working together across borders, nations, and organizations, we can pool resources, expertise, and diverse perspectives to tackle complex global challenges, such as climate change, poverty, and public health crises.

Embracing differences encourages us to recognize and celebrate diversity as a key driving force for progress and unity in our interconnected world.

A WORLD OF POSSIBILITIES

Tell me, what does a person want? said Aziza Idris Ahmed from Khartoum, Africa
"Peace and Safety. The rest comes after."

While in Dubai, I met with an amazing Sheik who said
"we all want the same thing, to make money, respect, and world peace!"
Ahh, I responded: "RESPECT" for our similarities and our differences. Respect."

And with that he gave me a thumbs up!

What is the value in diplomacy? Many of our politicians and leaders see little importance of democracy or human rights abroad. Yet, in ignoring these vital diplomatic and political foundations of America's global engagement, we risk undermining the effectiveness and legitimacy of using military force. After all, force on its own can only accomplish so much.

Lasting solutions require diplomatic engagement and long term support for building peaceful, safe societies.

IMAGINE THE POSSIBILITIES!

Democracy Unbound: Tocqueville's Insights in a Globalized Era

Alexis de Tocqueville, a French political thinker, and historian, is best known for his seminal work *Democracy in America*, published in 1835. While Tocqueville's writings were not directly related to modern globalization as we understand it today, his insights on democracy, liberty, and equality have had a profound and lasting influence on the understanding of political and societal dynamics in an interconnected world.

Tocqueville's observations in *Democracy in America*[240] focused on the emerging democratic experiment in the United States, examining the societal, political, and cultural implications of this form of government. He admired the principles of liberty and equality that underpinned American democracy, recognizing their potential to foster individual empowerment and social progress.

However, Tocqueville also expressed concerns about the potential challenges that democracy, particularly an emphasis on equality, could pose. He was wary of the tyranny of the majority and the potential for conformity and mediocrity in democratic societies. Tocqueville believed that excessive equality could lead to a "soft despotism" where the state, in its efforts to maintain uniformity, might undermine individual freedoms and initiative.

While Tocqueville's ideas on democracy were not explicitly related to modern globalization, his emphasis on the relationship between liberty, equality, and societal well-being has enduring relevance. In today's globalized world, where ideas, values, and cultures transcend borders, Tocqueville's insights offer valuable perspectives on how democratic principles and individual freedoms can be preserved and strengthened amidst the complexities and challenges of an interconnected world.

Tocqueville's work continues to inspire debates on the role of government, civil society, and individual agency in the context of globalization. His reflections on the importance of preserving liberty, advancing genuine equality, and maintaining vibrant civil associations remain relevant as societies navigate the complexities of a rapidly changing and interconnected global landscape. While Tocqueville did not directly engage with modern globalization, his intellectual contributions continue to shape discussions on democracy and governance in the globalized world.

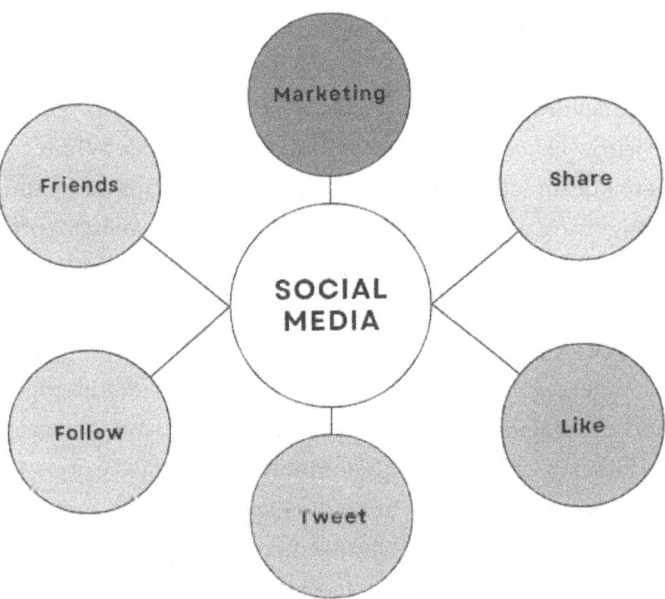

Hyperconnected yet Disconnected: The Internet's Social Media Paradox

The interesting conflict between technology and advancements is that both are meant to help us move forward but also push us backward at the same time.

One significant negative effect of technology is its potential to exacerbate social isolation and disconnect. Despite the promise of enhanced connectivity through social media platforms and virtual interactions, studies have shown that excessive reliance on technology can lead to decreased face-to-face communication and a sense of detachment from real-life interactions. The rise of social media has opened avenues for cyberbullying, online harassment, and the spread of misinformation, contributing to the erosion of trust and empathy within society.

Additionally, technology has sparked concerns over privacy and data security. The digital age has given rise to vast amounts of personal information being collected and stored, leading to potential data breaches and privacy violations. The exploitation of personal data for commercial purposes and the risks of identity theft have raised questions about the ethical use and protection of sensitive information in the digital era.

Furthermore, the rapid pace of technological advancements can result in job displacement and economic inequality. Automation and artificial intelligence are revolutionizing industries, leading to job losses in certain sectors and widening the income gap between skilled and unskilled workers. The challenge lies in ensuring that technological progress is accompanied by strategies to retrain and upskill the workforce, enabling individuals to adapt to the changing job market.

In the realm of environmental impact, the race for technological advancements has, in some cases, contributed to unsustainable practices and environmental degradation. The production and disposal of electronic devices, as well as the energy consumption of data centers, contribute to electronic waste and carbon emissions, posing challenges to sustainable development and environmental conservation.

Moreover, the proliferation of digital content and information overload can lead to decreased attention spans and cognitive overload. The constant bombardment of stimuli from multiple sources can hinder critical thinking and deep reflection, affecting individuals' ability to process information effectively and make well-informed decisions.

While technological advancements hold tremendous promise for progress, it is essential to recognize and address the potential negative effects they can bring. Striking a balance between harnessing technology for positive change while mitigating its adverse consequences requires thoughtful regulation, responsible use, and a keen understanding of the social, economic, and environmental implications. By approaching technology with a holistic perspective, we can harness its potential to bring about a better future while minimizing its drawbacks and challenges.

Using social media in a positive way can indeed lead to positive outcomes and create great connections with people we may have never met otherwise. Social media platforms provide us with a powerful tool to connect with individuals from diverse backgrounds, cultures, and geographic locations. By leveraging these platforms for constructive purposes, we can build meaningful relationships and foster a sense of community that transcends physical boundaries.

One of the significant benefits of social media is its ability to bring like-minded individuals together, creating networks of people who share similar interests, passions, or causes. Through online communities and groups, we can engage in discussions, exchange ideas, and collaborate on projects that have the potential to drive positive change in the world.

Additionally, social media enables us to access a vast pool of knowledge and expertise from experts and influencers across various fields. This democratization of information empowers individuals to learn, grow, and gain insights into subjects they may be curious about. It provides an opportunity for continuous learning and personal development, which can lead to great possibilities in terms of career growth, entrepreneurship, or creative endeavors.

Social media also serves as a platform for spreading positivity and inspiring others. By sharing uplifting stories, acts of kindness, and messages of hope, we contribute to a more optimistic and compassionate online environment. Such positivity can have a ripple effect, inspiring others to take positive actions and contribute to the well-being of others.

Moreover, social media has been instrumental in raising awareness about important social issues and promoting social justice causes. It has played a pivotal role in mobilizing communities for collective action and amplifying voices that may have previously been unheard. By utilizing social media as a tool for advocacy and activism, we can work together to address pressing global challenges and create a more equitable and just world.

Overall, social media's potential for connecting people, fostering relationships, and spreading positivity makes it a valuable and powerful tool in today's interconnected world. By embracing social media with a positive mindset and using it responsibly, we can unlock its transformative potential and contribute to building a better and more connected world.

Journeys of Connection: Unveiling the Transformative Power of Travel

Travel, in all its forms, has the incredible ability to connect us with people, cultures, and places in ways we never imagined. Beyond merely visiting new destinations, these journeys become profound experiences that shape our perspectives, broaden our horizons, and offer a deeper understanding of the world and its diversity.

When we embark on journeys of connection, we open ourselves to the beauty of human interaction. Meeting individuals from different backgrounds and sharing stories creates a sense of empathy and compassion that transcends language barriers and cultural divides. Through these encounters, we realize that despite our differences, there are shared values and aspirations that unite us as global citizens.

Travel also affords us the opportunity to immerse ourselves in unfamiliar environments, exposing us to new traditions, art forms, and culinary delights. These encounters with unique cultures spark a sense of wonder and appreciation for the richness of our collective heritage. The interactions we have during our travels serve as a gateway to understanding the interconnectedness of the global community.

Moreover, as we step out of our comfort zones, we discover a sense of adventure and resilience within ourselves. Embracing the unknown, we learn to adapt to different circumstances, building self-confidence and self-discovery along the way. Travel allows us to confront our preconceptions and reevaluate our assumptions, enabling personal growth and a greater sense of self-awareness.

Journeys of connection not only transform us as individuals but also contribute to positive change on a global scale. Through responsible and sustainable travel practices, we can support local communities and protect the environment. Engaging in meaningful interactions and collaborations with locals, we become catalysts for economic empowerment and cultural preservation.

In an era where technology connects us virtually, journeys of connection offer something unique and irreplaceable. They remind us of the beauty and complexity of the world, inspiring us to become better stewards of the planet and advocates for social justice.

Embrace the potential of travel to bridge disparities and establish a web of interlinked experiences. Together, we can build a global community united by compassion, understanding, and a shared commitment *step by step* into a more empathetic world for all.

> "We have different religions, different colored skin,
> but we all belong to one human race."
> Kofi A. Annan[241]

Global Unity through Connectivity: Promoting Understanding, Cooperation, and Compassion Among Nations

The complexity of the weakening of American hegemony on the global stage is multifaceted. During Harry Truman's time, the country benefited from greater unity, trust in the government, and bipartisan cooperation in Congress, which facilitated effective foreign affairs efforts. However, with the demise of the USSR, subsequent presidents faced challenges in establishing a new vision for the country, leading to America's decline on the world stage.

Despite these challenges, various examples of cultural diplomacy and cooperation between different countries highlight the significance of staying connected and having positive relationships with other nations.[242]

- **Austrian ambassador and Lebanon**: In 2022, the Austrian ambassador to Lebanon visited the Higher National Conservatory of Music in Lebanon to strengthen cultural relations between the two countries through a cooperation project with Austria.

- **Cambodia and India**: highly valued their cultural cooperation, focusing on ancient temple conservation, language studies, exchange programs, and museum enhancement.

- **China and Nigeria**: China aimed to strengthen its ties with Nigeria through cultural diplomacy and the exchange of arts and crafts.

- **Super Falcons and the US women's soccer team**: The friendly matches between the Super Falcons and the US women's soccer team aimed to prepare both teams for the 2023 FIFA Women's World Cup finals, promoting sports diplomacy.

- **China and Pakistan**: The Chinese government's donation to assist flood victims in Pakistan and their support for post-disaster reconstruction demonstrates the importance of disaster preparedness and mitigation as a form of international aid.

- **The 13th International Finnougrist Congress:** This event is held at the University of Vienna and brought together scholars from nineteen countries to exchange ideas on topics ranging from linguistics to cultural studies, promoting academic and cultural cooperation.

- **Arizona governor and Taiwan and South Korea:** The visit of the Arizona governor to Taiwan and South Korea to meet with business leaders and representatives highlights the importance of international economic cooperation and the global supply chain for high-end processor chips.

An inspiring historical example of the power of connection is Andree Guelen, a Belgian school teacher who saved numerous Jewish children during the Holocaust. She recognized the importance of connecting with each other and quietly rescued children, placing them in safe locations to protect them from deportation. Her actions exemplify the significance of staying connected and taking action to protect and support one another.[243]

Similarly, America's involvement in World War II as part of the Allies was driven by the defense of democracy and a commitment to saving lives. The Allied forces, including millions of American soldiers, played a pivotal role in defeating Nazi Germany and ending the Holocaust, highlighting the positive impact of international collaboration and connection.

Nurturing Diplomatic Ties: The Essence of Building Strong Collaborations with Countries

Establishing fruitful collaborations with other countries is a multifaceted endeavor that goes beyond mere logistical arrangements. While communication tools like phones and emails are essential for maintaining connections, they cannot replicate the depth of relationships brought about through consistent personal contact and interaction.

True diplomacy is more than just business transactions driven by economic interests. It entails a commitment to fostering bilateral relations, and having an embassy in another country signifies this dedication to connectivity and support. Having people on the ground provides invaluable insights into the host country's dynamics, culture, and developments, which is essential for effective diplomacy.

Information gathering, while possible through modern technology, cannot fully substitute the nuanced understanding gained through direct experience and engagement. An embassy's physical presence enhances the accuracy of assessments regarding local opportunities, risks, and developments, offering a competitive advantage in the diplomatic landscape.

Furthermore, extensive people-to-people contact facilitated by diplomats can foster deeper understanding and collaboration between nations. Moments shared over a round of golf, lunch, or coffee at a café often lead to more fruitful outcomes compared to mere exchanges of electronic messages.

Navigating international collaborations can present challenges, especially when countries fail to honor their agreements. Inconsistencies, such as discrepancies in embassy operating hours, can undermine effective communication and cooperation, raising concerns about fairness and reliability.

To handle these challenges, it is essential to establish clear and comprehensive agreements that outline the expectations and responsibilities of both parties. Diplomacy plays a crucial role in understanding and accommodating each country's preferences and norms. Therefore, mutual understanding and agreement on specific terms are crucial for a successful collaboration.

Effective Diplomacy: The Embassies' Framework for Diplomatic Engagements

- **Operating hours**: The embassy is open from 10 a.m. to 5 p.m. on weekdays according to respective time zones. National holidays will be observed, and the embassy will remain closed on those days.

- **Access to the embassy**: Any person may enter the embassy and register to visit, promoting open communication and engagement.

- **Language communication**: Recognizing potential language barriers, efforts will be made to ensure effective communication between parties.

- **Prohibited activities**: Storing illegal weapons, visiting brothels while on duty, and engaging in human trafficking are strictly prohibited to maintain integrity and adherence to international laws.

- **Employee identification**: All embassy employees must have proper identification for security and accountability purposes.

- **Technical issues**: Recognizing that technical glitches may occur, parties should be patient and understanding, acknowledging the possibility of occasional email delays.

- **Effective communication**: Both sides are encouraged to communicate any problems, concerns, or updates promptly to foster transparency and cooperation.

By adhering to well-defined agreements and open communication, countries can overcome challenges, foster meaningful connections, and work toward a more interconnected and harmonious world.

Celebrating Humanity: Embracing Diversity for a Connected World

Human nature has a fascinating way of gravitating toward like-minded individuals, creating familiar social circles that offer comfort, security, and a sense of belonging. This natural inclination for familiarity is deeply rooted in our evolutionary history, where forming cohesive groups helped ensure survival in ancient times.

However, this same mechanism can also give rise to anxiety and unease when confronted with people who are different from us. Our brain, body, hormones, nutrition, and nervous system all play a part in triggering a fear response in unfamiliar situations. As a result, our minds instinctively seek out the known and the familiar, reinforcing the bonds of cliques and social groups that uphold the status quo.

These social groups, with their unique ways of thinking, acting, and speaking, can create a sense of identity and cohesion among their members. Deviating from their norms can sometimes lead to social disapproval or exclusion, creating a barrier to embracing diversity.

As we grow and mature, some may find comfort in surrounding themselves with like-minded individuals in political or religious groups, seeking affirmation and validation. While this offers a sense of belonging, it can inadvertently lead to limited exposure to diverse perspectives and hinder personal growth.

Recognizing the profound value of embracing diversity is paramount for personal development and comprehending the world. Engaging with individuals from varied backgrounds, beliefs, and experiences enriches life, broadens horizons, and cultivates empathy and compassion.

By embracing differences and actively pursuing diverse interactions, we dismantle the barriers that divide us, fostering a more interconnected and harmonious society. Celebrating humanity's diversity enables the construction of bridges of understanding, compassion, and cooperation—transcending boundaries and engendering a truly united world. This celebration of our shared human journey lays the foundation for a more inclusive and radiant future.

In this captivating realm of boundless opportunities, the horizon stretches beyond imagination. As we unlock the secrets of diplomacy and embrace global connections, we embark on a thrilling journey where cultures merge, ideas collide, and innovation knows no bounds. Each step propels us closer to a future where unity prevails over division, where understanding conquers ignorance, and where empathy and compassion reign supreme.

With every heartbeat, we resonate with the potential of a world teeming with possibilities, awaiting harnessing and release. The prospects are limitless, and the expedition is exciting. Set forth on the journey of human existence, the vivid collage of experiences and dreams lights our path, *step by step*, guiding us toward greater summits.

So, let us dare to dream big, to envision a world where bridges of connection span the globe, where cultural exchanges introduce balance, and where diplomacy paves the way for collaboration and peace. In this world of infinite possibilities, we find hope, inspiration, and the power to transform lives.

As we conclude this exhilarating chapter, we invite you to take part in the unfolding saga of our interconnected world and to be the agents of change and catalysts of progress. Together, we create a balance of change, a unity that reverberates across continents, uniting us all in the pursuit of a brighter and more melodious tomorrow. Embrace the world of possibilities, for in it lies the key to unlocking the extraordinary and shaping a future beyond our wildest dreams.

"The Price of Greatness is Responsibility." [244]
Winston Churchill

Timeless Talks: Leaders Feasting on Ideas and Insights

With plates almost empty, the statesmen examine the endless possibilities for the future of the world.

> **Winston Churchill** "Gentlemen, as leaders of our respective nations, we must recognize the importance of cultural diplomacy in today's world. Building connections with other countries through the exchange of culture, ideas, and values can be a powerful tool for fostering understanding and cooperation."
>
> **George Washington** "I couldn't agree more, Winston. Cultural diplomacy can help to break down barriers and promote mutual respect between nations."
>
> **Abraham Lincoln** "Indeed, cultural diplomacy can be a powerful force for peace and progress. It allows us to connect with other countries on a deeper level and gain a greater understanding of their perspectives and experiences."
>
> **Mahatma Gandhi** "I believe that cultural diplomacy is essential for building a more peaceful and prosperous world. It allows us to appreciate the diversity of humanity and to find common ground with others."
>
> **Nelson Mandela** "I agree with my fellow leaders. Cultural diplomacy can be a powerful tool for promoting mutual understanding and cooperation between nations. It can also be an important means of fostering economic and social development."

Winston Churchill "As leaders, it is our responsibility to promote cultural diplomacy and encourage the exchange of ideas, values, and traditions between our nations. We must also work to create opportunities for young people to connect with other cultures, as they will shape the future of our world."

George Washington "I think we should focus on how to build bridges between cultures and how to use cultural diplomacy to promote peace and stability."

Abraham Lincoln "I concur. It is important to use cultural diplomacy to connect and engage with other cultures, to create a more peaceful and prosperous world. "

Mahatma Gandhi "I believe in the power of cultural diplomacy to bring people together and build bridges of understanding and cooperation."

Nelson Mandela "Indeed, cultural diplomacy is an essential element of building a more just and equitable world. We must work together to promote cultural understanding and cooperation between nations. "Bottom of Form

Winston Churchill "I recall my time as prime minister during World War II when we used cultural exchange programs to strengthen relationships with our allies and promote British culture abroad."

Mahatma Gandhi "I agree with Churchill. Cultural diplomacy can be a powerful means of connecting with other nations and fostering understanding. During my struggle for Indian independence, I advocated for the promotion of Indian culture and traditions as a way to build bridges with other nations and communities."

Nelson Mandela "As a leader who fought against racism and apartheid, I understand the importance of cultural diplomacy in promoting understanding and acceptance between different cultures and nations.

Through cultural exchange programs, we can break down barriers and promote a more just and equitable world."

Abraham Lincoln "Cultural diplomacy is a key to understanding the people of other countries. I believe that as we learn more about other cultures, we can work more closely with them and achieve a better understanding of the world. During my time as president, I understood the importance of establishing cultural and economic ties with other nations to promote peace and prosperity."

George Washington "I believe that cultural diplomacy is an effective way to foster greater understanding and cooperation between nations. As a leader of the American Revolution, I understand the importance of building relationships with other nations and cultures. Through cultural exchange programs, we can promote greater understanding and cooperation between nations."

IN CLOSURE

Timeless Talks: Leaders Feasting on Ideas and Insights

The Five Diplomats, representing diverse eras and diplomatic approaches, continued their discussion around the table. Each great leader brought their unique experiences and perspectives to the ongoing conversation about the world's direction and the means to bring nations and people closer together. With genuine concern, they addressed the noble goal of global connection, yet they also recognized the inevitable challenges ahead, especially in dealing with potential bad actors. Deeply engaged in the topic, these five eminent statesmen emphasized the significance of developing global connections and embracing cultural differences.

Winston Churchill "Gentlemen, we are here to discuss the direction of the world and how we can use diplomacy and politics to help the people. I firmly believe that a strong military and a powerful empire are the keys to maintaining peace and stability in the world."

Mahatma Gandhi "I disagree, Prime Minister Churchill. Violence and oppression only breed more violence and oppression."

Nelson Mandela "I agree with Gandhi that nonviolence is a powerful tool, but I also believe that we must be willing to fight for our rights and freedom. We must use diplomacy and politics to bring about justice and equality for all people, regardless of race or ethnicity."

Abraham Lincoln "I believe that diplomacy and politics must be used to preserve the union and abolish slavery. We must work together to ensure that all people are treated with dignity and respect."

George Washington "I agree with my fellow leaders that diplomacy and politics must be used to help the people, but we must also remember the importance of a strong military to protect our nation and its interests. We must use force and diplomacy to achieve our goals."

Winston Churchill "We must be strong and united as a world. Only by standing together can we hope to defeat the forces that threaten our peace and security."

Mahatma Gandhi "We must not rely on force alone. We must also rely on the power of nonviolence and diplomacy. We must connect with each other on a spiritual level and find common ground."

Nelson Mandela "Yes, we must find common ground, but we must also acknowledge and address past injustices. Only by addressing the root causes of conflict can we hope to achieve lasting peace."

Abraham Lincoln "We must also remember that our own nation is not perfect. We have our own history of division and injustice. We must work to bridge the divides within our own country before we can hope to do so on a global scale."

George Washington "We must also remember that diplomacy is a delicate balance. We must be able to stand firm in our principles while also being open to compromise and negotiation."

Winston Churchill "We must remember that the enemy of today may be the ally of tomorrow," he said. "We must be willing to engage with those who may seem like our foes and find common ground."

Mahatma Gandhi "For true peace to be achieved, we must understand and connect with those who may seem different from us," he said. "Nonviolence is the greatest force at the disposal of mankind. It is mightier than the mightiest weapon of destruction devised by the ingenuity of man."

Nelson Mandela "We must never give up on the possibility of reconciliation," he said. "We must strive to connect with those who have wronged us and find a way to forgive."

Abraham Lincoln "In our efforts to connect with the world, we must always remember that the true test of character is not how much we disagree but how we handle those disagreements," he said. "A house divided against itself cannot stand."

George Washington "We must remember that the world is constantly changing, and we must adapt and evolve to connect with it," he said. "We must always be willing to learn from others and work together for the common good. To truly unite this nation, we must understand and respect the diverse cultures that make it up."

Abraham Lincoln "It is through diplomacy that we can bridge the divide and bring about true unity."

Mahatma Gandhi "The fight for freedom and equality must extend beyond our borders and embrace all cultures."

Nelson Mandela "We must break down the barriers that separate us and build bridges of understanding through cultural diplomacy."

Winston Churchill "Only by standing together as a global community, can we hope to defeat the forces that seek to divide us."

Focused and determined, these historical figures remind us that diplomacy is not just about encouraging positive relationships between nations but about uniting humanity. It is through understanding and appreciating the cultures of others that we can create a more peaceful, just, and connected world.

The fire still burned warmly as the five statesmen discussed the importance of global connection despite their differences. They agreed on the necessity of engaging with other nations and cultures to advance peace and understanding. However, they also acknowledged the challenges that engaging with other nations and cultures presents. Open-mindedness, compassion, and forgiveness were deemed essential for successful diplomacy.

George Washington emphasized the need to respect and understand diverse cultures to unite the colonies. Abraham Lincoln recognized cultural diplomacy's role in bridging divisions during the Civil War. Gandhi extended his fight for freedom and equality beyond India, embracing all cultures. Nelson Mandela believed cultural diplomacy could break down apartheid's barriers. Winston Churchill urged a united global community against fascism, emphasizing that standing together is key to defeating divisive forces.

These leaders remind us that cultural diplomacy is an effective tool for a just and connected world. As this book concludes, let us remember their legacy and strive for a future where all cultures are valued.

The final pages may turn, but the powerful words of these leaders endure. They show us that unity is built through understanding and mutual appreciation. Their legacy urges us to continue the fight for a more equitable world.

As the fire dims and the book nears its conclusion, let us heed their call to action and embrace the profound significance of cultural diplomacy in uniting nations and people. We must wholeheartedly welcome the boundless opportunities that the future holds.

Through the lens of cultural diplomacy, we have the power to shape a more just and interconnected world. Let us ensure that the curtains of the world remain open, as we dream and labor toward a future enriched with endless possibilities of hope, joy, love, and peace. Our mission is clear: to construct a world that reflects our shared humanity.

As the candle's flame flickers and shadows lengthen, the five statesmen acknowledge the conclusion of their time. They hold steadfast in their belief that their legacy will endure through generations, and the pursuit of diplomacy's noble work will persist.

Drawing inspiration from the wisdom of great leaders like George Washington, Abraham Lincoln, Mahatma Gandhi, Nelson Mandela, and Winston Churchill, let us always remember that we are part of a shared humanity. We understand that through diplomacy, we can unite nations and pave the way for a brighter future for all.

INSIGHTS

The power of diplomacy lies in its ability to foster understanding, cooperation, and peace among nations, while the importance of connecting with each other transcends borders, cultures, and differences, ultimately paving the way for a harmonious and interconnected world.

Diplomacy has been hailed as the art of building bridges between nations, and forging relationships based on mutual respect and understanding. It is a means to resolve conflicts, promote cooperation, and build a better world for all.

As we share our experiences and perspectives, we are reminded of the power of connection and the positive impact it can have on our lives and the world we live in. So let us take this opportunity to celebrate the greatness of diplomacy and the importance of connecting with one another, for it is through these shared connections that we can build a brighter future together.

Through the step-by-step journey of global connection, I have gained profound insights about the commonalities that bind us together as human beings. Regardless of our differences, "people are people" and share similar hopes, fears, and aspirations.

On completion of this book, the ideas set forth therein have been confirmed by individuals throughout the world. Here is what "people" have to say.

It isn't possible to include every country in the world in this book, so here is a compiled collection of global perspectives on the significance of diplomacy. These statements are authentic and have been provided by individuals from around the world.

"It is important to have public diplomacy as a solution to one of the greatest weaknesses in US foreign policy that has exacerbated the unprecedented anti-Americanism of recent years–the US government's inability to conduct the "full spectrum" of diplomatic arts and integrate them with the other arts of statecraft at the level of grand strategy."—**John Lenczowski, Founder, President Emeritus, and Chancellor of The Institute of World Politics, an independent graduate school of national security, intelligence, and international affairs in Washington, DC**

"Being an Ambassador, Foreign Service Officer or working on behalf of the U.S. in official capacity, can certainly help advance relationships between countries. What this book focuses on is the significance of grassroots diplomacy: non-governmental individuals connecting with individuals from diverse cultures, to understand the inevitable differences, thereby enhancing cultural competence one person at a time. Communication, understanding, listening to other cultures and their experiences is a valuable tool to heighten diplomacy among people, and eventually countries." —**Armen Babajanian, Chief Executive Officer of the World Affairs Council of San Antonio**

"Conservation diplomacy helps promote peace and security, enhances economic growth and inclusion in conservation, factors that improve global social outcomes." —**Victoria Batesaki, Assistant project manager at Uganda Junior Rangers/ crocheter Kampala, Central Region, Uganda, Africa**

"The effective use of diplomacy to help change and improve the world can in fact be achieved on many levels and using a variety of different approaches. The answer is to carefully study and then use what opportunities are available and leverage it with the best approach or technique."— **John Wobensmith, Secretary of State of Maryland, former National Security Agency, US Dept. of Defense, and Development of the American Foreign Policy Council**

"The U.S. Department of Defense (DOD) and U.S. Agency for International Development (USAID) — the "foreign aid" arm of the State Department — collaborate effectively to respond to major disasters around the world. Such actions include quick responses to earthquakes, hurricanes, other natural disasters, and destruction caused by war. The goodwill generated by such humanitarian interventions is immeasurable. Thousands of lives have been saved and victims rescued by deployment of DOD logistics assets and USAID search and rescue teams, and funds, in the immediate aftermath of disasters, such as the Asian/Indonesia Tsunami and 2010 Haiti Earthquake. In the annals of diplomacy, heroic deeds speak louder than words."—**David R. Adams, Senior Foreign Service officer (Ret.)**

"On June 1, 1980, Ted Turner, in announcing the launch of CNN stated, 'We hope that the Cable News Network, with its international coverage . . . will bring . . . a better understanding of how people from different nations live and work together, so that we can perhaps, hopefully, bring together in peace and brotherhood and friendship . . . the people of this nation and world. It was a mission statement that rang true during the twenty-years I worked for CNN. It was a privilege to witness and cover some of the great stories of the last quarter of the twentieth century . . . the fall of the Berlin Wall, the birth of the new nation of Namibia, the election of the first black president of South Africa, Nelson Mandela. All of those were examples of bringing peoples together to strengthen democracy across the globe. It was an honor to be part of the global media company that brought the world to America, and America to the world." —**Chris Guarino, Former Executive Producer, CNN**

"The Kingdom of Bahrain is a small island nation located in the Arabian Gulf, just off the coast of the Kingdom of Saudi Arabia. Bahrain is a unique land with an ancient and storied culture that spans many centuries. Despite modernization and a cosmopolitan outlook, Bahrain is essentially an Arabic culture. Bahrain enjoys strong diplomatic ties with other countries for trade, security, and regional stability, highlighting its commitment to diplomacy and international engagement. Bahrain is part of the Gulf Cooperation Council and other international organizations such as the United Nations, the Arab League, World Health Organization, World Trade Organization, World Intellectual Property Organization, among others. Additionally, Bahrain enjoys Free Trade, Investment Protection, and Double Taxation Avoidance Agreements with numerous countries around the globe and is a signatory of the Abraham Accords." —**Rose Sager, Trade Representative, Embassy of the Kingdom of Bahrain**

"The Dominican Republic has a rich cultural heritage, influenced by its indigenous Taíno population, Spanish colonizers, and African slaves. Today, the country is known for its music, dance, cuisine, and art. The government of the Dominican Republic has recognized the potential of cultural diplomacy to promote the country's image abroad and build relationships with other nations." —**Johanny Lindskog, Dominican Republic**

"We are all so alike & yet so different." —**Sandy Danoff, My Mom**

"There is a lot of hate in the world, so we need to be friendly and kind with each other. Monaco meets people all over the world and important to be nice." —**Lorenzo Gherardi, Monte Carlo, Monaco**

"Hong Kong has plenty to see for people. So much to do, all people friends." —**Titi Ko, Hong Kong**

"We should all be friends in my opinion." —**Esther Freðeriks Reykjanesbaer, Iceland**

"Thank you for your great work, it's so important now. When the world is struggling from the wars, conflicts and misunderstanding it's so important to understand the main principles of the Diplomatic relationships and to respect our differences, cultural, mental, educational. First of all, I think that you wouldn't find right definition of Ukrainian style diplomacy. Our people are learning fast, they are flexible and easy-going, but they won't let someone get something theirs if they are not ready to share it. The same principle will be working for communication, you will need time and patience to understand Ukrainians, but if you do and they become your friends you won't find someone else who can be so much helpful and secure. Modern Ukrainian Diplomacy has proved the whole world that telling people the truth and being equal to everyone are the main principles to speak and be heard. The whole world is standing with Ukraine, because of consistent and grammatical diplomacy, in which the main thing is the transparency of information and the willingness to provide direct evidence. People do not believe in beautiful fairy tales; people need truth and facts." —**Bodrova Daria, Adviser to the Honorary Consul, Consular Office of the Slovak Republic, Odesa, Ukraine**

"As a young single mother and sole support of my two young sons, I learned early on and personally that if I just listened to them growing up, they would be my best teachers in life. Concurrently, this familial life lesson paid countless dividends being a professional woman in a predominantly male field. Proactive listening from the spirit, heart, and mind is an art that transcends toxic relationships, communities, generations, and cultures. As a noted expert, activist and professional, this book is undoubtedly the transcendent 'super glue' for all who walk the path with any diplomacy from familial to countries." —**Dr. Jo Dee Baer, PhD "America's Top Foundational Health Coach" Certified Health Coach/ Holistic Nutritionist PhD Author/Speaker/Trainer/Philanthropist**

"Cuba is magical with the music and the people, and we want to be friends with the world." —**Lea Diaz, Havana, Cuba**

"Yes, diplomacy is an important part of Dutch culture, as we are known for cooperation with other nations. Dutch people are known for our direct communication style, and we value honesty and openness in our interactions." —**Chyrl Heyworth, Holland**

"Ireland's 50-year history of being a member of the European Union has contributed to shared peace as well as shared prosperity in Europe and throughout the post WWII world." —**Alyson Byrne, Ireland**

"We all need friends, Important! persahabatan di seluruh dunia" friendships in the world." **—Ellas Mahinda Jakarta, Indonesia**

"We are all human beings, and we happen to speak different languages, and we are all looking for the same thing." **—Gary Soto Lima, Peru**

"In the beauty of Finland . . . we know to have friends and connect with the world, to bridge hearts and include everyone." **—Lilja Virtanen, Ivalo, Finland**

"It is about people, nice, open, ready to help, friendly that makes Venezuela understand how we need to connect with each other." **—Soham Sier Caracas, Venezuela**

"Diplomacy is of great importance to Brazil as it helps the country to maintain strong relationships with other nations, promote its interests and project its image globally. Brazil's foreign policy is guided by the principles of peaceful coexistence, non-intervention, and respect for national sovereignty." **—Fernanda Oliveira, Brazil**

"In the North Pole we meet people from all over the world. We treat people the way each of us wants to be treated!" **—Aly Batres, North Pole**

"Although Korea emits dynamic energy in its spirit, it has maintained an inclusive diplomatic approach due to the nature of the pacifist Peninsula. South Korea builds strong relationships with key partners around the world. Through its emphasis on soft power and cultural diplomacy, South Korea has been successful in promoting its economic, spiritual and cultural interests on the global stage, and is widely regarded as a leader in the field of international relations." **—Laura Yang, South Korea**

"Puerto Rico is a small island that has an unusual situation. When you are born in Puerto Rico you are born with the concept that is normal and necessary to share and connect with others. We party to celebrate and share with others our traditions, thinking, political views, food and many other things that represent our country." —**Hazel Mercado, Puerto Rico**

"It is very nice to be reminded of the power and importance of a dialogue in these very difficult times, where the willingness to have a dialogue is fading quickly away. One can only wish this book is read by all the world leaders before is too late." —**Otakar Hevler, Switzerland**

"Connecting with each other is to have wisdom to be human and knowing each other's culture around the world." —**Chan Saisut, Sydney, Australia**

"We connect through food and bites." —**Juliana Lichenko, Russia**

"If it were not for the things that we are moving away from, We would not be moving in the direction that we are going. There is no progress without change." —**Dr. James Marinakis, United States of America**

"Suriname is a small country located on the northeastern coast of South America. We are a member of the United Nations and the Union of South American Nations, Suriname has engaged in diplomacy to promote regional integration, economic development, and human rights." —**Ron Kasiman, Suriname/South America**

"In Argentina we need diplomacy! As we seek to build relationships with other nations and promote our interests in the global arena, we need to focus on many issues including trade, human rights, and regional stability." —**Lili Oppizi, Argentina**

"We need to help each other and be like a family, so in times of need we are helping each other." —**Kenneth Lem, Singapore**

"South Africa is a prominent player in African diplomacy, advocating for regional integration, peace, and stability. We play a significant role in global diplomacy, particularly in issues such as climate change, human rights, and nuclear disarmament." —**Jill Jacobson, South Africa**

"Sweden is known for its long history of neutrality and active participation. in international diplomacy, particularly in promoting peace and human rights." —**Magnus Andersson, Sweden**

"Spain has a long history of diplomacy and has played an important role in shaping international affairs." —**Ingrid Tournant, Spain**

"Diplomacy plays a critical role in France's foreign policy, as we promote its values, interests, and influence around the world. Connecting with people is also a key part of French diplomacy, as it promotes understanding with other nations and cultures. —**Katiana Tournant, France**

"Cultural Diplomacy is an important building block in sustaining a democracy, especially in a society susceptible to clashes between groups. The goals of equality and security for all groups and individuals are hopefully achieved within a strong democracy." —**Claire Ziva Kabilou, Jerusalem, Israel**

"In Tokyo we are international. We are kind, very welcoming, very good and open to everybody. It is important to talk to each other." —**Daiki Nagashima, Tokyo, Japan**

"The importance of cultural diplomacy cannot be overstated. We live in a globalized world and being able to broaden our horizons through exposure to different cultures and perspectives is important. Education abroad is a great way to do so. Education enhances our critical thinking and problem-solving skills, and doing it abroad prepares us to be global citizens who can contribute positively to the world. It also promotes social and economic mobility, empowers individuals and communities, and drives innovation and progress across all fields and sectors." —**Håkon Johansen Syrrist, Norway**

"Diplomacy is important because you can meet international people and new cultures get to know people from all over." —**Borbala, Porth, Hungary**

"You don't have enemies with diplomacy." —**Ivan Lucic, Vienna, Austria**

"Diplomacy is about the importance of peaceful relations in the world."
—**Maciey Kadzinski, Poland**

"Diplomacy in Scotland has played a big role in our history and is very important today. Scotland's diplomatic relations with other nations has helped our culture and economy. We love our friends around the world!"
—**Beverly Shaw, Scotland**

"We need more understanding and respect for our world." —**Sara Pavoncello, Rome, Italy**

"The relationship between Armenia and Turkey has been strained for over a century due to historical conflicts, including the Armenian Genocide of 1915. However, there have been recent efforts towards reconciliation and normalization of relations between the two countries, including the signing of a peace deal in November 2020 following a war over the Nagorno-Karabakh region. Diplomacy matters!" —**Maryam Kiviroglu, Armenia**

"Sikhs have a rich history of diplomacy and have made significant contributions to the field. The principles of Sikhism, such as equality and social justice, have been central to their diplomatic efforts, which include promoting peace and human rights around the world. Sikh diplomacy has also focused on building connections with other cultures and religions through interfaith dialogue and community service." —**GP Singh and Simran Jeet Singh, United States of America**

"Taiwan engages in a wide range of activities to connect with the international community. We realize how important it is to include cultural exchanges, economic partnerships, and people-to-people diplomacy. Taiwan is successful in building relationships with many countries around the world." —**Hsiao-chi Chen, Taiwan**

"Iran, as a big part of the Persian empire, has a long complex diplomatic history due to its strategic situation in Middle East throughout the centuries. However, as historical memory of people cannot recall old times, it is mostly known for recent challenges such as the governance issues, nuclear agreements, and their impact on sanctions against the country which will has led to weakening the economic power of most of the population. Furthermore, media propaganda has led to exacerbation of cultural isolation as well as political ones. This has caused a gap between Iranian people and other nations. If we discard the media lens and see reality for its true meaning, it will become clear that there is more in common amongst people rather than differences. It just takes an open heart and mind to see through the fog created by governments and discover the power of Iranian people which lies in their big hearts, kindness, compassion, and the willingness to be free." —**Name withheld per request, Iran**

"Connecting with each other is important for society to work as it gives us "peace of mind." —**Rosa Soros, Athens, Greece**

"Slovakia is a member of the United Nations, the European Union, NATO, and other international organizations, and has a long history of diplomacy and foreign relations and being a civil society. A world leader in technical innovation. We are committed to promoting peace and stability around the world, and diplomatic relations with many countries." —**Dr. Cecilia Rokusek, EdD, MSc, RDN Slovakia**

"In Argentina it is fun to have democracy and to be good with yourselves and others, and we need to make peace in the world." —**Leandro Valentuela, Buenos Aires, Argentina**

"When people meet each other on each other's home ground they visit each other's language, culture, and values. When people are away from their familiar territory, they become more childlike and need the help and guidance of others to find their way around. The stranger who has to trust the host in this way is more innocent and vulnerable, allowing them to read the environment with all the senses and thereby live more intensely.

They may, if they let themselves, be humbled and see and accept the other´s point of view more easily, as it becomes more experiential. Those who have ever really tried to get to know another culture, will become a changed person. And this new and changed person will more deeply know the people and culture and will be less easily be pitted against them. Herein lies the opportunity for a peaceful co-existence." —**Sarah Poralla MPhil European Politics and Society (Oxon) and BSc Sociology (London School of Economics) Cologne, Germany**

"Cultural diplomacy is the science of recognizing in the Other His /Her intrinsic values." —**Carmen Ospino Parejo, La Arcadia Institute for Languages and Yoga, Ernakulam, Kerala, India**

"Awareness of global trends and developments is the key to successful investment strategies and opens the door to tremendous opportunities. Staying ahead involves monitoring economic, political, cultural and technological developments and can prove rewarding on many levels from the personal to the financial." —**Jeremy Bradshaw, London, United Kingdom**

"Being open minded and respecting people's beliefs is important to all people in our world." —**Sarah Abalos, Philippines**

"Those moments of connection create new pathways in our memories, crossing timelines, setting up greater possibilities for us to solve the mysteries that we find each day. These experiences become a wealth of knowledge which turns to wisdom having been influenced by so many. We are who we have known and who knows us. Connect today." —**Tim Curry, Czech Republic**

"Dubai is an emirate that transformed into an epicenter of trade and culture and proved itself to be a key facilitator for global diplomacy between Nations spanning from the east to west. Dubai's framework for diplomacy is built on interconnectedness and understanding of eastern and western traditions and has entered its existence on peace, security, and economic diplomacy statesmanship." —**Adam Roosevelt, Dubai, United Arab Emirates**

"Diplomacy has played a significant role in Vietnam's history. Today, Vietnam maintains diplomatic relations with countries around the world and has become an important player in regional politics and economics." —**Kevin Le, Vietnam**

"Connecting with others, even those who may look and sound just like you, provides an opportunity to grow, examine similarities, appreciate unique differences, and celebrate the reasons for the disparities. Embracing the differences between our cultures...welcoming their unique stories and histories... only helps to inform us. The more we learn, the more we know. The more we know, the greater our understanding, empathy, compassion, and respect. These two nations, Canada, and the United States, share far more than a border, common languages, and similar politics... we share common morals, ethics, and philosophy. Our similarities, like our unique differences, work in conjunction to support, honor, and protect the independent nature of our two nations." —**Sarah Lester, Canada**

"We all need friends to communicate with others to not be in that empty world." —**Pascual Pedro, Guatemala**

"We need to all be friends." —**Hanli Wong, Chongqing, China**

"Communication and connectivity are essential for facilitating diplomatic efforts towards peaceful resolutions. Syria prides itself on how important it is to build strong international relationships in promoting international cooperation and understanding." —**Elias Mahfoud, Syria**

"Diplomacy is the way to have friends and to not be alone." —**Mauricio Mora, Costa Rica**

"In New Zealand we have so much diversity and are open to one another and we understand how important it is to learn about other cultures in the world." —**Tiffany Pukarta, Auckland, New Zealand**

"The Czech Republic is an important country in Central Europe with a rich cultural heritage of diplomacy. It plays a crucial role in connecting Western and Eastern Europe, both geographically and economically, and is a member of the European Union and NATO." —**Dagmar Hejda, Czech Republic**

"We should be connected to the world with foreign affairs because it enables us to understand and engage with the complexities of the global community, foster cooperation and collaboration among nations, promote peace and stability, and address shared challenges such as climate change, terrorism, and economic inequality. It also allows us to expand our knowledge and perspectives, and contribute to the development of a more interconnected, interdependent, and prosperous world." —**Adriana Colback, Colombia**

"If I can see you as a human being, you will be protected." —**Freder Jean, Haiti**

"I live in Estonia and connecting with people makes us smarter and widens our horizons." —**Julia Avrhnenko, Tallinn, Estonoia**

"Cultural diplomacy takes many shapes and forms. Connecting the world through the power of the Romanian Blouse! The forms and ornaments found on Romanian folk blouses, called '*ia*' a part of what cultural diplomacy can be. June 24 was declared the Universal Day of the Romanian Blouse. The celebration started in 2013 as a Facebook initiative 'La Blouse Roumaine.' The 'Universal Day of the Romanian Blouse' has become a truly global event celebrated on six continents, 48 countries, 109 cities, and 143 events." —**Bogdan Banu, Romania**

"In Finland we have multicultural and diverse people, and all get along and why connecting is important." —**Ramina Korhonen, Vantaa, Finland**

"This we know: the earth does not belong to man; man belongs to the earth. All things are connected like the blood that unites us all. Man did not weave the web of life; he is merely a strand in it. Whatever he does to the web, he does to himself." [245]

—**Chief Seattle of the Duwamish and Suquamish, Born: 1790–Died: June 7, 1866**

(Indigenous communities are present in over 70 countries across the world.)

EPILOGUE

Promoting Positive Growth through Respectful Connections: The Future of Cultural Diplomacy

THE FUTURE OF cultural diplomacy holds promise as a powerful means of bringing people together and encouraging understanding between nations. By embracing and respecting our differences, we can cultivate a positive mindset that encourages growth and development on a global scale.

The evolving landscape of international relations, marked by increasing globalization and interconnectedness, presents opportunities for cultural exchange and cooperation to thrive. Technology and travel enable more people to experience different cultures and traditions, leading to greater mutual understanding and appreciation.

If diplomacy falters and proves ineffective, allowing conflicts to escalate, the resulting consequences can be profound and far-reaching. It signifies a breakdown in attempts to find a peaceful resolution through negotiation, dialogue, and compromise. The transition from diplomacy to armed conflict often represents a failure to bridge differences, address grievances, or build trust between parties. It underscores the complexity of international relations and the need for a deeper understanding of the underlying factors that hinder successful diplomatic resolutions. This shift necessitates a reevaluation of strategies, a renewed emphasis on conflict prevention, and a commitment to learning from these tragic and costly experiences to strive for a more peaceful future.

In a world where conflicts can escalate to war, and attempts at diplomacy seem futile, questioning the efficacy of diplomacy as a conflict resolution tool is natural. However, dismissing diplomacy based on specific failures would be an oversimplification. Diplomacy, a nuanced and multifaceted process, entails negotiation, dialogue, communication, and finding common ground to address differences peacefully.

The epilogue of cultural diplomacy will be shaped by how it is harnessed and the objectives it seeks to achieve. When conducted with sincerity and genuine intent, cultural diplomacy has the potential to foster peace, harmony, and empathy between nations, contributing to a more peaceful and interconnected world. As we navigate the future, embracing cultural exchange and respecting each other's differences can pave the way for a brighter and more harmonious global community.

CHOCOLATE CAN SAVE THE WORLD!

Chocolate has had an impact on every continent on the globe except Antarctica.

You'd be hard-pressed to find anyone who doesn't like chocolate. While it's mostly known for its taste, it's also a good source of nutrients when in its pure form and eaten in moderation. Chocolate is believed to contain high levels of antioxidants and contains anandamide, a chemical also found in the brain that makes people feel good.

Chocolate holds such a high level of global importance that September 13th is officially designated **International Chocolate Day**[246] America inherited its love of chocolate through its European immigrants, and the top four countries responsible to produce the world's chocolate are Germany, Belgium, Italy, and Poland.

We all have the Mayans to thank chocolate as we know it, even though the chocolate they consumed was nothing like confection we eat today. After bringing cocoa trees up from the northern tropics of South America and farming them on the Yucatan Peninsula,[247] the Mayans developed cocoa into a warm drink. It was good enough for the Aztecs, though, because they stole the idea for the drink and cocoa farming from their Mayan neighbors in what is now Mexico, turning chocolate into such a luxury good that it was used as money.

Chocolate is still an important part of Mexican culture, and in America, almost every holiday has some sort of chocolate association: heart-shaped boxes of chocolate for Valentine's Day, bunny-shaped chocolate to fill Easter baskets, buckets of foil-coated candy for trick-or-treaters, and piping hot mugs of hot chocolate during Christmastime. A global idea connected with chocolate is the universal love and appreciation for this delectable treat, transcending cultural boundaries and bringing people together in a shared indulgence of sweetness and joy. **In conclusion, can our world connect with itself, with others, as we are so divided, so disconnected? It is yet to be seen. Hopefully, we can work together, and we can learn to connect; we can at least try.**

And eat a piece of chocolate together!

Anyone for chocolate?

ABOUT THE AUTHOR

Marjorie Hope graduated from Salisbury University and obtained post graduate certifications from the London School of Economics and Harvard University. As a competitive gymnast, she owned and operated a large gymnastics school, embracing the synergy between mind, body, and spirit while incorporating the importance of being "fit for life" and that "more is possible."

In 2016, she founded America Connected, an international non-profit and non-partisan organization teaching people around the world how to connect through cultural diplomacy.

Appendix

INTERNATIONAL ORGANIZATIONS

We need organizations that can promote peace and unity[248] and bring us together to respect and grow our world.

    These are examples of the many international organizations that exist to promote diplomacy and cooperation among countries. Each organization has its own specific goals and areas of focus, but they all play an important role in shaping the international community and addressing global issues.[249]

United Nations (UN)–an intergovernmental organization that aims to promote international cooperation and maintain peace and security around the world.

World Trade Organization (WTO)–an intergovernmental organization that regulates and promotes international trade.

International Monetary Fund (IMF)–an organization that works to ensure the stability of the international monetary system by providing financial assistance to countries in need.

World Bank–an international organization that provides financial assistance and support to developing countries for the pursuit of economic development and poverty reduction.

North Atlantic Treaty Organization (NATO)–a military alliance of countries from North America and Europe, established to provide collective defense against potential aggressors.

Organization for Security and Co-operation in Europe (OSCE)–an intergovernmental organization that aims to promote dialogue and cooperation on security and other issues between countries in Europe, North America, and Asia.

Organization of American States (OAS)–an inter-American organization that promotes cooperation and dialogue among countries in the Americas.

African Union (AU)–an intergovernmental organization that aims to promote unity and cooperation among countries in Africa.

Asia-Pacific Economic Cooperation (APEC)–an intergovernmental forum that promotes economic cooperation and free trade among countries in the Asia-Pacific region.

Association of Southeast Asian Nations (ASEAN)–an intergovernmental organization that promotes cooperation and dialogue among countries in Southeast Asia.

European Union (EU)–a political and economic union of European countries that aims to promote cooperation and integration among its member states.

Arab League–an organization of Arab countries that aims to promote cooperation and dialogue among its members.

Organization of Islamic Cooperation (OIC)–an inter-governmental organization that aims to promote cooperation and dialogue among countries with a majority Muslim population.

League of Arab States–an organization that promotes cooperation and dialogue among Arab countries.

Commonwealth of Nations–a voluntary association of 54 countries, mostly former territories of the British Empire, that promotes cooperation and dialogue among its members.

INTERNATIONAL ORGANIZATIONS

America Connected–a non-profit, non-partisan organization bringing nations and peoples of the world closer together. By connecting people and developing the building blocks of relationships, focusing on world economic growth solutions, pressing health challenges, and promoting peaceful world societies.

Union for the Mediterranean–an intergovernmental organization that aims to promote cooperation and dialogue among countries in the Mediterranean region.

International Atomic Energy Agency (IAEA)–an intergovernmental organization that promotes the peaceful use of nuclear energy and works to prevent the spread of nuclear weapons.

World Health Organization (WHO)–an intergovernmental organization that promotes global public health and works to combat diseases.

International Telecommunication Union (ITU)–an intergovernmental organization that promotes cooperation and dialogue on issues related to information and communication technologies.

United Nations Children's Fund (UNICEF)–an agency of the United Nations that aims to promote the rights and well-being of children around the world.

International Labour Organization (ILO)–an agency of the United Nations that promotes and sets international labor standards and works to improve working conditions and promote social justice.

International Monetary Fund (IMF)–an international organization that promotes international monetary cooperation and aims to stabilize the exchange rate of currencies.

World Intellectual Property Organization (WIPO)–an agency of the United Nations that promotes the protection of intellectual property rights and works to ensure that inventors and creators are compensated.

World Meteorological Organization (WMO)–an intergovernmental organization that promotes international cooperation on weather, climate, and water-related issues.

United Nations Framework Convention on Climate Change (UNFCCC)–an international treaty that aims to address the issue of climate change and promote cooperation among countries to reduce greenhouse gas emissions.

United Nations Industrial Development Organization (UNIDO)–an agency of the United Nations that promotes industrial development and cooperation among countries.

United Nations Development Programme (UNDP)–an agency of the United Nations that promotes sustainable development and works to reduce poverty and promote human rights.

United Nations High Commissioner for Refugees (UNHCR)–an agency of the United Nations that provides protection and assistance to refugees and internally displaced persons.

United Nations Population Fund (UNFPA)–an agency of the United Nations that promotes reproductive health and rights and works to reduce maternal and child mortality.

United Nations Office for Project Services (UNOPS)–an operational arm of the United Nations that provides project management and support services to other UN agencies, governments, and organizations.

United Nations Relief and Works Agency for Palestine Refugees in the Near East (UNRWA)–an agency of the United Nations that aids Palestinian refugees and works to promote their rights.

International Atomic Energy Agency (IAEA)–an intergovernmental organization that promotes the peaceful use of nuclear energy and works to prevent the proliferation of nuclear weapons.

International Telecommunication Union (ITU)–an agency of the United Nations that promotes cooperation among countries in the field of telecommunications.

International Civil Aviation Organization (ICAO)–an agency of the United Nations that promotes cooperation among countries in the field of civil aviation and sets international standards for air traffic control and safety.

International Maritime Organization (IMO)–an agency of the United Nations that promotes cooperation among countries in the field of maritime transportation and sets international standards for the safety and security of ships and the protection of the marine environment.

International Hydrographic Organization (IHO)–an intergovernmental organization that promotes cooperation among countries in the field of hydrography and sets international standards for the survey and charting of the world's oceans and coastal areas.

World Tourism Organization (UNWTO)–an agency of the United Nations that promotes sustainable tourism and works to improve access to tourism opportunities around the world.

International Monetary Fund (IMF)–an international organization that promotes international monetary cooperation and works to stabilize exchange rates and promote economic growth.

World Economic Forum (WEF)–an independent international organization that works to improve the state of the world by engaging leaders in business, politics, and civil society to shape global, regional and industry agendas.

The Global Partnership for Sustainable Development Data (GPSDD)–an international organization that focuses on improving data access and use to support sustainable development goals.

International Atomic Energy Agency (IAEA)–an international organization that promotes the peaceful use of nuclear energy and works to prevent the proliferation of nuclear weapons.

The Global Forum on Transparency and Exchange of Information for Tax Purposes–an organization that works to improve international tax transparency and cooperation to combat tax evasion.

The Global Partnership for Education (GPE)–an international organization that works to ensure that all children have access to quality education.

International Renewable Energy Agency (IRENA)–an international organization that works promote the use of renewable energy and support sustainable development.

The United Nations Framework Convention on Climate Change (UNFCCC)–an international organization that works to address the issue of climate change and promote sustainable development.

The United Nations Convention to Combat Desertification (UNCCD)–an international organization that works to combat desertification and promote sustainable land management.

The United Nations Convention on Biological Diversity (UNCBD)–an international organization that works to promote the conservation of biodiversity and the sustainable use of natural resources.

The United Nations Framework Convention on Climate Change (UNFCCC)–an international organization that works to address the issue of climate change and promote sustainable development.

International Telecommunication Union (ITU)–an international organization that works to promote cooperation among countries in the field of telecommunications and information technology.

INTERNATIONAL ORGANIZATIONS

International Atomic Energy Agency (IAEA)–an international organization that promotes the peaceful use of nuclear energy and works to prevent the proliferation of nuclear weapons.

International Civil Aviation Organization (ICAO)–an international organization that works to promote cooperation among countries in the field of civil aviation and improve air traffic management and safety.

International Labour Organization (ILO)–an international organization that works to promote and protect workers' rights and improve working conditions around the world.

The International Maritime Organization (IMO)–an international organization that works to promote cooperation among countries in the field of maritime safety and the protection of the marine environment.

International Monetary Fund (IMF)–an international organization that promotes international monetary cooperation and works to stabilize exchange rates and promote economic growth.

The International Telecommunication Union (ITU)–an international organization that works to promote cooperation among countries in the field of telecommunications and information technology.

Meridian Center for Global Leadership (MCGL)–administers professional and educational exchange programs that enhance Meridian's vision of a more secure and prosperous world.

Servas International is an international, non-profit, non-governmental federation of national Servas groups, encompassing an international network of hosts and travelers to help build world peace, and goodwill.

World Food Program (WFP)–an international organization that works to combat hunger and malnutrition and improve access to food and nutrition for people in need around the world.

World Bank–an international organization that provides financial and technical assistance to developing countries for economic development and poverty reduction.

International Atomic Energy Agency (IAEA)–an international organization that promotes the peaceful use of nuclear energy and works to prevent the proliferation of nuclear weapons.

International Organization for Migration (IOM)–an international organization that works to promote safe and orderly migration and improve the lives and opportunities of migrants around the world.

International Renewable Energy Agency (IRENA)–an international organization that promotes the use of renewable energy and supports sustainable development.

International Seabed Authority (ISA)–an international organization that regulates the exploration and mining of the seabed and ocean floor beyond national jurisdiction.

International Union for Conservation of Nature (IUCN)–an international organization that promotes the conservation of nature and biodiversity and supports sustainable development.

United Nations Industrial Development Organization (UNIDO)–an international organization that supports sustainable industrial development and works to reduce poverty and promote economic growth.

United Nations Framework Convention on Climate Change (UNFCCC)–an international organization that works to address the issue of climate change and promote sustainable development.

United Nations Capital Development Fund (UNCDF)–an international organization that provides financial and technical assistance to help build the economic and social infrastructure of developing countries.

United Nations Development Programme (UNDP)–an international organization that supports sustainable development and works to reduce poverty and promote economic growth.

United Nations Environment Programme (UNEP)

United Nations High Commissioner for Refugees (UNHCR)–an international organization that aids and protection to refugees, asylum seekers, and stateless persons around the world.

United Nations Human Settlements Programme (UN-Habitat)–an international organization that promotes sustainable urbanization and supports the development of livable and inclusive cities and communities.

United Nations Office for Disaster Risk Reduction (UNDRR)–an international organization that works to reduce the risk of disasters and promote resilience to natural and human-induced hazards.

United Nations Office for Outer Space Affairs (UNOOSA)–an international organization that promotes the peaceful use of outer space and supports the development of space-based technologies and applications.

United Nations Office on Drugs and Crime (UNODC)–an international organization that works to combat the illicit drug trade, transnational organized crime, and corruption.

United Nations Population Fund (UNFPA)–an international organization that promotes sexual and reproductive health and rights and works to reduce poverty and promote gender equality.

United Nations Relief and Works Agency for Palestine Refugees in the Near East (UNRWA)–an international organization that provides humanitarian assistance and support to Palestinian refugees.

United Nations System Staff College (UNSSC)–an international organization that provides training and capacity-building for staff of the United Nations and its agencies.

United Nations University (UNU)–an international organization that conducts research and education on global issues and supports the work of the United Nations and its agencies.

Universal Postal Union (UPU)–an international organization that facilitates the exchange of mail and other postal items between countries and supports the development of postal services around the world.

World Meteorological Organization (WMO)–an international organization that promotes cooperation among countries in the field of meteorology and weather forecasting and works to improve our understanding of the Earth's atmosphere and climate.

World Organization of the Scout Movement (WOSM)–an international organization thatpromotes the development of young people through non-formal education, and encourages the values of peace, respect, and friendship.

World Veterans Federation (WVF)–an international organization that supports the welfare and rights of veterans and promotes peace and understanding among nations.

World Vision International–an international humanitarian and development organization that aims to provide long-term assistance to children and families in need, and work to end poverty, promote education, and protect human rights.

World Wildlife Fund (WWF)–an international conservation organization that works to protect endangered species and their habitats and promote sustainable use of natural resources.

International Committee of the Red Cross (ICRC)–an international humanitarian organization that aids victims of armed conflicts and other situations of violence and promotes respect for international humanitarian law.

International Criminal Court (ICC)–an independent, permanent court that investigates and prosecutes individuals for genocide, crimes against humanity, war crimes, and the crime of aggression.

International Criminal Police Organization (INTERPOL)–an international organization that supports cooperation among national law enforcement agencies to combat transnational crime and promote public safety.

International Labour Organization (ILO)–an international organization that promotes decent working conditions and rights for all workers and supports the development of social protections and social dialogue.

International Maritime Organization (IMO)–an international organization that promotes cooperation among countries to ensure safe, secure, and efficient shipping, and to protect the marine environment.

International Telecommunication Union (ITU)–an international organization that promotes cooperation among countries in the field of telecommunication and information technology and supports the development of new technologies and applications.

International Union for Conservation of Nature (IUCN)–an international organization that works to protect and conserve nature and promote the sustainable use of natural resources. It also provides a global platform for the exchange of knowledge and expertise in conservation, and supports the work of governments, NGOs, and other organizations in this field.

United Nations Children's Fund (UNICEF)–an international humanitarian and development organization that works to promote the rights and well-being of children, and support their survival, development, and protection.

United Nations Development Programme (UNDP)–an international development organization that supports countries in their efforts to achieve sustainable development and reduce poverty.

United Nations High Commissioner for Refugees (UNHCR)–an international humanitarian organization that provides protection and assistance to refugees and other persons of concern and promotes respect for their rights and dignity.

United Nations Industrial Development Organization (UNIDO)–an international organization that promotes industrial development and sustainable economic growth in developing countries and supports the development of small and medium-sized enterprises.

United Nations Institute for Disarmament Research (UNIDIR)–an international research organization that supports the work of the UN in the field of disarmament and non-proliferation, and promotes dialogue and cooperation among governments, NGOs, and other stakeholders.

United Nations Office for the Coordination of Humanitarian Affairs (OCHA)–an international organization that coordinates the response of the UN and other humanitarian partners to emergencies and crises, and supports the work of governments, NGOs, and other organizations in this field.

United Nations Office on Drugs and Crime (UNODC)–an international organization that supports the work of governments, NGOs, and other partners in the fight against drugs, crime, and terrorism, and promotes the rule of law and respect for human rights.

United Nations Population Fund (UNFPA)–an international development organization that supports the rights and well-being of women and girls and promotes sexual and reproductive health and rights.

United Nations Relief and Works Agency for Palestine Refugees in the Near East (UNRWA)–an international humanitarian organization that aids and supports the rights of Palestine refugees in the Middle East and promotes their well-being and self-reliance.

United Nations University (UNU)–an international research and training organization that supports the work of the UN in the field of education, science, and culture, and promotes dialogue and cooperation among governments, NGOs, and other stakeholders.

World Food Program (WFP)–an international humanitarian organization that provides food assistance to people affected by conflict, natural disasters, and other crises, and supports the work of governments, NGOs, and other organizations in this field.

International Atomic Energy Agency (IAEA)–an international organization that promotes the safe and peaceful use of nuclear energy and technology, and supports the work of governments, NGOs, and other partners in this field.

International Civil Aviation Organization (ICAO)–an international organization that promotes the safe and efficient operation of civil aviation, and supports the work of governments, NGOs, and other partners in this field.

International Labour Organization (ILO)–an international organization that promotes the rights and well-being of workers, and supports the work of governments, NGOs, and other partners in this field.

International Maritime Organization (IMO)–an international organization that promotes the safe and efficient operation of shipping, and supports the work of governments, NGOs, and other partners in this field.

International Monetary Fund (IMF)–an international organization that promotes the stability of the international monetary system, and supports the work of governments, NGOs, and other partners in this field.

International Olympic Committee (IOC)–an international organization that promotes the Olympic movement and supports the work of governments, NGOs, and other partners in this field.

International Telecommunication Union (ITU)–an international organization that promotes the development of telecommunications and information technology, and supports the work of governments, NGOs, and other partners in this field.

International Union for Conservation of Nature (IUCN)–an international organization that promotes the conservation of nature, and supports the work of governments, NGOs, and other partners in this field.

International Union of Railways (UIC)–an international organization that promotes the development of rail transport, and supports the work of governments, NGOs, and other partners in this field.

International Union of Pure and Applied Chemistry (IUPAC)–an international organization that promotes the development of chemistry, and supports the work of governments, NGOs, and other partners in this field.

International Union of Pure and Applied Physics (IUPAP)–an international organization that promotes the development of physics, and supports the work of governments, NGOs, and other partners in this field.

International Union of Pure and Applied Biology (IUPAB)–an international organization that promotes the development of biology and supports the work of governments and NGOs.

The Royal Over-Seas League (ROSL)–a not-for-profit institution founded in 1910, dedicated to promoting international friendship pursuant to its Royal Charter, an ethos which binds its global membership. Promotes a public affairs series which focusses on geo-political issues, concerts, art exhibitions.

ENDNOTES

1. Washington Post, Nov. 19, 2021, Africa's Rising Cities

2. Korea Peace Summit. (2018, April 27). Panmunjom Declaration for Peace, Prosperity and Unification of the Korean Peninsula. Retrieved from https://www.un.org/sg/en/content/sg/statement/2018-04-27/secretary-generals-remarks-the-panmunjom-declaration-peace-prosperity-and-unification-the-korean-peninsula

3. George Washington, letter to Benjamin Harrison, 27 October 1784, in The Writings of George Washington from the Original Manuscript Sources, 1745-1799, ed. John C. Fitzpatrick, vol. 28 (Washington, DC: U.S. Government Printing Office, 1939), 310.

4. Albright, Madeleine. "The Mighty and the Almighty: Reflections on America, God, and World Affairs." Harper Perennial, 2007, p. 130.

5. The United States Department of State https://www.state.gov/

6. United States Department of State's website provides a wealth of information on U.S. foreign policy and international relations. Its website includes news updates, reports, policy statements, and other resources on a range of topics, from country-specific information to diplomatic initiatives and cultural exchanges. You can access the website here: https://www.state.gov/

7. NATO (North Atlantic Treaty Organization) https://www.nato.int/

8. The United Nations (UN) https://www.un.org/

9. The Economist https://www.economist.com/

10. The Council on Foreign Relations (CFR) https://www.cfr.org/

11. America Connected: a non-profit that connects nations and people of the world closer together. America Connected https://americaconnected.org/

12. "Democracy." Encyclopædia Britannica. Encyclopædia Britannica, Inc., n.d. Web. 18 Mar. 2023. https://www.britannica.com/topic/democracy.

13   "The Capitol Riot: How the Insurrection Unfolded." The New York Times, 11 Jan. 2021, https://www.nytimes.com/interactive/2021/01/11/us/capitol-riot-timeline.html.

14   Gandhi: An Autobiography–The Story of My Experiments with Truth

15   Gandhi, Mahatma. Encyclopædia Britannica, Encyclopædia Britannica, Inc., 24 Feb. 2022, https://www.britannica.com/biography/Mahatma-Gandhi.

16   "Chemistry: The Central Science" by Brown, LeMay, and Bursten (14th edition)

17   Democritus "To a wise and good man the whole earth is his fatherland." "The World's Great Speeches" by Lewis Copeland and Lawrence W. Lamm, and "A History of Greek Philosophy" by John Burnet. The specific source of the quote is often cited as Fragment 121 from the writings of Democritus, which can be found in various collections of his fragments, including "The Fragments of the Presocratics" edited by John Mansley Robinson.

18   "The United States and the Origins of the Cold War, 1941-1947" by John Lewis Gaddis. This is a classic work on the origins of the Cold War, focusing on the policy decisions and actions of the United States during this period.

19   UNESCO (https://en.unesco.org/online-services/library),

20   Ancient Greece Perseus Digital Library (http://www.perseus.tufts.edu/hopper/)

21   Ancient Rome Metropolitan Museum of Art (https://www.metmuseum.org/toah/hd/roma/hd_roma.htm)

22   Byzantine era: website of the Byzantine Studies Association of North America (https://www.bsana.net/)

23   Procopius and Anna Komnene: excellent source for Procopius and Anna Komnene is the website of the Internet History Sourcebooks Project (https://sourcebooks.fordham.edu/medsource.asp). This website offers a collection of primary sources on medieval and ancient history, including works by Procopius and Anna Komnene. It includes English translations of Procopius' "Secret History" and "The Wars of Justinian," as well as Anna Komnene's "The Alexiad," a chronicle of the reign of her father, Byzantine Emperor Alexios I Komnenos.

24   Islamic Golden Age: Metropolitan Museum of Art (https://www.metmuseum.org/toah/hd/igma/hd_igma.htm). The website provides an overview of the period, which saw significant advances in science, mathematics, medicine, and the arts in the Islamic world. It includes information on specific historical figures and their contributions, as well as images of art and artifacts from the period.

25   Renaissance: British Library (https://www.bl.uk/renaissance). This website offers a virtual tour of the British Library's Renaissance manuscripts and printed books, featuring works by Leonardo da Vinci, Michelangelo, William Shakespeare, and other notable figures of the period.

26   Pablo Casals Museum (http://www.museupablocasals.cat/en)

27   Toni Morrison Society (https://tonimorrisonsociety.org/)

28   "Yo-Yo Ma: A Life in Music" by Jim Whiting. publisher's website, Mitchell Lane Publishers (https://mitchelllane.com/products/yo-yo-ma-a-life-in-music).

29   Muhammad Ali: Champion of Peace" (Al Jazeera article): https://www.aljazeera.com/opinions/2016/6/4/muhammad-ali-champion-of-peace

30   "The Musical Diplomat: Mstislav Rostropovich" (US Department of State archive): https://2001-2009.state.gov/r/pa/ei/bgn/5378.htm

31   "Youssou N'Dour: The Voice of Africa" (NPR article): https://www.npr.org/templates/story/story.php?storyId=5221812

32   "Andres Segovia: The Man Who Reinvented the Guitar" (NPR article): https://www.npr.org/2011/02/10/133626446/andres-segovia-the-man-who-reinvented-the-guitar

33   "Martha Graham and American Modernism" (Smithsonian American Art Museum exhibition): https://americanart.si.edu/exhibitions/graham

34   "Ravi Shankar: A Life in Music" (BBC article): https://www.bbc.com/culture/article/20201209-ravi-shankar-a-life-in-music

35   Mahatma Gandhi "Gandhi: An Autobiography" by Louis Fischer "Gandhi: The Man, His People, and the Empire" by Rajmohan Gandhi

36   Mahatma Gandhi "Gandhi: An Autobiography" by Louis Fischer "Gandhi: The Man, His People, and the Empire" by Rajmohan Gandhi

37   Winston Churchill "Churchill: A Life" by Martin Gilbert

"The Last Lion: Winston Spencer Churchill" by William Manchester

"Winston Churchill: The Wilderness Years" by Martin Gilbert

"My Early Life: A Roving Commission" by Winston Churchill

"The Gathering Storm" by Winston Churchill

38. Martin Luther King, Jr. "A Testament of Hope: The Essential Writings and Speeches of Martin Luther King Jr." "The Autobiography of Martin Luther King Jr." edited by Clayborne Carson

39. Abraham Lincoln "Team of Rivals: The Political Genius of Abraham Lincoln" by Doris Kearns Goodwin, "Abraham Lincoln: A Life" by Michael Burlingame

40. "Mother Teresa: Come Be My Light–The Private Writings of the Saint of Calcutta" by Mother Teresa, edited by Brian Kolodiejchuk

41. Napoleon Bonaparte was a military leader and statesman who rose to prominence during the French Revolution and went on to become the Emperor of France.

42. "Washington: A Life" by Ron Chernow

43. "The Art of Happiness" by Dalai Lama and Howard Cutler

44. "The Twelve Caesars" by Suetonius

45. "Franklin D. Roosevelt: A Political Life" by Robert Dallek

46. "Ashoka the Great: India's Mauryan Emperor" by Subhadra Sen Gupta

47. Alexander The Great "Alexander the Great: A Very Short Introduction" by Hugh Bowden

    The British Museum website's section on Alexander the Great (https://www.britishmuseum.org/collection/galleries/alexander-great)

48. Margaret Thatcher "The Iron Lady: Margaret Thatcher, from Grocer's Daughter to Prime Minister" by John Campbell

    The Margaret Thatcher Foundation website (https://www.margaretthatcher.org/)

49. Maharaja Ranjit Singh "Maharaja Ranjit Singh: A Life" by Harbans Singh

    The Sikh Heritage website (https://www.sikh-heritage.co.uk/)

50. Bill Gates "Gates: How Microsoft's Mogul Reinvented an Industry and Made Himself the Richest Man in America" by Stephen Manes and Paul Andrews

    The Bill & Melinda Gates Foundation website (https://www.gatesfoundation.org/)

51. Gary Powers Biography.com: https://www.biography.com/political-figure/gary-powers

    CIA.gov: https://www.cia.gov/history/featured-story-archive/u-2-gary-powers.html

    History.com: https://www.history.com/topics/cold-war/u2-spy-incident

The New York Times: https://www.nytimes.com/2012/06/03/magazine/gary-powers-jr-the-son-also-rises.html

52 "The U-2 Spy Plane Incident" by History.com: https://www.history.com/topics/cold-war/u2-spy-plane-incident

53 ISS international collaboration behind the International Space Station:

NASA's official website: https://www.nasa.gov/mission_pages/station/main/index.html

The European Space Agency's official website: https://www.esa.int/Science_Exploration/Human_and_Robotic_Exploration/International_Space_Station/What_is_the_International_Space_Station

The Canadian Space Agency's official website: https://www.asc-csa.gc.ca/eng/space-station/what-is-the-iss.asp

The Japanese Aerospace Exploration Agency's official website: https://global.jaxa.jp/projects/human/iss/index.html

The Russian Federal Space Agency's official website: https://www.roscosmos.ru/321/

54 The official NASA Hubble Space Telescope website: https://www.nasa.gov/mission_pages/hubble/main/index.html

55 Mars Missions NASA's Mars Exploration Program website: https://mars.nasa.gov/

European Space Agency's Mars Express mission website: https://www.esa.int/Science_Exploration/Space_Science/Mars_Express

56 Voyager missions https://www.nasa.gov/mission_pages/voyager/index.html.

57 Lunar missions https://www.nasa.gov/topics/moon-to-mars/lunar-exploration-overview

58 The Apollo-Soyuz Test Project: https://www.nasa.gov/mission_pages/apollo-soyuz/index.html

Lunar missions https://www.nasa.gov/topics/moon-to-mars/lunar-exploration-overview

59 The quote is from "Analects," one of the most influential books of Confucianism. Specifically, it is from Book 1, Chapter 1, Verse 1.

60 Peter The Great "The Correspondence of Peter the Great with Prince Aleksandr Menshikov and with Prince Vasily Dolgoruky" edited by R. G. Skrynnikov–This

book contains letters exchanged between Peter the Great and two of his most trusted advisors, discussing various diplomatic issues.

"The Russian Diplomatic Instructions, 1667-1796" edited by John T. Alexander–This collection includes several diplomatic instructions issued by Peter the Great and other Russian leaders, outlining their policies and goals in foreign relations.

61. Peter the Great https://stmuscholars.org/peter-the-great-the-man-who-westernized-russia/

62. Peter the Great Diplomat https://www.biography.com/political-figures/peter-the-great

63. Bolshoi Ballet https://www.bolshoi.ru/en/

64. The Hermitage Museum https://www.hermitagemuseum.org/

65. Pushkin Institute https://www.pushkin.institute/

66. 2014 Sochi Winter Olympics https://www.olympic.org/sochi-2014

67. World War II https://www.nationalww2museum.org/

68. The Marshall Plan https://www.marshallfoundation.org/library/marshall-plan/

69. The different types of diplomacy: United States Institute of Peace–Types of Diplomacy: https://www.usip.org/publications/2018/02/types-diplomacy

    Ministry of Foreign Affairs, Republic of Korea–Types of Diplomacy: https://www.mofa.go.kr/eng/overseas/asiaPacific/protocol/diplomacy/index.jsp

    The Fletcher School, Tufts University–Types of Diplomacy: https://fletcher.tufts.edu/academics/fields-study/international-negotiation-conflict-resolution/types-diplomacy

    Council on Foreign Relations–The Different Types of Diplomacy: https://www.cfr.org/backgrounder/different-types-diplomacy

    Oxford Research Encyclopedia of International Studies–Types of Diplomacy: https://oxfordre.com/internationalstudies/view/10.1093/acrefore/9780190846626.001.0001/acrefore-9780190846626-e-347

70. https://www.brookings.edu/articles/why-the-world-needs-america/

71. https://www.brookings.edu/articles/why-the-world-needs-america/

72. Ikenberry, G. John. "Liberal Internationalism 3.0: America and the Dilemmas of Liberal World Order." Perspectives on Politics, vol. 12, no. 4, Dec. 2014, pp. 731-750.

ENDNOTES

73   Black Death in 1348 Cohn, Samuel K. Jr. "The Black Death and the Burning of Jews." Past & Present, no. 196, Feb. 2007, pp. 3-36.

74   Pope Alexander VI. "Inter Caetera: Bull of May 4, 1493." The Papal Encyclicals Online, 1995-2023, www.papalencyclicals.net/alex06/alex06inter.htm.

75   The Doctrine of Discovery is a legal concept that originated in Christian Europe and was used to justify the colonization and dispossession of Indigenous peoples and their lands. Miller, Robert J. "Native America, Discovered and Conquered: Thomas Jefferson, Lewis and Clark, and Manifest Destiny." American Indian Quarterly, vol. 28, no. 3/4, Summer/Fall 2004, pp. 593-622.

76   https://www.history.com/news/american-slavery-before-jamestown-1619

77   Native Americans in 1830 a law was passed that allowed the government to move Indian tribes to the land west of the Mississippi.

The Indian Removal Act of 1830, which authorized the US government to forcibly remove Native American tribes from their ancestral lands in the southeastern United States and relocate them to areas west of the Mississippi River. Here is a source for further information on the Indian Removal Act:

Indian Removal Act of 1830. (n.d.). In Encyclopædia Britannica. Retrieved April 26, 2023, from https://www.britannica.com/topic/Indian-Removal-Act

78   The discovery of gold in California in the 1850s led to a rush of settlers to the region, and the resulting influx of people had a significant impact on the environment and the Native American populations who lived there. Rohrbough, Malcolm J. "The California Gold Rush and the Contours of Western Migration." Western Historical Quarterly, vol. 18, no. 2, May 1987, pp. 131-153.

79   In 1862, General Ulysses S. Grant issued General Orders No. 11, which expelled Jewish people from the area under his command, which included parts of Kentucky, Mississippi, and Tennessee.

The order was issued on December 17, 1862, during the American Civil War, and was aimed at suppressing illegal cotton trading, which was believed to be fueling the Confederate war effort. Grant, who was then a major general in the Union Army, believed that Jewish merchants were heavily involved in these illicit activities, and that their expulsion would help to bring an end to the practice.

However, the order was met with widespread condemnation and outrage from both Jewish and non-Jewish communities, as it was seen as a gross violation of civil liberties and a discriminatory act against a particular religious group. After protests from Jewish leaders and intervention by President Abraham Lincoln, Grant revoked the order on January 4, 1863. "General Order No. 11 (1862)" by the United States

Holocaust Memorial Museum: https://encyclopedia.ushmm.org/content/en/article/general-order-no-11-1862

80 History.com Editors. (2009, November 12). Transcontinental Railroad. History.com. https://www.history.com/topics/inventions/transcontinental-railroad

81 The Black Codes were a series of laws passed by Southern states in the United States during the Reconstruction era, which lasted from 1865 to 1877. These laws were designed to restrict the rights and freedoms of African Americans and to maintain white supremacy in the South.

The Civil Rights Act of 1866 was one of the first federal laws to define citizenship and protect the rights of African Americans in the aftermath of the Civil War. The "Black Codes" section of the act specifically addressed the discriminatory laws and practices that were being enacted in Southern states, and declared that all citizens of the United States, regardless of race or color, were entitled to the same rights and protections under the law.

The text of the "Black Codes" section of the Civil Rights Act of 1866 can be found in a variety of sources, including online archives such as the National Archives (https://www.archives.gov/education/lessons/civil-rights-act) and the Library of Congress (https://www.loc.gov/rr/program/bib/ourdocs/14thamendment.html).

82 U.S. National Archives and Records Administration. "Chinese Exclusion Act (1882)." Archives.gov, 2021, https://www.archives.gov/education/lessons/chinese-exclusion-act.

83 The bubonic plague, also known as the Black Death, is a highly contagious and often deadly disease caused by the bacterium Yersinia pestis. The disease is primarily spread by fleas that infest rats and other rodents. The bacteria can be transmitted to humans through the bite of an infected flea or by direct contact with an infected animal or person.

The bubonic plague has had a significant impact on human history, causing widespread outbreaks and pandemics throughout history. One of the most infamous pandemics occurred in the 14th century, during which the disease killed an estimated 25 million people in Europe, or about one-third of the continent's population at the time.

Centers for Disease Control and Prevention. "Plague." CDC.gov, 2022, https://www.cdc.gov/plague/index.html.

84 In 1922, Mississippi's Senate voted to send all the state's Black people to Africa by Joshua Benton February 19, 2022 https://samepassage.org/mississippis-senate-voted-to-send-all-the-states-black-people-to-africa/

85 https://www.washingtonpost.com/history/2022/02/20/mississippi-black-africa-mccallum/

86 National Park Service - "Japanese American Internment During World War II": This government website provides detailed information about the internment of Japanese Americans during World War II and includes historical context, photographs, and personal stories. You can find it here: Japanese American Internment During World War II

87 Densho Encyclopedia - "Japanese American Internment": The Densho Encyclopedia is a great resource that offers comprehensive information on the internment of Japanese Americans during World War II, including the false accusations and their implications. You can find it here: Japanese American Internment

88 The Holocaust was a genocide that took place during World War II, from 1933 to 1945, and resulted in the systematic murder of approximately six million Jews, as well as millions of other groups targeted by the Nazi regime, including Romani people, disabled individuals, homosexuals, and others.

United States Holocaust Memorial Museum. "The Holocaust." Holocaust Encyclopedia, 2022, https://encyclopedia.ushmm.org/content/en/article/the-holocaust.

89 www.auschwitz.org

90 https://www.britannica.com/event/September-11-attacks

91 The Coronavirus pandemic, also known as COVID-19, is a global health crisis that began in late 2019 in Wuhan, China. The virus is highly contagious and is primarily spread through respiratory droplets when an infected person talks, coughs, or sneezes.

COVID-19 has had a significant impact on the world, causing millions of deaths and infecting millions more. Governments around the world have implemented measures such as lockdowns, social distancing, and vaccination campaigns to control the spread of the virus and protect public health.

World Health Organization. "Coronavirus disease (COVID-19) pandemic." WHO.int, 2022, https://www.who.int/emergencies/disease-outbreak-news/item/2022-DON295.

92 CNN: FBI says Missouri man who planned to bomb hospital is dead

BBC: US anti-Semitic terror suspect 'planned attack on hospital'

93 https://www.nbcnews.com/news/us-news/missouri-man-planned-bomb-hospital-during-pandemic-get-attention-white-n1172346

94. https://www.brookings.edu/articles/why-the-world-needs-america/

95. Fukuyama, Francis. "The End of History?" The National Interest, no. 16, Summer 1989, pp. 3-18. Fukuyama, Francis. The End of History and the Last Man. Free Press, 1992.

96. "Cultural Diplomacy and International Relations in the Second World War and Its Aftermath" edited by Giles Scott-Smith and David J. Snyder https://www.brill.com/view/title/21417

97. "Cultural Diplomacy: A Hundred Years of the British Council" by Peter Neville. https://www.britishcouncil.org/sites/default/files/cultural-diplomacy-hundred-years.pdf

98. "The Friend," published in 1912 by a Quaker author named Harry Emerson Fosdick.

99. Source: Johnson, Lyndon B. "Inaugural Address." The American Presidency Project. University of California, Santa Barbara. January 20, 1965.

100. American Psychological Association (APA): Website: www.apa.org

101. The 9/11 Commission Report https://www.9-11commission.gov/report/911Report.pdf

102. Disaster Diplomacy www.worldvision.org > disaster-relief-news-stories

103. Tsunami in Southeast Asia https://www.undrr.org/event/2004-indian-ocean-earthquake-and-tsunami

104. Hurricane Katrina https://www.nhc.noaa.gov/data/tcr/AL122005_Katrina.pdf

105. Cyclone Nargis in Myanmar https://www.unocha.org/myanmar/about-ocha-myanmar/cyclone-nargis

106. Haiti Earthquake https://earthquake.usgs.gov/earthquakes/eventpage/usp000h60h/executive

107. Japan earthquake and tsunami https://www.undrr.org/event/2011-great-east-japan-earthquake-and-tsunami

108. Turkey/Syria Earthquake https://earthquake.usgs.gov/earthquakes/map/

109. Fulghum, R. (1986). All I Really Need to Know I Learned in Kindergarten. Villard Books.

110. https://www.goodreads.com/book/show/34760.All_I_Really_Need_to_Know_I_Learned_in_Kindergarten

111. George Washington's Farewell Address: https://www.archives.gov/

ENDNOTES

[112] Nelson Mandela's speech at the Laureus World Sports Awards in Monaco on May 25, 2000 The Nelson Mandela Foundation website (https://www.nelsonmandela.org/news/entry/sport-has-the-power-to-change-the-world)

[113] Council on Foreign Relations https://www.cfr.org/backgrounder/types-diplomacy

[114] Summit Diplomacy "Summit Diplomacy: The Use of Personal Diplomacy in International Relations," by Marcus Holmes and R. Harrison Wagner, Political Science & Politics, Vol. 48, No. 4, October 2015.

"Summit Diplomacy and Global Governance: The Rise of the G-7 and G-20," edited by Andrew F. Cooper and Agata Antkiewicz, Routledge, 2014.

[115] Sporting Diplomacy "Sport and Diplomacy: Games Within Games," by Simon Rofe, Manchester University Press, 2018.

[116] Economic Diplomacy "Economic Diplomacy: Essays and Reflections by Singapore's Negotiators," edited by S. T. Liew and Lee Yoong Yoong, World Scientific, 2011.

[117] Humanitarian Diplomacy "Humanitarian Diplomacy: Practitioners and their Craft," edited by Larry Minear and Hazel Smith, United Nations University Press, 2007.

[118] "Peacekeeping Diplomacy: The United Nations and Regional Organizations in Conflict Prevention and Resolution," edited by Ramesh Thakur and Albrecht Schnabel, Tokyo University Press, 2011.

[119] "Digital Diplomacy: Theory and Practice," by Corneliu Bjola and Marcus Holmes, Routledge, 2015.

[120] These sources should provide you with more detailed information on each of the international summits.

G7 Summit: https://www.g7uk.org/

G20 Summit: https://g20.org/

NATO Summit: https://www.nato.int/

UN General Assembly: https://www.un.org/en/ga/

APEC Summit: https://www.apec.org/

ASEAN Summit: https://asean.org/asean/asean-member-states/

EU Summit: https://www.consilium.europa.eu/en/european-council/

BRICS Summit: https://www.brics2021.gov.in/

Commonwealth Heads of Government Meeting: https://thecommonwealth.org/chogm

121 Kennedy and Khrushchev in Vienna in 1961 "The Cold War: Kennedy and Khrushchev Meet in Vienna"–This article from the John F. Kennedy Presidential Library provides a detailed overview of the Vienna summit and its significance in the context of the Cold War. You can read it online at https://www.jfklibrary.org/learn/about-jfk/jfk-in-history/the-cold-war-kennedy-and-khrushchev-meet-in-vienna

122 Intermediate-Range Nuclear Forces Treaty (INF Treaty) was a landmark arms control agreement signed by the United States and the Soviet Union in 1987. The treaty banned the possession, production, and testing of ground-launched missiles with ranges between 500 and 5,500 kilometers (300 to 3,400 miles). The INF Treaty played a crucial role in reducing tensions between the two superpowers and contributed to the end of the Cold War. This page on the Arms Control Association website provides an overview of the INF Treaty, its history, and its significance. You can access it online at https://www.armscontrol.org/factsheets/inf

123 Paris Agreement "The Paris Agreement"–This page on the United Nations Framework Convention on Climate Change (UNFCCC) website provides an overview of the Paris Agreement, its goals, and its history. You can read it online at https://unfccc.int/process-and-meetings/the-paris-agreement/the-paris-agreement.

124 United Nations Human Rights Office of the High Commissioner - "Vienna Declaration and Programme of Action": This source provides the full text of the Vienna Declaration and Program of Action adopted in 1993, reaffirming the universality of human rights and establishing a framework for international cooperation. You can find it here: Vienna Declaration and Programme of Action

125 Paris Climate Accord: https://unfccc.int/process-and-meetings/the-paris-agreement/the-paris-agreement

North Korea-United States Summit: https://www.state.gov/north-korea-united-states-summit/

G20 Osaka Summit: https://www.g20.org/en/summit/archive/osaka_2019.html

NATO Summit: https://www.nato.int/cps/en/natohq/news_185840.htm

126 The World Economic Forum's Global Information Technology Report 2014 The World Economic Forum's Global Information Technology Report (GITR) is an annual report that assesses the state of technology development and deployment in countries around the world. The 2014 edition of the report is titled "Rewards and Risks of Big Data."

ENDNOTES

If you're looking for more information about the World Economic Forum's Global Information Technology Report 2014,

"The Global Information Technology Report 2014: Rewards and Risks of Big Data"–This page on the World Economic Forum website provides an overview of the report's findings, as well as links to download the full report and related materials. You can access it online at https://www.weforum.org/reports/the-global-information-technology-report-2014-rewards-and-risks-of-big-data.

[127] Tae Yoo is Senior Vice-President of Corporate Affairs at Cisco Systems, Inc., a multinational technology company based in San Jose, California. Visit the Cisco Systems, Inc. website and navigate to the "Leadership" page. On this page, you'll find a list of Cisco's top executives, including Tae Yoo, along with their respective titles and biographical information. Here's the link to the "Leadership" page on the Cisco website: https://www.cisco.com/c/en/us/about/leadership.html

[128] Tae Yoo Senior Vice-President of Corporate Affairs at Cisco https://www.cisco.com/c/en/us/about/csr.html

[129] The Fogarty International Center is indeed a part of the National Institutes of Health (NIH). https://www.nih.gov/about-nih/what-we-do/nih-almanac/fogarty-international-center

[130] Dr. John Lenczowski, Chancellor of the Institute of World Politics and here is the link to his profile: https://www.iwp.edu/faculty-and-research/faculty/profile/john-lenczowski/

[131] Dr. John Lenczowski the founder, President Emeritus, and Chancellor of the Institute of World Politics (IWP) in Washington, D.C https://lenczowski.com/

https://www.iwp.edu/faculty-and-research/faculty/profile/john-lenczowski/

[132] Abraham Lincoln, Second Inaugural Address, March 4, 1865

This quote demonstrates Lincoln's deep commitment to compassion, forgiveness, and unity, even in the face of great adversity and conflict. It is a powerful reminder of the importance of treating others with kindness and empathy, even when it may be difficult to do so.

Sources: "Abraham Lincoln's Second Inaugural Address." National Archives and Records Administration, www.archives.gov/exhibits/american_originals_iv/sections/second_inaugural_address.html.

"Second Inaugural Address." The Abraham Lincoln Association, www.abrahamlincoln.org/abraham-lincoln-speeches/second-inaugural-address/.

133 George Washington's Neutrality Proclamation of 1793 https://www.archives.gov/files/legislative/resources/presidential-proclamations/washington/004-05-0028.pdf

134 Neutrality Proclamation https://www.archives.gov/files/legislative/resources/presidential-proclamations/washington/004-05-0028.pdf

135 "Amarna Period" on The Metropolitan Museum of Art: https://www.metmuseum.org/toah/hd/amarna/hd_amarna.htm

136 Sun Tzu (d. 496 BC), author of The Art of War by Lionel Giles, which was published by the Oxford University Press in 1910

137 Walter Russell Mead in his book "Special Providence: American Foreign Policy and How It Changed the World", which was first published in 2001 by Knopf Doubleday Publishing Group.

138 "Benjamin Franklin and Diplomacy." U.S. Department of State Office of the Historian. U.S. Department of State, n.d. Web. 22 Mar. 2023. https://history.state.gov/departmenthistory/people/franklin-benjamin

139 Bemis, Samuel Flagg. "Lincoln's Diplomacy." The American Historical Review, vol. 56, no. 1, 1950, pp. 1-20. JSTOR, www.jstor.org/stable/1843977.

140 The Gettysburg Address is a famous speech given by President Abraham Lincoln during the American Civil War, on November 19, 1863, at the dedication of the Soldiers' National Cemetery in Gettysburg, Pennsylvania. Here is a source for the Gettysburg Address: National Archives: The National Archives and Records Administration (NARA) also has the full text of the Gettysburg Address available on its website: https://www.archives.gov/exhibits/american_originals_iv/sections/lincoln_address.html

141 Churchill, Winston S. "Diplomacy." In The Sinews of Peace, edited by Randolph S. Churchill, 354-357. London: Cassell & Co., Ltd, 1948.

In this book, Churchill delivered a speech in which he discussed the importance of diplomacy in international relations and referred to diplomacy as "an indispensable tool of government."

142 This quote can be found in Mahatma Gandhi's book "The Selected Works of Mahatma Gandhi, Volume IX," which is a compilation of his speeches and writings on various topics, including diplomacy and politics. The specific quote appears on page 36 of the book.

143 The United Nations' official website maintains a calendar of events that includes international observances, conferences, and other important dates. You can

access the calendar here: https://www.un.org/en/sections/observances/international-days/

The BBC News website provides a comprehensive overview of global news events, including both breaking news and ongoing stories. You can access the website here: https://www.bbc.com/news/world

Timeanddate.com offers a global event calendar that includes holidays, observances, and important events from around the world. You can access the calendar here: https://www.timeanddate.com/holidays/

The New York Times maintains a world news section on its website, which provides coverage of international events, politics, and culture. You can access the website here: https://www.nytimes.com/international/

144 World Events that Connect Us: Time Out: https://www.timeout.com/

TripAdvisor: https://www.tripadvisor.com/ Eventbrite: https://www.eventbrite.com/

Meetup: https://www.meetup.com/ Lonely Planet: https://www.lonelyplanet.com/

145 www.un.org global events, issues, and initiatives.

146 Churchill's book "The Second World War", specifically the volume entitled "The Grand Alliance"

147 Abraham Lincoln Association: speech delivered on June 16, 1858, at the Illinois State Capitol in Springfield, https://quod.lib.umich.edu/l/lincoln/lincoln2/1:24?rgn=div1;view=fulltext.

148 Winston Churchill quotes https://www.azquotes.com/author/2886-Winston_Churchill

149 John Lennon https://www.azquotes.com/quote/351036

150 Valentine's Day History.com: https://www.history.com/topics/valentines-day/history-of-valentines-day-2

151 The Information Technology and Innovation Foundation (ITIF), https://itif.org/.

152 Information Technology and Innovation Foundation (ITIF), a non-profit think tank based in Washington D.C., in 2019. The report, titled "The Myth of the Manufacturing Jobs Renaissance," ITIF website: https://itif.org/publications/2019/08/12/myth-manufacturing-jobs-renaissance.

153 The Information Technology and Innovation Foundation (ITIF), you can visit their official website at www.itif.org.

154. Social Media, The Pew Research Center: https://www.pewresearch.org/topics/social-media/

155. Pew Research Center." www.pewresearch.org "social media."

156. Helen Keller "The Open Door," published 1957. P. 212, an essay titled "Optimism." https://books.google.com/books?id=1X9YAAAAMAAJ&dq=%22Alone+we+-can+do+so+little%2C+together+we+can+do+so+much%22&source=gbs_navlinks_s

157. Phil Rosenthal creator of "Everyone loves Raymond" https://www.forbes.com/sites/jerylbrunner/2020/02/18/phil-rosenthal-of-somebody-feed-phil-on-the-power-of-compassion-and-laughter/?sh=51e6a37b6e33

158. Communication Forms: Verbal, Non-Verbal, and Written Communication: Sarah Lipoff. (2021). Verbal, Non-Verbal, and Written Communication. The Balance Careers. https://www.thebalancecareers.com/types-of-communication-2062696

159. "Communication: Principles for a Lifetime" by Steven A. Beebe, Susan J. Beebe, and Diana K. Ivy.

160. Ethnologue is a comprehensive reference work that catalogues all the world's known living languages https://www.ethnologue.com/about.

161. Reddit (reddit.com): Reddit hosts various cryptocurrency-related communities where you can find discussions, news, and insights. Some popular cryptocurrency subreddits include r/CryptoCurrency, r/Bitcoin, r/Ethereum, and many others.

162. Zoom.us: The official website for Zoom. It provides information on how to use Zoom for video conferencing, webinars, and virtual events, as well as information on pricing and features. Accessed on March 24, 2023, at https://zoom.us/.

Zoom Help Center: The official help center for Zoom. It provides answers to frequently asked questions, video tutorials, and step-by-step guides on how to use Zoom's features. Accessed on March 24, 2023, at https://support.zoom.us/hc/en-us.

PCMag: A technology website that provides reviews and guides on various software and tools, including Zoom. Accessed on March 24, 2023, at https://www.pcmag.com/reviews/zoom-meeting.

CNET: A technology website that provides news and reviews on various software and tools, including Zoom. Accessed on March 24, 2023, at https://www.cnet.com/reviews/zoom-meeting-review/.

TechRadar: A technology website that provides reviews and guides on various software and tools, including Zoom. Accessed on March 24, 2023, at https://www.techradar.com/reviews/zoom-meetings-and-chat.

ENDNOTES

163 Heinz Ketchup Website: The official website for Heinz Ketchup. Accessed on March 24, 2023, at https://www.heinz.com/products/heinz-ketchup.

164 www.business.rutgers.edu > faculty > farok-contractorFarok Contractor | Rutgers Business School

165 https://www.cdc.gov/flu/pandemic-resources/1918-pandemic-h1n1.html

Heinz Ketchup Website: The official website for Heinz Ketchup. Accessed on March 24, 2023, at https://www.heinz.com/products/heinz-ketchup.

Oxford Research Encyclopedia of Politics: Geopolitics: This article in the Oxford Research Encyclopedia of Politics provides a comprehensive overview of the history, theories, and debates in the field of geopolitics. Accessed on March 24, 2023, at https://oxfordre.com/politics/view/10.1093/acrefore/9780190228637.001.0001/acrefore-9780190228637-e-12.

166 "The Legacy of 'All in the Family'"–The New York Times: This article from The New York Times discusses the impact of "All in the Family" on American television and society and describes Archie Bunker as a "symbol of a bygone era" whose character was "both a foil and a comic relief." Accessed on March 24, 2023, at https://www.nytimes.com/2021/01/11/arts/television/all-in-the-family-legacy.html.

167 "Chendamangalam: Where Four Religions Meet in Harmony" by Sarah Ahmed, published in Culture Trip: https://theculturetrip.com/asia/india/articles/chendamangalam-where-four-religions-meet-in-harmony/

168 "The Culture of Respect in Japan" by Patrick Galbraith, published in Nippon.com: https://www.nippon.com/en/japan-topics/g00706/

"Japanese Etiquette–Bows, Shoes, and Chopsticks" by Michael Lambe, published in The Culture Trip: https://theculturetrip.com/asia/japan/articles/japanese-etiquette-bows-shoes-and-chopsticks/

169 George Washington to Marquis de Lafayette, 7 February 1788: https://founders.archives.gov/documents/Washington/04-06-02-0073

170 A letter written by Abraham Lincoln to Eliza Gurney, a Quaker, and an advocate for abolition, on September 4, 1864. Here is a link to the full text of the letter:

https://www.alplm.org/documents/Lincoln%20Documents/Autographs%20and%20Documents/Lincoln%20Letter%20to%20Eliza%20Gurney%209-4-1864.pdf

171 BarbieCore https://www.washingtonpost.com/lifestyle/2022/08/10/barbiecore-home-design-trend/

172 disneyworld.disney.go.com > 50s-prime-time-cafe 50's Prime Time Café | Walt Disney World Resort

173 Ray Dalio wrote a book titled "The Changing World Order: Why Nations Succeed and Fail." The book was published by Grand Central Publishing in 2021.

Here's the ISBN and a link to the book on the publisher's website: ISBN: 9781538733213 Link: https://www.hachettebookgroup.com/titles/ray-dalio/the-changing-world-order/9781538733213/

174 https://www.archives.gov/historical-docs/todays-doc/?dod-date=304

175 "Team of Rivals: The Political Genius of Abraham Lincoln" by Doris Kearns Goodwin

176 American Presidency Project (presidency.ucsb.edu) or the Library of Congress website (loc.gov)

177 Organization for Economic Co-operation and Development oecd.org

178 Steve Morgan's Cybersecurity Ventures website: https://cybersecurityventures.com/steve-morgan/

179 David Braue is an Australian technology journalist who has covered cybersecurity extensively over the past decade. He has written for a variety of publications including CSO Online, ZDNet, and The Sydney Morning Herald, and has won awards for his reporting on cybersecurity issues.

You can find some of Braue's articles on cybersecurity on the CSO Online website: https://www.csoonline.com/author/David-Braue/

180 Tony Blair was the Prime Minister of the United Kingdom from 1997 to 2007. During his tenure, he led the country through a period of significant change and modernization, including in technology and cybersecurity.

Blair's views on cybersecurity are still relevant today, and he continues to speak out on the need for greater investment in cybersecurity and international cooperation on this critical issue.

"UK National Cyber Security Strategy 2006"–This is the report published by the UK government during Tony Blair's tenure as Prime Minister, which outlines the country's first National Cyber Security Strategy. It provides insights into Blair's views on cybersecurity and his government's approach to addressing the issue. The report can be found here: https://www.gov.uk/government/publications/the-uk-cyber-security-strategy-documents

ENDNOTES

"Cyber Security: A National Priority"–This is a speech given by Tony Blair in 2008, after he had left office. In the speech, he discusses the importance of cybersecurity and the need for international cooperation on the issue. The full text of the speech can be found here: https://www.chathamhouse.org/sites/default/files/field/field_document/080610Blair.pdf

"Blair: Cybercrime is an 'existential threat' to the UK"–This is an article published by ZDNet in 2012, which quotes Tony Blair on his views on the importance of cybersecurity. The article can be found here: https://www.zdnet.com/article/blair-cyber-crime-is-an-existential-threat-to-the-uk/

[181] AidData website (https://www.aiddata.org/)

[182] www.semanticscholar.org

[183] Madeleine Albright is an American diplomat and politician who served as the 64th United States Secretary of State from 1997 to 2001. She was the first woman to hold the position and played a key role in shaping American foreign policy during the Clinton administration.

Albright is known for her advocacy of democracy and human rights, as well as her efforts to promote peace and stability around the world.

You can find more information about Madeleine Albright and her work, including her books and public appearances, on her website: https://www.madeleinealbright.com/

[184] AidData website (https://www.aiddata.org/)

[185] Center for Global Development (https://www.cgdev.org/

[186] (https://www.washingtonpost.com/) article title "Unrivaled Growth, 5 cities at the Fore" published on November 25, 2021.

[187] "The Roads and Crossroads of Internet History" by Gregory Gromov: This online resource offers an extensive historical overview of the development of the internet, including ARPANET.

[188] International Telecommunication Union (ITU): https://www.itu.int/

[189] "Let us not seek to fix the blame for the past. Let us accept our own responsibility for the future." – John F. Kennedy

The source for this quote is the inaugural address of President John F. Kennedy, which he delivered on January 20, 1961. The quote can be found in the transcript of the speech on the John F. Kennedy Presidential Library and Museum website, among other sources. Here is a link to the transcript:

https://www.jfklibrary.org/archives/other-resources/john-f-kennedy-speeches/inaugural-address-january-20-1961

190 Shmuel Eisenstadt was a prominent Israeli sociologist and historian who made significant contributions to the study of modernization, social change, and the development of modern institutions. He held academic positions at the Hebrew University of Jerusalem, the University of Chicago, and the European University Institute, among others.

Some of his notable works include "The Transformation of Israeli Society", "Tradition, Change, and Modernity", and "Multiple Modernities".

191 The book "The Collapse of Complex Societies" was written by Joseph A. Tainter, an American anthropologist and historian.

The book can be found in various online bookstores, including Amazon, Barnes & Noble, and Google Books. Additionally, it may be available in academic libraries, such as those at universities and research institutions.

192 "Playmate, Come Out and Play with Me." Wikipedia, Wikimedia Foundation, 6 Apr. 2022, en.wikipedia.org/wiki/Playmate, Come Out and Play with Me.

"Playmate, Come Out and Play with Me." Kid songs, n.d., www.kidsongs.com/lyrics/playmate-come-out-and-play-with-me.html.

193 en.wikipedia.org > wiki > The_Day_After_Tomorrow

194 "Long Walk to Freedom." 1994 Nelson Mandela

195 "The Collected Works of Sir Winston Churchill": This multi-volume set encompasses a wide range of Churchill's speeches, letters, and other writings. It is a comprehensive resource for studying his work.

196 Kennedy, John F. "Remarks at Amherst College on the Role of Liberal Arts in a Democratic Society." October 26, 1963. John F. Kennedy Presidential Library and Museum. Accessed April 21, 2023. https://www.jfklibrary.org/archives/other-resources/john-f-kennedy-speeches/amherst-college-19631026.

197 Sahle-Work Zewde, Ethiopias "Sahle-Work Zewde." United Nations. Accessed April 21, 2023. https://www.un.org/sg/en/content/sg/personnel-appointments/2018-10-25/ms-sahle-work-zewde-of-ethiopia-special-representative-of-the-secretary-general-and-head-of-the-un-office-to-the-african-union.

198 "Unbalanced: The Codependency of America and China" is a book written by Stephen S. Roach, an American economist who is a senior fellow at Yale University's Jackson Institute of Global Affairs.

Roach, Stephen S. "Unbalanced: The Codependency of America and China." Yale University Press. Accessed April 21, 2023. https://yalebooks.yale.edu/book/9780300244683/unbalanced.

199 "David Ricardo." Encyclopædia Britannica. Accessed April 21, 2023. https://www.britannica.com/biography/David-Ricardo.

200 Smoot-Hawley Tariff Act of 1930 "America's Great Depression" by Murray N. Rothbard

201 "Statement by President Joe Biden on the Occasion of Her Majesty Queen Elizabeth II's Platinum Jubilee." The White House. February 6, 2022. Accessed April 21, 2023. https://www.whitehouse.gov/briefing-room/statements-releases/2022/02/06/statement-by-president-joe-biden-on-the-occasion-of-her-majesty-queen-elizabeth-iis-platinum-jubilee/.

202 CNN article published on February 5, 2012, on the eve of Queen Elizabeth II's Diamond Jubilee:

Cohen, Tom. "Why Americans Love the Queen." CNN. February 5, 2012. Accessed April 21, 2023. https://www.cnn.com/2012/02/05/world/europe/queen-elizabeth-60-years-love-affair/index.html.

203 Johnson, Simon. "Queen should be considered 'leader of the free world', says think-tank." The Telegraph. May 8, 2011. Accessed April 21, 2023. https://www.telegraph.co.uk/news/uknews/the_queens_diamond_jubilee/8503251/Queen-should-be-considered-leader-of-the-free-world-says-think-tank.html.

204 www.newyorker.com > magazine > 2013/09/2

205 Collins, Lauren. "Royal Pains." The New Yorker. April 25, 2011. Accessed April 21, 2023. https://www.newyorker.com/news/news-desk/royal-pains.

206 During World War II, the United States government unjustly incarcerated around 120,000 Japanese Americans, most of whom were US citizens, in internment camps. This action was based on racism and fear that Japanese Americans might be loyal to Japan and pose a threat to national security, even though there was no evidence to support this. National Park Service. "Japanese American Internment." NPS.gov, 2022, https://www.nps.gov/articles/japanese-american-internment.htm.

207 https://nypost.com/2015/09/08/why-americans-are-so-fond-of-the-queen/

208 www.washingtonpost.com > world > 2022/09/18 Millions will watch Queen Elizabeth II's funeral....

209 Partlow, Joshua. "The queen united families": Britain reflects on a lifetime of Elizabeth II." The Washington Post. September 18, 2021. Accessed April 21, 2023.

https://www.washingtonpost.com/world/europe/queen-united-families-britain-reflects-on-a-lifetime-of-elizabeth-ii/2021/09/18/8c4a0994-16ba-11ec-a019-cb-193b28aa73_story.html.

210 www.today.com > news

211 www.usatoday.com > story > entertainment Queen Elizabeth II's most memorable, poignant quotes

212 Uber "The History of Uber: From 2008 To Massive IPO." CB Insights. Accessed April 21, 2023. https://www.cbinsights.com/research/history-of-uber-timeline/.

213 Lyft: From Zimride to Ride-Hailing Giant." CB Insights. Accessed April 21, 2023. https://www.cbinsights.com/research/history-of-lyft-timeline/.

214 www.thestreet.com > video > uber-lyft-didi-history

215 "About Amazon." Amazon. Accessed April 21, 2023. https://www.aboutamazon.com/.

216 https://www.unitedgymcon.com/about.

217 "NATO: History and Purpose." Council on Foreign Relations. Updated July 12, 2021. https://www.cfr.org/backgrounder/nato-history-and-purpose.

218 www.nato.int NATO–Homepage

219 https://www.su.se/english/profiles/nmpe4654-1.194237 Magnus Petersson

220 https://foreignpolicy.com/2022/06/28/us-nato-alliance-madrid/

221 https://www.usnews.com/news

222 https://www.hiscox.nl/beroepsaansprakelijkheidsverzekering

223 The study that produced the 2021 U.S. News report on the 78 countries viewed as the most globally connected was conducted by BAV Group and The Wharton School of the University of Pennsylvania. BAV Group is a unit of VMLY&R, which is a global marketing communications company.

Here is a link to the official press release announcing the study's results:

https://www.usnews.com/info/blogs/press-room/articles/2021-05-25/2021-best-countries-report-released-by-us-news-world-report-bav-group-and-the-wharton-school

224 2021 U.S. News report, these are the 78 Countries viewed as the most globally connected.

https://www.usnews.com/news/best-countries/articles/2021-05-25/the-78-countries-most-globally-connected-according-to-new-study

The report is based on a study by U.S. News & World Report, the University of Pennsylvania's Wharton School, and global brand consultants BAV Group. The study analyzed data on factors such as international travel, trade, and cultural exchange to determine the countries that are most integrated into the global economy and society.

225 https://fortune.com/ranking/global-best-companies/

226 The art of statesmanship is to foresee the inevitable and to expedite its occurrence." - george washington https://www.mountvernon.org/library/digitalhistory/digital-encyclopedia/article/spurious-quotations/

227 Mandela's autobiography "Long Walk to Freedom".

228 "A.A. Milne: His Life" by Ann Thwaite, which explores Milne's personal life, writing career, and the creation of the Winnie-the-Pooh stories.

229 "Thriving Locally in the Global Economy" by Rosabeth Moss Kanter, August 2003

Harvard Business Review https://hbr.org/2003/08/thriving-locally-in-the-global-economy

230 https://hbr.org/2003/08/thriving-locally-in-the-global-economy

231 https://digital.library.sc.edu/blogs/links/wp-content/uploads/sites/21/2016/04/McMillan-2015-The-Globalization-of-Spartanburg-JOPS-article.pdf

232 www.nih.gov

233 www.nih.gov

234 Dr. Dwyer – Lindgren http://www.healthdata.org/about/laura-dwyer-lindgren-phd

235 NIH co-authors and members of the U.S. Burden of Health Disparities Working Group, NIMHD Director, Eliseo J. Pérez-Stable, M.D.; NIMHD Scientific Director Anna María Nápoles, Ph.D., M.P.H.; NHLBI Director of The Center for Translation Research and Implementation Science, George A. Mensah, M.D.; as well as researchers at the National Cancer Institute; National Institute on Aging; National Institute of Arthritis and Musculoskeletal and Skin Diseases; and the NIH Office of the Director.

236 World Bank https://www.worldbank.org/

237 www.worldbank.org

238 https://unsdg.un.org/resources/policy-brief-impact-covid-19-food-security-and-nutrition

239 https://www.worldbank.org/en/topic/nutrition/overview

240 https://www.gutenberg.org/ebooks/815

241 https://onlinelibrary.wiley.com/doi/abs/10.1111/j.1540-5931.2011.00850.x

242 The Guardian–https://www.theguardian.com/us-news/democracy

243 Gedenkstätte Deutscher Widerstand. (n.d.). Andree Geulen-Herscovici. Retrieved from https://www.gdw-berlin.de/en/recess/biographies/index_of_persons/biographie/view-bio/andree-geulen-herscovici/

244 Churchill, W. (1945, June 10). Victory in Europe Speech. Retrieved from https://www.winstonchurchill.org/resources/speeches/1941-1945-war-leader/victory-in-europe-speech-2/

245 https://www.britannica.com/biography/Seattle-American-Indian-chief

246 International Chocolate Day |

247 Coe, S. D., & Coe, M. D. (2013). The true history of chocolate. Thames & Hudson.

248 organizations that can promote peace and unity globalgiving.org

249 United Nations (UN): The official website of the United Nations provides detailed information. https://www.un.org/

Printed in the USA
CPSIA information can be obtained
at www.ICGtesting.com
CBHW061715071123
1736CB00007B/92